Differences in Identity in Philosophy and Religion

Also available from Bloomsbury

Comparative Philosophy without Borders, edited by Arindam Chakrabarti and Ralph Weber
Comparative Studies in Asian and Latin American Philosophies, edited by Stephanie Rivera Berruz and Leah Kalmanson
Faith and Reason in Continental and Japanese Philosophy, by Takeshi Morisato
Imagination: Cross-Cultural Philosophical Analyses, edited by Hans-Georg Moeller and Andrew Whitehead
Nonexistent Objects in Buddhist Philosophy, by Zhihua Yao

Differences in Identity in Philosophy and Religion

A Cross-Cultural Approach

Edited by
Sarah Flavel and Russell Re Manning

Assistant Editor:
Lydia Azadpour

BLOOMSBURY ACADEMIC
LONDON • NEW YORK • OXFORD • NEW DELHI • SYDNEY

BLOOMSBURY ACADEMIC
Bloomsbury Publishing Plc
50 Bedford Square, London, WC1B 3DP, UK
1385 Broadway, New York, NY 10018, USA
29 Earlsfort Terrace, Dublin 2, Ireland

BLOOMSBURY, BLOOMSBURY ACADEMIC and the Diana logo are trademarks of
Bloomsbury Publishing Plc

First published in Great Britain 2020
This paperback edition published in 2021

Copyright © Sarah Flavel, Russell Re Manning, Lydia Azadpour and Contributors, 2020

Sarah Flavel, Russell Re Manning and Lydia Azadpour have asserted their right under the
Copyright, Designs and Patents Act, 1988, to be identified as Editors of this work.

For legal purposes the Acknowledgements on p. x constitute an extension
of this copyright page.

Cover image: © exxorian/Getty Images

All rights reserved. No part of this publication may be reproduced or transmitted
in any form or by any means, electronic or mechanical, including photocopying,
recording, or any information storage or retrieval system, without prior
permission in writing from the publishers.

Bloomsbury Publishing Plc does not have any control over, or responsibility for,
any third-party websites referred to or in this book. All internet addresses given in this
book were correct at the time of going to press. The author and publisher regret any
inconvenience caused if addresses have changed or sites have ceased to exist,
but can accept no responsibility for any such changes.

A catalogue record for this book is available from the British Library.

A catalog record for this book is available from the Library of Congress.

ISBN: HB: 978-1-3500-7650-1
PB: 978-1-3502-9017-4
ePDF: 978-1-3500-7651-8
eBook: 978-1-3500-7652-5

Typeset by Deanta Global Publishing Services, Chennai, India

To find out more about our authors and books visit www.bloomsbury.com and
sign up for our newsletters.

Contents

List of Figures		vi
List of Contributors		vii
Acknowledgements		x

	Introduction: Different differences in identity in philosophy and religion *Sarah Flavel, Russell Re Manning and Lydia Azadpour*	1
1	Souls, stars and shadows *Stephen R. L. Clark*	7
2	Confucian philosophy as a universal approach to integrated living: A contemporary interpretation *Geir Sigurðsson*	21
3	Realizing virtues: Plato and Buddhism *Chiara Robbiano and Shalini Sinha*	41
4	Application of tradition in Gadamer and the sameness-otherness of Islamic philosophy *Selami Varlik*	69
5	'The mind is more like matter, the body more like the form': Geulincx against Descartes (and the scholastics) on the sources of difference in minds *Michael Jaworzyn*	91
6	My identity differs: On why I am not myself in light of Hume, Beauvoir and Zen Buddhist writings *Andrew K. Whitehead*	113
7	Individual identity and cultural practice: Relationalism in modern protestant theology *Harald Matern*	129
8	One's other self: Contradictory self-identity in Ueda's phenomenology of the self *Raquel Bouso*	149
9	Events of excess, being and existence in Jean-Luc Nancy and Jean-Luc Marion's philosophies *Robert Luzar*	175
Index		201

Figures

8.1 *Both Man and Ox Forgotten*, traditionally attributed to
Tenshō Shūbun (active ca. 1423–60), fifteenth century. Ink and
light colours on paper handscroll (32 × 181.5 cm). Museum
of Shokoku-ji Temple, Kyoto, Japan — 156

8.2 *Returning to the Fundamental, Back to the Source*, traditionally
attributed to Tenshō Shūbun (active ca. 1423–60), fifteenth century.
Ink and light colours on paper handscroll (32 × 181.5 cm).
Museum of Shokoku-ji Temple, Kyoto, Japan — 157

8.3 *Entering the City with Hands Hanging Down*, traditionally
attributed to Tenshō Shūbun (active ca. 1423–60), fifteenth
century. Ink and light colours on paper handscroll (32 × 181.5 cm).
Museum of Shokoku-ji Temple, Kyoto, Japan — 157

Contributors

Lydia Azadpour is a postgraduate research scholar at Royal Holloway, University of London. She is currently completing her PhD project on the concept of species in philosophies of nature between 1790 and 1810. She holds degrees from the University of Warwick (UK) and KU Leuven (Belgium).

Raquel Bouso Garcia is an associate professor at the Universitat Pompeu Fabra in Barcelona, where she received her PhD with a thesis on the notion of emptiness in the thought of Nishitani Keiji (1900–90). She has translated works by Nishitani Keiji, Ueda Shizuteru and Toshihiko Izutsu into Spanish, along with other works in Japanese philosophy. Besides various articles, she has published *El zen* (Catalan, 2008; Spanish, 2012), co-edited FJP vol. 6, *Cross-Currents and Confluences* (2009), and *La filosofía japonesa en sus textos*, with J. W. Heisig, T. P. Kasulis and J. C. Maraldo (2016).

Stephen R. L. Clark is Emeritus Professor of Philosophy at the University of Liverpool, and Honorary Research Fellow in the Department of Theology at the University of Bristol. He continues to manage an international e-list for philosophers, and to serve as Associate Editor of the *British Journal for the History of Philosophy*. His books include *The Mysteries of Religion* (1984), *A Parliament of Souls* (1990), *God, Religion and Reality* (1998), *Biology and Christian Ethics* (2000), *Understanding Faith: Religious Belief and Its Place in Society* (2009), *Ancient Mediterranean Philosophy* (2013) and *Plotinus: Myth, Metaphor and Philosophical Practice* (2016). His chief current interests are in the philosophy of Plotinus, the understanding and treatment of non-human animals, philosophy of religion and science fiction.

Sarah Flavel is Reader in Asian and Comparative Philosophy at Bath Spa University in the UK. She obtained her PhD as an Irish Research Council Scholar at University College Cork, Ireland, where she researched the relationship between the thought of Japanese philosopher Nishitani Keiji and the German philosopher Friedrich Nietzsche. She is founder of the Annual Bath Spa Colloquium for Global Philosophy and Religion, and is Academic Director of the International Academy for Chinese Thought and Culture, a collaborative summer school in China as part of the Global Academy of Liberal Arts. Her expertise lies in continental European and East Asian philosophies, in particular Daoism and Buddhism.

Michael Jaworzyn is currently writing a doctoral dissertation on Arnold Geulincx's legacy at KU Leuven, supported by a PhD Fellowship from the Fonds Wetenschappelijk Onderzoek (Research Foundation Flanders). He is the author of various articles on the early reception and transformation of Descartes's work.

Robert Luzar is an artist, writer and educator. He is Senior Lecturer in Fine Art at Bath Spa University, and holds a PhD from Central Saint Martins. He investigates 'event', 'trace' and 'subjectivity' in practices of drawing that combine with performance, video and space. He exhibits his works internationally in venues, which have included *Palazzo Loredan Venice* (IT), *Torrance Art Museum* (USA), *Talbot Rice Gallery* (UK), and *Katzman Contemporary* (CA). His writings are published in books and journals such as *Nancy and Visual Culture* (Edinburgh University Press 2016), *Drawing: Research, Theory, Practice* (Intellect) and *Theatre and Performance Design* (Routledge).

Harald Matern Dr theol., is Senior Lecturer at the Faculty of Theology, University of Basel. He studied Theology and Philosophy at Freiburg (GER), Basel (CH), Buenos Aires (ARG) and Heidelberg (GER). Harald completed his MTh (2009) and PhD (2013) at the University of Basel and has been researching and teaching at Basel and Erlangen. In 2017/18 he was a Visiting Scholar at St Edmund's College and the Faculty of Divinity, University of Cambridge. His main research interests are the History of Theology in the modern age (mainly continental); Bioethics and Creation Theology; Christianity and Culture, and the work of Paul Tillich.

Russell Re Manning is Reader in Religions, Philosophies and Ethics at Bath Spa University, UK and Visiting Fellow of St Edmund's College, University of Cambridge. He is Series Editor of *The Collected Works of Paul Tillich in English* and a member of the Executive Committee of the International Society for Science and Religion. Publications include *The Cambridge Companion to Paul Tillich*, *The Oxford Handbook of Natural Theology* and *30-Second Religion*. He is currently working on a book about Nietzsche.

Chiara Robbiano (PhD Greek philosophy, Leiden University, the Netherlands) is Assistant Professor of Philosophy, Honours Director and Tutor at University

College Utrecht. In spring 2019 she was Visiting Professor at Tohoku University (Sendai, Japan). After the publication of *Becoming Being. On Parmenides' Transformative Philosophy*, Akademia Verlag, 2006, she published widely in peer-reviewed journals (*Philosophy East and West, Ancient Philosophy, Journal of World Philosophies*) and in books on Greek and cross-cultural philosophy.

Geir Sigurðsson (PhD philosophy, University of Hawai'i) is professor of Chinese studies at University of Iceland. He is author of *Confucian Propriety and Ritual Learning* (SUNY Press, 2015) and of a forthcoming annotated translation into Icelandic of *Master Sun's Art of Warfare* (*Hernaðarlist Meistara Sun*).

Shalini Sinha is Lecturer in non-Western philosophy at the University of Reading, UK. She grew up in India and Canada and then studied and taught in Canada and the UK. Her research interests include Buddhist, Hindu and Jaina metaphysics and ethics of the self, Buddhist and Hindu philosophy of mind and action, and topics in cross-cultural philosophy. She teaches courses in cross-cultural metaphysics, ethics, political philosophy and philosophy of religion, and the application of these to contemporary social and political issues. She has contributed articles to various collections on Indian and cross-cultural philosophy and is working on a monograph on the self in Indian philosophy.

Selami Varlik is Assistant Professor of philosophy at Istanbul 29 Mayis University in Turkey. He received his PhD on a Gadamerian criticism of Fazlur Rahman's Quranic hermeneutics at the Ecole des Hautes Etudes en Sciences Sociales in Paris. He mainly works on the relationship between phenomenological hermeneutics – especially Gadamer and Ricoeur – and Islamic philosophy and spirituality. He is currently working on a study of the interconnection between poetic and speculative discourse in Paul Ricoeur and Islamic thought.

Andrew K. Whitehead is presently Associate Professor of Philosophy at Kennesaw State University in the United States. His recent publications include the co-edited volumes *Imagination: Cross-Cultural Philosophical Analyses* (2018), *Wisdom and Philosophy: Contemporary and Comparative Approaches* (2016) and *Landscape and Travelling East and West: A Philosophical Journey* (2014), all of which are published by Bloomsbury Academic.

Acknowledgements

Some of the material in Chapter 1 also appears, with the editors' permission, within a larger discussion in Stephen R. L. Clark, 'Classical Mediterranean Conceptions of the Afterlife', in *The Palgrave Handbook of the Afterlife*, eds. Yujin Nagasawa and Benjamin Matheson (London: Palgrave Macmillan 2017), 41–57.

Chapter 8 is part of a research project on Japanese Philosophy, supported by the Spanish Ministry of Economy and Competitiveness, Grant FFI2015-65662-P.

Introduction: Different differences in identity in philosophy and religion

Sarah Flavel, Russell Re Manning and Lydia Azadpour

This collection presents a different interpretation of the different accounts of identity in global philosophy and religion. The chapters engage different philosophical and religious traditions and all seek to advance distinct arguments; all are equally united in their rejection of what we might call 'the myth of different identities' in global philosophy and religion. As so often in the study of global philosophy and religion, this myth of different identities conceals orientalist assumptions about the differences between Eastern and Western traditions; assumptions that this collection rejects. More specifically, we reject what has become established as the 'typical' or 'ordinary' narrative of identity in diverse traditions: that is to say the unsustainable yet widely held view that 'Western' philosophies and religions approach identity by positing discrete and self-sufficient entities, while by contrast, 'Eastern' traditions seek to explain identity in terms of relations. In slogan form, this 'standard narrative' holds that Western thought about identity is essentialist and that Eastern thought about identity is relational. Western thinkers, the story goes, seek to make sense of identity by looking for what makes a particular thing that thing – its essence; whereas Eastern thinkers seek to make sense of identity by looking at how a particular thing differs from others – its relations.

The basic claim of the chapters in this volume is that this standard narrative is not adequate to the complexities of religious and philosophical thinking about identity in global contexts. Further, instead of seeking to identify distinctively 'Western' and 'Eastern' approaches to identity, this collection suggests that, first, the division of all thought into two monolithic traditions does not reflect the complexity and variety of traditions and philosophies across the globe, of which we have only been able to mention a few here. Second, that consideration of difference cuts across the conventional boundaries of traditions. In other words, this book's overall argument is that difference matters cross-culturally for thinking about identity and how identity is defined. As such, the problematic assumption of sameness versus difference (essentialism vs. relationalism) is misguided and unhelpful – and at times harmful. What is required – and what this book starts to develop – is not a new framework for entrenching the differences in conceptions of identity between traditions, but instead a recognition of the different differences in identity within traditions. This book begins the process of examining the ways in which identity differs across a number of philosophical and religious traditions and of the (divergent) ways in which ideas of alterity are at work in thinking about identity across regional philosophical and religious divides.

Far from repeating the orientalist construction of the non-Western 'other' that differs not only in its substantive identity (being different from the privileged Western norm) but also in the very notion of identity per se (the non-Western other as a different sort of other), the thesis of this collection is that difference is at work in thinking about identity in various traditions across different cultures – including many where this is less well known. We wish to suggest that far from the traditional claim that Western philosophy and religion are premised on an original assumption of identity, instead these traditions in many ways are as much dependent on ideas of difference or relationality as those better known for emphasizing such ideas. Of course, this is not meant to promote some kind of 'occidentalism' or orientalism in reverse, in which the differentializing traditions of the East are taken as normative and read back into their Western counterparts. Furthermore, we acknowledge that the very words at our disposal, in talking about cultural distinctions, to some extent reinforce this very problem. Our claim is at once more simple and more complex: difference is differently constitutive for identity in various traditions. We can therefore say that it would neither be possible to extinguish the differences that conceptual frameworks seem to exhibit in different cultural contexts nor be desirable to reify them into absolute distinctions.

The chapters that follow seek to illustrate this thesis via a broad historical arc, beginning with multi-identity and non-essentialism in ancient Egypt and Greece. In 'Souls, Stars and Shadows', Stephen R. L. Clark examines what he refers to as a 'two self' theory of identity in the ancient world. He finds in the ancient Egyptian distinction between two kinds of soul: *ka*, which remains as the shadow of a mortal life, and *ba*, which can join the gods as a star – a precursor to the views of the Neoplatonist Plotinus in the third century CE. In exploring the complex relation between these two selves in Antiquity, Clark shows that the Platonists could conceive of a kind of identity that goes beyond and does not depend on the memories of the particular individual, but equally does not necessarily mean a dissolution of the self in one indistinguishable spirit.

Geir Sigurðsson argues for the persisting relevance of Confucian thought to other traditions. After an elucidation of the cosmological view in which medieval developments of Confucianism emerged, Sigurðsson asserts that this cosmology can be made compatible with contemporary scientific modes of thought. Given this foundation, he goes on to explain the Confucian model of education as a life-long process which involves adopting traditional practices. In Sigurðsson's account, not only the relational self but also the understanding of individualism that Confucianism suggests is developed as of particular import.

Chiara Robbiano and Shalini Sinha explore commonalities between two schools of thought traditionally interpreted as having very little in common – the Buddhist and the Platonic. In their chapter, 'Realizing Virtues: Plato and Buddhism', Robbiano and Sinha rethink the notion of identity by exploring the role of three shared themes in Buddhist and Platonic thought: the changeable character of the everyday world, the orientation of desires towards the apparent and reorientation to the true good and the transformation of self and world as the goal of philosophy as a way of life. In rethinking the boundary between self and world, they show that the resultant conceptions of identity – though different in many ways – both allow us to think of self-transformation as world-transformation.

In his chapter, 'Application of Tradition in Gadamer and the Sameness-Otherness of Islamic Philosophy', Selami Varlik questions the presuppositions of engaging in comparative philosophy. Regarding the case of Islamic philosophy, he argues that the idea of comparative philosophy often reaffirms the notion that there are two fundamentally different traditions to be bridged. Suggesting a new approach to intercultural philosophy, he argues that what is needed in this context is to acknowledge the dialectic of sameness and otherness in the origins of both thinkers. Thinking Gadamer and Avicenna together, for example, is discussed not as an exercise in comparative philosophy but as an exercise requiring a common conceptual language to connect the various works addressed, so that each philosopher can learn from and be understood in light of the other.

Michael Jaworzyn uses the case of early Cartesian Arnold Geulincx to suggest that the Cartesian tradition is more varied than this standard picture of the Cartesian self might indicate. According to his account of Geulincx's work, everything that allows us to understand ourselves as particular individuals we owe not to the fact that we are thinking things but to what for Geulincx is the only source of difference: body in motion. Despite the fact that much of what Geulincx claims seems implicitly to go against standard readings of Descartes, a good deal of it is based on genuinely Cartesian principles. He claims that Geulincx's views in fact echo aspects of Descartes's thought that have been highlighted, sometimes critically, by recent scholars of Descartes.

Andrew K. Whitehead's contribution argues that it is more appropriate to compare the Zen Buddhist no-self doctrine to existentialist accounts of the self, particularly that of Simone de Beauvoir, than to the Humean views to which it is more often linked. Despite the ostensible proximity between Hume's work and the Buddhist no-self doctrine, Whitehead shows that there are just as many points of disagreement, and accordingly provides a summary and critique of Hume's views from the perspective of Zen Buddhism. He suggests in turn that Simone de Beauvoir's existentialist view of the self as a project makes for a more promising avenue for understanding the Zen view of no-self from a comparative perspective.

Harald Matern addresses the concept of identity in difference from the perspective of modern protestant theology. He argues, with reference to Schleiermacher and Tillich, that a particular German-speaking tradition provides a point of view that can affirm individual identity without having to view such identities in isolation from their social setting. It can do so by conceiving human individuality as a 'performative process', and that one of the roles of religion is to make us aware of the various, fragmentary relations that have continually to be enacted and integrated into our identities. As a result, he suggests both that we should be wary of too quickly rejecting theological perspectives in public discourse or segregating religious communities, and that the Christian tradition has resources which might be more broadly useful in the global discussion of the extent to which religion can or should play a role in the constitution of identities.

In 'One's Other Self: Contradictory Self-Identity in Ueda's Phenomenology of the Self', Raquel Bouso illuminates Ueda Shizuteru's understanding of the human being. In particular, Bouso gives an account of Ueda's discussion of the process of reaching one's true identity or true self, stressing the openness to the other and self-negation involved in this process. Her account shows how Ueda draws on a variety of influences – Nishida Kitarō, European Existential Phenomenology and Hermeneutics – to further develop the Zen Buddhist insight of the true self as no-self.

Finally, in 'Events of Excess, Being and Existence in Jean-Luc Nancy and Jean-Luc Marion's Philosophies', Robert Luzar illuminates Marion's phenomenological and Nancy's post-phenomenological conceptualizations of the event. His analysis shows how both Nancy and Marion develop accounts of the event that put in question the established distinction between empiricism and revelation, and once again that challenge the assumption that Western thought is premised on the assertion of an essential 'I', of substantial core of identity.

From ancient Egypt to contemporary France, via traditions as varied as Confucianism, Platonism, Buddhism, existentialism, Islamic philosophy, hermeneutics and modern Protestant theology, the chapters in this volume show forth the different differences in identity in global philosophy and religion and, we hope, open up new – and different – conversations about this most pressing and perennial question.

1

Souls, stars and shadows

Stephen R. L. Clark

Introduction

In what follows I aim to expound and to examine the 'two self' theory of identity, from Ancient Egypt to Plotinus: on the one hand, there is a psycho physical unity, whose mere shadow remains in the afterlife; on the other, the real self, *nous* or *ba*, that is native to the stars, and need not remember (perhaps should not remember) its merely earthly history.[1] It was possible, or so Platonists believed, that we could awaken, even in this life, to our real identity. But there is a sense in which what wakens is not (for example) just *Plotinus* – a particular third-century Egyptian. It is worth noticing that caterpillars, in one ancient and respectable account, are not *turned into* butterflies, but they only lay the eggs (the chrysalides) from which the butterflies will hatch! Plotinus even identifies our present corporeal selves, exactly, as *grubs* in the tree of nature (*Ennead* IV.3 [27].4, 26-30). And '*psyche*' means both soul and butterfly. On the other hand, there must be some real connection between the shadow-self and the real or star-like self. What sort of identity or quasi-identity is this? And what are its practical effects or its practical content? Following the Egyptian clue, we have at least two 'souls' – on the one hand, the mere shadow or image of a sometime mortal life (*ka*), and on the other, a spirit who may join the gods in glory (*ba*), becoming in its turn one of the transfigured dead (*akh*). We may hope that we are all like Heracles, to be freed from memory of past follies and misadventures.

Heracles and Heracles

According to Plotinus's exegesis of Homer's *Odyssey* 11.601-2, Heracles's image or shadow is in Hades, but he himself is among the gods (*Ennead* I.1

[53].12; see also IV.3 [27].32).[2] Most commentators suggest that some copyist, desperate to reconcile entirely conflicting traditions, had added the line about 'Heracles himself', distinct from the shade of Heracles. In the earlier text or oral recitation, it is supposed, Heracles was no more than another mortal hero, whose 'afterlife' was no real life at all. At death, *The Iliad* repeatedly declares, our force (*menos*), will (*thumos*), guts (*phrenes*) and breath (*psyche*) itself all leave the bodily remains behind, but not so as to constitute a real surviving entity. All that can be found in the Unseen, in Hades, are memories and images of 'the departed', perhaps to be given momentary life by the blood of sacrifice, but best walled off from the life of the survivors.[3] If there is any conscious experience there at all it is a life of regretful memory – a notion that in later years amounts to eternal damnation, whether or not particular punishments are imagined.[4] A quite different notion of our 'soul' (still *psyche*) permitted the idea that we *are* souls, able to wander away even during this mortal life, and destined for real life hereafter. In Homeric or pre-Homeric times, such 'life souls' may be reserved for the special few, who are being raised to life immortal, even to godhead (like Heracles himself, or Dionysus), or granted a unique escape from death, an everlasting home in Elysion, as Zeus's son-in-law (a fate prophesied for Menelaus). In *The Odyssey* even the great hero Achilles was left in Hades, though an alternative tradition suggested that his mother took him away instead to the White Island.[5] That Island may be Elysion – or it may be merely an island in the Black Sea, his putative burial place. Another editor might have added a gloss to Achilles's gloomy conversation with Odysseus to accommodate the story.

But these differing accounts need not have had different sources, as though one tradition or poetic lineage firmly supposed that even heroes only survived as shadows, and another insisted rather that they were raised immortal. The likelier story is that we have always held apparently conflicting views about the present whereabouts of those we can no longer touch or hold. The dead still exist at least 'in our mind's eye', in dreams or sudden reminiscences: Do they also exist in an Otherworld in the far, imaginary West, or the Underworld, or heaven, independent of our memory? Do they grow and change there, or remain forever what they were, or simply fade to be forgotten? Is there some chance that they may grow to life immortal? There need have been no rationalizing copyist to distinguish shadow-Heracles and Heracles-the-god: gods and heroes (i.e. well remembered persons whether for good or evil) differ from the rest of us – but there may be and may always have been the same uncertainty, the same ambivalence, even about the non-heroic dead.

But even if these ambiguities are familiar ones, and need no special explanation, they may also provide the seeds of more developed theories. On the one hand, the dead are shadows, *eidola*, dream images of the real bodily beings that have real effects in the world, and real choices. On the other, perhaps they can be counted – or some of them can be counted – alongside really immortal beings, tangible divinities. The ancient Egyptian story suggested that 'one aspect of the god's nature, his *ba*, is in heaven; another one, his body, rests in the realm of the dead'.[6] Even the human dead may have at least two modes of 'survival': the *ka* is given form through the body's mummification, the array of funeral goods, and seems to persist simply as an echo of the once living being; the *ba*, represented as a bird with a human head, can be expected to join the sun in his progress across the heavens, maybe as a star, probably in the constellation Orion (the sidereal home of Osiris).[7] There may, in short, be a systematic theory of the Afterlife, developed in Egypt, and persisting (perhaps) in Homer, and (more certainly) in Plotinus.

Gods and transformations

A consistent materialist must be committed to the view that each of us is no more than a single wave of the sea, and that wisdom lies in identifying ourselves with the whole: it is that world that guides or determines all our thoughts and actions, quite as much as it guides or determines the path of planets, falling rocks or chemical reactions. There is nothing more to us, materialists must suppose, than that. The transformation of this particular body here into other bodies is all that I can expect, and need not fear. Anything – or so many in the Classical world believed – could be transformed into another shape – women into trees, or birds, or oxen – and the gods could take on any shape they pleased to beget their offspring upon mortal women. Nor was this so unfamiliar: tadpoles become frogs, and caterpillars turn into – or perhaps give birth to – butterflies. So it is not so obvious that each of us here-now is *essentially* and *distinctively* a human animal: humans are only a transient subset of 'lifekind', even if – on staunchly anthropocentric principles – we are somehow the most *typical* or *natural* of living creatures, the form from which all other things diverge.[8] Nowadays we can add that each living creature is itself a *colony*, a more or less cooperative assembly of other creatures, and dependent also on a wider living world for its continued being. This is not so distant from the Empedoclean speculation that – with some good reasons – Aristotle disparaged[9]: living organisms cannot be simply chance-met aggregates of hands, feet and internal organs (as though such things could ever survive *outside* an existing, goal-directed organism). But they can be – since they are – associations of smaller creatures whose ancestors surrendered an 'independent' life to be part of the larger whole, just as individual humans are normally and naturally to be found in *poleis*, or some similar collectivity.

If we could abandon or overlook our usual conviction that we are significantly and essentially *human*, and independent, beings we might find ourselves in agreement with the Stoic or Daoist view. 'No mortal thing has a beginning, nor does it end in death and obliteration; there is only a mixing and then a separating of what was mixed.'[10] But there was also an alternative. The very thinkers who most emphasized the transformative possibilities of living nature were also known to believe in distinct and immortal souls, of another sort than the souls which were the life of individual bodies. Long ago we were gods, and some of us – Empedocles said – remember this. In realizing our imprisonment he presented himself to Acragas in Sicily as 'an immortal god, mortal no more'.[11] Hesiod's gods are condemned to lie frozen by the Styx when they break their oath, and Zuntz's aphorism is almost correct: 'the banished god described by Hesiod is – Man'.[12] Almost correct, but not exactly: for the point Empedocles is making is that the banished god isn't essentially human, even if it may be born among humans 'as prophets, singers of hymns, healers and leaders'[13] – and among beasts as lions, or laurels among trees.[14]

The banished god that finds itself embodied here is not necessarily tied down to its body, even while that body lives. Hermotimus of Clazomenae, for example, set his soul roaming round the world while his body lay seemingly lifeless (till his treacherous wife, bored with his long silence, had the body cremated).[15] He was, it was said, an earlier incarnation of the soul that was also Pythagoras, and he himself claimed to have had the same soul as a hero of the Trojan War, Euphorbus.[16] An even odder character, Aristeas of Proconnesus (an island *polis* in the Propontis, between the Mediterranean and the Black Sea), in the seventh century BCE, is said to have vanished from his home after seeming to fall dead, and reappeared seven years later to deliver a poem, the *Arimaspea*, about his travels, 'possessed by Apollo', in the North. More oddly still, he reappeared 240 years later, in southern Italy, claiming to have been with Apollo, as a raven.[17]

Some later Platonists, like Iamblichus, were wary of the notion that our human soul could ever be incarnate as an 'animal', but it seems clear that others – from Plato to Plotinus – were content that we might be embodied as ants or bees or eagles, depending on the form of life we had chosen.[18] Plato, in his 'myth of Er', suggested that we all had *chosen* the lives we had to live (though in that story, the choice indeed seems only to be between different sorts of human life[19]), and must make the best of it. Perhaps, Plotinus added, we might hope for a better part next time – as actors hope for a more significant role once they have shown their talents.[20] The story would be easier to comprehend if all of us – not simply the favoured few like Hermotimus or Empedocles – could *remember* being 'a boy and a girl, a shrub and a bird and the fish that leaps from the sea'.[21] Memory is not the criterion of identity here: on the contrary, the stories about past events that come into my mind here-now are only *memories* if it was I that was their subject or their agent. Conversely, there are many true stories about 'my own' past actions that I do not now recall. At least, if I were to *seem* to remember being (say) Hermotimus I would have some slight reason to consider it might be true. But the story about our life hereafter actually emphasizes that hardly anyone will remember – and that this is as it should be: Euphorbus, Hermotimus and Pythagoras are different lives, with different duties. Each life we live has its own time and reason, even if those lives do, somehow, share 'a soul'.

Criteria of identity

So what criterion of identity is relevant? Plotinus reckoned that we could simply *recognize* our friends, as Pythagoras recognized his friend, in the sound of a beaten dog.[22] 'For here below, too, we can know many things by the look in people's eyes when they are silent; but There all their body is clear and pure and each is like an eye, and nothing is hidden or feigned, but before one speaks to another that other has seen and understood.'[23] 'There', that is, we apparently have recognizable, and naked, bodies – or at least we have some public presence, even if that presence is not so easily locatable, nor yet as divisible, as our present corporeal being. Are these 'bodies' merely the shadowy images that Homer led us to expect, even though we can expect to be more like Teiresias than the common Homeric mass? But images of what? Precisely because these souls – or better, perhaps, these *daimones* or *spirits* – are not identical with any one of their earthly lives, we cannot expect to recognize (say) Socrates merely from the *look* of things: his spirit is not snub-nosed, even symbolically. But if there were no individualized public presence we might have to expect that there is just *one* spirit for all of us, wholly indistinguishable and therefore wholly identical. That indeed seems, sometimes, to be the implication of the philosophers' account: 'mind is the god in us – whether it was Hermotimus or Anaxagoras who said so – and mortal life contains a portion of some god.'[24] And maybe this is common knowledge: 'all men are naturally and spontaneously moved to speak of the god who is in each one of us *one and the same.*'[25]

But this cannot be all that is intended by this story: there may be only one absolute *Nous* (at once Mind and Being), and it still be true that each living spirit is a distinct face of *Nous*, a really distinct individual not identical with any ordinarily earthly being.

> If one likens it [that is, Reality] to a living richly varied sphere, or imagines it as a thing all faces, shining with living faces, or as all the pure souls running together into the same place, with no deficiencies but having all that is their own, and universal Intellect seated on their summits so that the region is illuminated by intellectual light – if one imagined it like this one would be seeing it somehow as one sees another from outside; *but one must become that, and make oneself the contemplation.*[26]

Just occasionally, Plotinus remarked, we may glimpse that possibility, when the world we see grows shadowy. 'Often I have woken up out of the body to myself, and have entered into myself, going out from all other things; I have seen a beauty wonderfully great and felt assurance that then most of all I belonged to the better part.'[27] But what wakens is not just *Plotinus*, a particular third-century Egyptian. Remember that caterpillars, in one ancient and respectable account, are not *turned into* butterflies, but they only lay the eggs (the chrysalides) from which the butterflies will hatch![28] And *psyche* means both 'soul' and 'butterfly'. Our present selves are grubs in the great tree of nature.[29]

The immortal soul or spirit, then, is effectively a *daimon*, with an unearthly body that somehow still reveals an abiding character and form of life. In the stories that Plato appends several times to his dialogues these spirits will be sorted out in Hades: most may have to endure purgatorial torments, a few will pass on – for a while – to the Elysian Fields.[30] Almost all will be returned to natural existence, in whatever form best suits them. A very few will be discarded forever, or else break free forever from the wheel. In later developments of the story – echoing the Egyptian myth – our spirits must ascend through seven planetary spheres, shedding the qualities or vices we acquired in our earlier descent, and so return at last to heaven as stars[31] – which are themselves indivisible points. Free so to pass through space we must have a sort of local presence, an *okhema*, a vehicle or 'astral body' – though *Plotinus* flatly denied that we had any need of this to manage our immediate return.[32]

As stars, so Plotinus also insisted, we have no need of memory: everything of importance will then be immediately present, and we shall have no more need than Heracles to recall our earthly lives. This will be our longed-for return:

> Even before this coming to be we were there, men [that is, *anthropoi*] who were different, and some of us even gods, pure souls and intellect united with the whole of reality; we were parts of the intelligible, not marked off or cut off but belonging to the whole; and we are not cut off even now.[33]

How different is this hope from the Stoic suggestion that the wise at least, by identifying with or attaching to their idea of the cosmos, are effectively immortal as the single Mind all really rational beings share? This would seem to be at odds with Plotinus's declaration that we shall recognize our – plural – friends, as well as with Socrates's hope of conversing with past heroes if he survives his execution.[34] According to Porphyry the oracle at Delphi declared that Plotinus, freed 'from the wave of this blood-drinking life' and from 'the tomb (*sema*) that held [his] daimonic soul', had joined 'the dance of immortal love', alongside Minos, Rhadamanthus, Aeacus, Plato and Pythagoras.[35] Such confusions, as I pointed out before, are commonplace, and do not signify that Socrates (or Plato or Plotinus or the Oracle) is being 'ironic'. Whatever the world we wake to at our deaths may be, they are confident at any rate that we shall wake,[36] and waking realizes that we are none of us what we once thought we were. Our earthly deaths will be an initiation into a sacred reality[37] – but what that is like, God knows.

Following the Egyptian clue, we have at least two 'souls' – on the one hand, the mere shadow or image of a sometime mortal life (*ka*), and on the other, a spirit who may join the gods in glory (*ba*). We may hope that we are all like Heracles, to be freed from memory of past follies and misadventures. This does require us to rethink some of what we supposed we know.

> Modern scholars, deprived of all theurgic imagination and grace, may still insist on their rejection of Egyptian philosophy, but the fact remains that Pythagoras and Plato brought something important from Egypt, connected with the theory of Ideas, the divine Archetypes and their images and symbols, the mathematical sciences, regarded in a mystical sense, and the conception of the immortal winged soul (*ba*) wandering in search of her true identity and thereby following the precept of Horus-Ra (Apollo): Know Thyself, The soul seeks to know truth (*maat*) and live by it. When her ascent is completed, the soul, turned into the luminous intellect (*akh*), contemplates the Forms in the solar barque of Ra.[38]

An interesting analogy (at least) has recently surfaced in psychological study: a woman who has no 'first-person, episodic' memory of her own life, though she may know many facts about it.[39] Just so most of us can acknowledge that we were born at such and such a time and place, had an unremembered infancy, and have since done many things we don't ourselves recall. Losing all our episodic memory does not necessarily render us incapable. And maybe we can get some comfort even in this earthly life from the story told of Proclus: in his last illness 'though he forgot almost all human things as the paralysis advanced … he completed the hymns [he had asked to be chanted] and the greater part of the Orphic verses … read out in his presence'.[40] Those suffering from dementia and losing their personal memories, even their autobiographical memories, may still be able to sing.[41] Our predecessors would have inferred that this is what was worth remembering: 'A shadow's dream (*skias onar*) is man, but when (a) god sheds a brightness, shining light is on earth and life is as sweet as honey.'[42] The context of Pindar's ode is a celebration of Success – the crown of physical strength and skill, as mainstream 'Classical' culture most admired. But 'a man has not failed if he fails to win beauty of colours or bodies, or power or office or kingship even, but if he fails to win this and only this'[43] – the vision of immortal beauty. The hidden message may instead be that it is here and now that is the dream, the fantasy, the vapour, and that – if we were only to open 'another way of seeing'[44] – we could see, and join, the stars. And I end with Eckhart Tolle's sudden insight:

> 'I cannot live with myself any longer.' This was the thought that kept repeating in my mind. Then suddenly I became aware of what a peculiar thought it was. 'Am I one or two? If I cannot live with myself, there must be two of me: the "I" and the "self" that "I" cannot live with.' 'Maybe', I thought, 'only one of them is real'.[45]

Notes

1 Originally presented at Prometheus Conference in Manchester, 10–12 July 2015, and subsequently at the Bath Spa University for Global Philosophy and Religion, 29–30 April 2016. Some of the material also appears, with the editors' permission, within a larger discussion of classical conceptions of 'life after death' in Stephen R. L. Clark, 'Classical Mediterranean Conceptions of the Afterlife', in *The Palgrave Handbook of the Afterlife,* ed. Yujin Nagasawa and Benjamin Matheson (London: Palgrave Macmillan 2017), 41–57.

2 See further, on the double nature of Heracles, Algis Uzdavinys, *Philosophy as a Rite of Rebirth from Ancient Egypt to Neoplatonism* (Westbury and Wiltshire: Prometheus Trust 2008), 28–9.

3 See John Heath, 'Blood for the Dead: Homeric Ghosts Speak Up', *Hermes* 133, no. 4 (2005): 389–400.

4 See James Hillman, *The Dream and the Underworld* (New York: Harper: New York, 1979), 56.

5   See Jonathan S. Burgess, *The Death and Afterlife of Achilles* (Baltimore: Johns Hopkins Press, 2009), 78–110 and Anthony T. Edwards, 'Achilles in the Underworld: *Iliad, Odyssey,* and *Aethiopis*', *Greek, Roman, and Byzantine Studies* 26 (1985): 215–27.
6   Siegfried Morenz, *Egyptian Religion,* trans. Ann E. Keep (New York: Cornell University Press, 1973 [1960]), 151, after the Leiden Hymns (thirteenth century BCE).
7   R. Drew Griffith, 'Sailing to Elysium: Menelaus' Afterlife (*Odyssey* 4.561-569) and Egyptian Religion', *Phoenix* 55 (2001): 213–43, 215, after Pyramid Text utterances (twenty-fourth century BCE).
8   Aristotle, *De Partibus Animalium* 656a7 in Aristotle, *Parts of Animals: Movement of Animals. Progression of Animals*, trans. A. L. Peck and E. S. Forster. Loeb Classical Library 323 (Cambridge, MA: Harvard University Press, 1937); see Stephen R. L. Clark, *Aristotle's Man: Speculations upon Aristotelian Anthropology* (Oxford: Clarendon Press 1975), 28–9.
9   Aristotle, *Physics* 2.198b29ff in Aristotle, *Physics, Volume I: Books 1-4*, trans. P. H. Wicksteed and F. M. Cornford. Loeb Classical Library 228 (Cambridge, MA: Harvard University Press, 1957).
10 Empedocles, 31B8DK in Robin Waterfield, ed., *The First Philosophers: The Presocratics and Sophists* (New York: Oxford University Press, 2000), 145.
11 Empedocles, 31B112DK in Waterfield, *First Philosophers,* 140.
12 Hesiod, *Theogony,* in Hesiod, *Theogony. Works and Days. Testimonia*, ed. and trans. Glenn W. Most, 775–806. Loeb Classical Library 57 (Cambridge, MA: Harvard University Press, 2018); Günter Zuntz, *Persephone: Three Essays on Religion and Thought in Magna Graecia* (Oxford: Clarendon Press, 1971), 267.
13 Empedocles, 31B146DK in Waterfield, *First Philosophers,* 141.
14 Empedocles, 31B127DK in Waterfield, *First Philosophers,* 141.
15 Pliny, 7.174 in *Natural History Volume I: Books 1-2*, ed. H. Rackham. Loeb Classical Library 330 (Cambridge, MA: Harvard University Press, 1938).
16 Diogenes Laërtius, *Lives and Opinions of Eminent Philosophers. Volume II: Books 6-10*, trans. R. D. Hicks. Loeb Classical Library 185 (Cambridge, MA: Harvard University Press, 1925).
17 See Ioan Petru Culianu, *Psychanodia I: A Survey of the Evidence Concerning the Ascension of the Soul and Its Relevance* (Leiden: Brill 1983), 37; see also J. D. P. Bolton, *Aristeas of Proconnesus* (Oxford: Oxford University Press, 1962).
18 See Giannis Stamatellos, 'Plotinus on Transmigration: A Reconsideration', *Journal of Ancient Philosophy* 7 (2013): 49–64.
19 Plato *Republic* 10.614b-621b.
20 Plotinus, *Ennead* III.2 [47] in Plotinus, *Ennead, Volume III*, trans. A. H. Armstrong. Loeb Classical Library 442 (Cambridge, MA: Harvard University Press, 1967), 17, 45–53.

21 Empedocles DK31B117 in Waterfield, *First Philosophers*, 154.
22 According to Xenophanes of Colophon, DK21B7 in Laërtius *Lives*, 8.36. For a less literal interpretation of the story see my essay 'Can Animals Be Our Friends?', *Philosophy Now* 67 (May/June 2008): 13–16.
23 Plotinus, *Ennead* IV.3 [27] in Plotinus, *Ennead, Volume IV*, trans. A. H. Armstrong. Loeb Classical Library 443 (Cambridge, MA: Harvard University Press, 1984), 18, 19–24.
24 Aristotle, *Protrepticus* in W. D. Ross, ed., *Works of Aristotle. Vol. 12: Select Fragments* (London: Oxford University Press, 1952), 42 [fr.10c]; see Gábor Betegh, *The Derveni Papyrus: Cosmology, Theology and Interpretation* (Cambridge: Cambridge University Press 2004), 284.
25 Plotinus, *Ennead* VI.5 [23] in Plotinus, *Ennead VI: 1–5*, trans. A. H. Armstrong. Loeb Classical Library 445 (Cambridge, MA: Harvard University Press, 1988), 1 (my emphasis).
26 Plotinus, *Ennead* VI.7 [38], 15, 25–16, 3 (my emphasis).
27 Plotinus, *Ennead* IV.8 [6], 1.
28 Aristotle, *De Historia Animalium*, 5.551a3.
29 Plotinus, *Ennead* IV.3 [27], 4, 26–30. The notion is given an explicit science fiction shape in Eric Frank Russell, *Sentinels from Space* (New York: Bouregy & Curl, Inc. 1952).
30 Plato, *Phaedo* 107a-115a in Plato, *Euthyphro. Apology. Crito. Phaedo*, trans. and ed. Christopher Emlyn-Jones and William Preddy. Loeb Classical Library 36 (Cambridge, MA: Harvard University Press, 2017); Plato, *Republic* 10.614-21 in Plato, *Republic. Volume 2: Books 6-10*, ed. and trans. Christopher Emlyn-Jones and William Preddy. Loeb Classical Library 276 (Cambridge, MA: Harvard University Press, 2013); Plato, *Gorgias* 523a-525a in Plato, *Lysis Symposium: Georgias*, trans. W. R. M. Lamb. Loeb Classical Library 166 (Cambridge, MA: Harvard University Press, 1925).
31 Proclus, *Elements of Theology*, 2nd edn, ed. E. R. Dodds (Oxford: Clarendon Press 1963), 307n2; on Proposition 209 see also J. M. Rist, *Plotinus: The Road to Reality* (Cambridge: Cambridge University Press 1967), 190–1; see also Plotinus, *Ennead* IV.3 [27], 15; II.3 [52], 9, 7ff.
32 Plotinus, *Ennead* I.6 [1], 8, 16–28: Plotinus, *Enneads, Volume I*, trans. A. H. Armstrong. Loeb Classical Library 440 (Cambridge, MA: Harvard University Press, 1969); see John Finamore, *Iamblichus and the Theory of the Vehicle of the Soul*. American Philological Association (Chico: Scholars Press, 1985). Uzdavinys, *Philosophy as a Rite of Rebirth from Ancient Egypt to Neoplatonism*, 85 notes, after a New Kingdom writing, *The Book of the Heavenly Cow* (c. 1350 BCE), that Egyptian initiates 'must ascend on the back of the heavenly Cow (a sort of *okhema*) and reach the intelligible realm'!

33 Plotinus, *Ennead* VI.4 [22].14, 18ff.
34 Plato, *Apology* 40c5-41c7.
35 Porphyry, *Life of Plotinus* 22 in Plotinus, *Ennead* I, 34, 45, 53–7.
36 Plotinus, *Ennead* IV.8 [6].1.
37 Plutarch fr.165 (Stobaeus 4.52.49), cited in Alan F. Segal, *Life after Death: A History of the Afterlife* (New York: Doubleday, 2004), 217.
38 Uzdavinys, *Philosophy as a Rite of Rebirth from Ancient Egypt to Neoplatonism*, 21.
39 Erika Hayasaki, 'In a Perpetual Present', *Wired Magazine* (April 2016): http://www.wired.com/2016/04/susie-mckinnon-autobiographical-memory-sdam/.
40 Marinus, *Life of Proclus*, in *Neoplatonic Saints: The Lives of Plotinus and Proclus by their Students*, ed. M. J. Edwards (Liverpool: Liverpool University Press 2000), 89.
41 See Oliver Sacks, *Anthropologist on Mars: Seven Paradoxical Tales* (New York: Alfred A. Knopf, 1995) and *Musicophilia: Tales of Music and the Brain*, 2nd edn (New York: Vintage Books, 2008), 371–86.
42 Pindar *Pythian* 8.95ff in Pindar, *Olympian Odes: Pythian Odes*, ed. and trans. William H. Race. Loeb Classical Library 56 (Cambridge, MA: Harvard University Press, 1997).
43 Plotinus, *Ennead* I.6 [1].7, 34–5.
44 Plotinus, *Ennead* I.6 [1].8, 16–28. For further details of the Plotinian or Neo-Platonic way see Stephen R. L. Clark, *Plotinus: Myth, Metaphor and Philosophical Practice* (Chicago: University of Chicago Press 2016).
45 Eckhart Tolle, *The Power of Now* (London: Hodder & Stoughton, 2005 [1999]), 1.

Bibliography

Aristotle. *Parts of Animals: Movement of Animals. Progression of Animals*. Translated by A. L. Peck and E. S. Forster. Loeb Classical Library 323. Cambridge, MA: Harvard University Press, 1937.

Aristotle. *Physics. Volume I: Books 1-4*. Translated by P. H. Wicksteed and F. M. Cornford. Loeb Classical Library 228. Cambridge, MA: Harvard University Press, 1957.

Betegh, Gábor. *The Derveni Papyrus: Cosmology, Theology and Interpretation*. Cambridge: Cambridge University Press 2004.

Bolton, J. D. P. *Aristeas of Proconnesus*. Oxford: Oxford University Press, 1962.

Burgess, Jonathan S. *The Death and Afterlife of Achilles*. Baltimore: Johns Hopkins Press, 2009.

Clark, Stephen R. L. *Aristotle's Man: Speculations upon Aristotelian Anthropology*. Oxford: Clarendon Press, 1975.

Clark, Stephen R. L. 'Can Animals be our Friends?' *Philosophy Now* 67 (May/June 2008): 13–16.

Clark, Stephen R. L. 'Classical Mediterranean Conceptions of the Afterlife'. In *The Palgrave of the Afterlife*. Edited by Yujin Nagasawa and Benjamin Matheson, 41–57. London: Palgrave Macmillan, 2017.

Clark, Stephen R. L. *Plotinus: Myth, Metaphor and Philosophical Practice*. Chicago: University of Chicago Press, 2016.

Culianu, Ioan Petru. *Psychanodia I: A Survey of the Evidence Concerning the Ascension of the Soul and Its Relevance*. Leiden: Brill, 1983.

Edwards, Anthony T. 'Achilles in the Underworld: *Iliad, Odyssey*, and *Aethiopis*'. *Greek, Roman, and Byzantine Studies* 26 (1985): 215–27.

Edwards, Mark J., ed. *Neoplatonic Saints: The Lives of Plotinus and Proclus by their Students*. Liverpool: Liverpool University Press, 2000.

Finamore, John. *Iamblichus and the Theory of the Vehicle of the Soul*. American Philological Association. Chico: Scholars Press, 1985.

Griffith, R. Drew. 'Sailing to Elysium: Menelaus' Afterlife (Odyssey 4.561-569) and Egyptian Religion'. *Phoenix* 55 (2001): 213–43.

Hayasaki, Erika. 'In a Perpetual Present'. *Wired Magazine* (April 2016): http://www.wired.com/2016/04/susie-mckinnon-autobiographical-memory-sdam/

Heath, John. 'Blood for the Dead: Homeric Ghosts Speak Up'. *Hermes* 133, no. 4 (2005): 389–400.

Hesiod, *Theogony* in Hesiod, *Theogony. Works and Days. Testimonia*. Edited and translated by Glenn W. Most. Loeb Classical Library 57. Cambridge, MA: Harvard University Press, 2018.

Hillman, James. *The Dream and the Underworld*. New York: Harper: New York, 1979.

Laërtius, Diogenes. *Lives and Opinions of Eminent Philosophers. Volume II: Books 6–10*. Translated by R. D. Hicks. Loeb Classical Library 185. Cambridge, MA: Harvard University Press, 1925.

Morenz, Siegfried. *Egyptian Religion*. Translated by Ann E. Keep. New York: Cornell University Press 1973 [1960].

Pindar. *Olympian Odes: Pythian Odes*. Edited and translated by William H. Race. Loeb Classical Library 56. Cambridge, MA: Harvard University Press, 1997.

Plotinus. *Ennead, Volume I: Porphyry on the Life of Plotinus. Ennead I*. Translated by A. H. Armstrong. Loeb Classical Library 440. Cambridge, MA: Harvard University Press, 1969

Plotinus. *Ennead, Volume III*. Translated by A. H. Armstrong. Loeb Classical Library 442. Cambridge, MA: Harvard University Press, 1967.

Plotinus. *Ennead, Volume IV*. Translated by A. H. Armstrong. Loeb Classical Library 443. Cambridge, MA: Harvard University Press, 1984.

Plotinus. *Ennead, Volume VI: 1–5*. Translated by A. H. Armstrong. Loeb Classical Library 445. Cambridge, MA: Harvard University Press, 1988.

Plato. *Euthyphro. Apology. Crito. Phaedo*. Edited and translated by Christopher Emlyn-Jones and William Preddy. Loeb Classical Library 36. Cambridge, MA: Harvard University Press, 2017.

Plato. *Lysis Sumposium. Georgias*. Translated by W. R. M. Lamb. Loeb Classical Library 166. Cambridge, MA: Harvard University Press, 1925.

Plato. *Republic. Volume 2: Books 6–10*. Edited and translated by Christopher Emlyn-Jones and William Preddy. Loeb Classical Library 276. Cambridge, MA: Harvard University Press, 2013.

Proclus. *Elements of Theology*, 2nd edn. Edited by E. R. Dodds. Oxford: Clarendon Press 1963.

Rist, J. M. *Plotinus: The Road to Reality*. Cambridge: Cambridge University Press 1967.

Ross, W. D., ed. *Works of Aristotle. Vol. 12: Select Fragments*. London: Oxford University Press, 1952.

Russell, Eric Frank. *Sentinels from Space*. New York: Bouregy & Curl, Inc. 1952.

Sacks, Oliver. *Anthropologist on Mars: Seven Paradoxical Tales*. New York: Alfred A. Knopf, 1995.

Sacks, Oliver. *Musicophilia: Tales of Music and the Brain*. 2nd edn. New York: Vintage Books, 2008.

Segal, Alan F. *Life after Death: A History of the Afterlife*. New York: Doubleday 2004.

Stamatellos, Giannis. 'Plotinus on Transmigration: A Reconsideration', *Journal of Ancient Philosophy* 7 (2013): 49–64.

Tolle, Eckhart. *The Power of Now*. London: Hodder & Stoughton, 2005 [1999].

Waterfield, Robin, ed. *The First Philosophers: The Presocratics and Sophists*. New York: Oxford University Press, 2000.

Zuntz, Günter. *Persephone: Three Essays on Religion and Thought in Magna Graecia*. Oxford: Clarendon Press, 1971.

2

Confucian philosophy as a universal approach to integrated living: A contemporary interpretation

Geir Sigurðsson

Introduction

Asian traditions of thought have tended to be regarded by Western philosophers as parochial, that is, too restricted to their particular cultural traditions and too dependent upon idiosyncratic world views to merit serious attention by Westerners, who, on the contrary, are presumed to be fully capable of producing valid universal thought structures. For instance, in a preface to his 1972 publication *Mysticism and Morality* Arthur C. Danto argued that the 'fantastic architectures of Oriental thought … are open to our study and certainly our admiration, but they are not for us to inhabit'.[1] In the very same year, Herbert Fingarette also published a book, incidentally in the very same book series, that became and continues to be quite influential: *Confucius – The Secular as Sacred*. Fingarette advanced the exact opposite view, namely, as he argues in his preface, that 'Confucius can be a teacher to us today – a major teacher, not one who merely gives us a slightly exotic perspective on the ideas already current'.[2] These two contrasting views that of parochialism and of universalism are the two polar opposites between which Euro-American explorations of Chinese and perhaps in particular Confucian thought have oscillated during the last four decades.

In this chapter, I intend to show that Confucianism can indeed be interpreted, formulated and developed as a universal philosophy that can not only be learnt *about* but also and more importantly be learnt *from*. This important distinction of approaches, that of learning 'about' and of learning 'from', is originally taken from Gottfried Wilhelm Leibniz (1646–1716) in his various writings on China, where he claims that while European civilization has scientific, technological and even metaphysical advantages over China, the Chinese are superior 'in practical philosophy, that is, in the precepts of ethics and politics adapted to the present life and use of mortals'.³ Thus, Leibniz is among the first canonical philosophers of the European tradition to claim that Chinese thought and philosophy should not merely be an object of scholarly curiosity, but ought to be studied because of what they have to offer.

My focus will be on the Confucian conceptions of education and self-cultivation, both of which can arguably also be understood as the central endeavours of Confucian philosophy. However, a meaningful discussion of this philosophy also requires that it be placed within a broader cosmological framework with an appeal to contemporary thinkers. My exposition will follow in three necessarily broad strokes: Firstly, I will briefly outline the cosmological or, as I prefer to call it, 'daological' view against the background of which the medieval developments of Confucian philosophy eventually emerge, and argue that this cosmology can be made compatible with contemporary scientific conceptions of world-operations. Secondly, I will provide an overview of the Confucian understanding of education as a life-long process of humanization through the adoption and appropriation of traditional modes of practice. Thirdly, I shall indicate how Confucianism, despite having a strong commitment to the 'relational self' emanating from its cosmological background, gives rise to a certain kind of 'individualism', albeit one rather different from what we usually understand with the term. In this sense I show that the final aims of Confucian philosophy may be rather more individual-centred than has been thought.

One objective here is to show how the seemingly archaic and thus culture-specific Confucian customs, often called 'ritual propriety' (*li* 禮), function as pedagogical forms of behaviour and gestures that entail both the interpersonal respect necessary for successful associated living and facilitating growth and development in the individual, while always socially embedded, human being, or, to use Henry Rosemont's and Roger Ames's much more suitable term, 'human becoming'.⁴ Such devices can really be found in any given culture, but the Confucian thinkers realized their importance for the construction of a healthy, vibrant and well-functioning society. Thus, I argue, the Confucian approach is universal in the sense that it can be applied to any culture or society – even without the assumption of any fixed valuations or dogmas that are restricted to a circumscribed Confucian world and thus 'not for us to inhabit'.

Due to its long history and diverse manifestations, Confucianism is notoriously difficult to define. Some scholars have even coined the term in its plural form, 'Confucianisms', to emphasize the wide conceptual diversity in the history of Confucianism.⁵ This is one of the more important reasons why the attitude to Confucianism can likewise be so varied. Many tend to understand Confucianism on the basis of its status as the official ideology in China during the Ming and Qing dynasties. In this chapter, however, Confucianism is first and foremost understood as a philosophy or a philosophical stream of thought building upon certain ideas or principles of what constitutes the good life and the good society. Moreover, my approach assumes a hermeneutic stance, one that allows and even calls for a certain flexibility in interpretation according to the circumstances to which it is meant to apply. I have argued elsewhere that such stance is in fact quite in line with the approach to tradition taken by at least the early Confucians, where, while certainly foundational in some sense, tradition is understood as a path to be constantly forged rather than as a place to be discovered once and for all.⁶ Confucianism in this understanding is therefore a historically conscious endeavour to continuously revise and re-evaluate the more concrete aspects of its own teachings. In this sense, it engages in a continuous overcoming of itself, which at the same time entails its constant reformation. This approach has direct bearing on interpreting the role of the individual person in Confucianism, and we shall therefore return to this topic in Section 'Confucian "individualism"'.

The daological framework

What role does ontology or cosmology play in our lives? At first, it might seem to be insignificant. After all, the makeup of the world and our status within it are philosophical issues that we do not often raise in everyday conversation. In some parts of the world, however, we often talk about the weather, not only because we are desperately looking for a possible discussion topic but because the weather has such strong impact on our everyday life, the scope of possible activities and our general emotional condition. In other words, the weather affects our emotional well-being in daily life in a most direct and felt manner. But however vague our beliefs may be about our ultimate cosmic status, it would be perfunctory to dismiss the impact of cosmological affairs on our daily lives. With their lack of immediacy, the wider cosmic picture may not be an everyday issue of concern. Nevertheless, while we might not always and even rarely be fully aware of it, the cosmological context provides the deepest ground on which we stand in all our valuations, significant decisions and, indeed, general emotional attitude to life and world. We only need to think of the vast philosophical, religious and existential consequences of the paradigm shift from a geocentric to a heliocentric world view in Western culture during the post-Renaissance period to fathom the extent of the impact of our cosmological world view on the human being's self-understanding.[7] Immanuel Kant's philosophy, for instance, is an attempt to construct a metaphysics consistent with both the then rather new scientific world view emerging from Newton's theories and the Enlightenment ethical outlook grounded on universal reason. The following passage from Kant's *Critique of Practical Reason* is arguably his most celebrated one:

> Two things fill the mind with ever new and increasing admiration and awe, the more often and steadily reflection is occupied with them: the starry heaven above me and the moral law within me. Neither of them need I seek and merely suspect as if shrouded in obscurity or rapture beyond my own horizon; I see them before me and connect them immediately with my existence.[8]

We may not agree with Kant's own particular version of how the world should be conceptualized. But among his most acute insights was the inevitable reliance of ethics on metaphysics. How we think of and approach our co-existence with other human beings, with other living beings in the world and our environment at large will largely depend on our understanding of the totality of things and their correlation with each other. There is a certain consistency between how we lead our mundane life and how we comprehend the world as a totality, even though that comprehension may be vague or liminal.

While Confucius himself may not have paid much attention to issues beyond the social context, his followers seem to have realized that the Confucian social and ethical teachings would receive weightier accreditation if provided with a cosmological dimension. The *Zhongyong* 中庸, a short but vastly influential text that was to become a part of the Confucian canon, begins by stating that human beings have a natural inborn propensity to improve themselves through education and self-cultivation – a normative propensity received by *tian* 天 or nature as a whole.[9] Mengzi 孟子, the second great Confucian, also argues that our natural propensity contains the seeds or sprouts of the most sophisticated Confucian 'virtues' of wisdom (*zhi* 知), appropriateness (*yi* 義), propriety (*li* 禮) and humanness (*ren* 仁).[10] In other words, it is due to being an integral part of the holistically conceived natural makeup that human beings have a normative social task and function.

These early Confucian explorations, seeking to establish clear links between everyday living and the natural realm as a whole, were later assimilated with and cemented in broader cosmological elaborations largely based upon the ancient

Classic of Changes (*Yijing* 易經), but enriched and expanded by a number of Daoist and even Buddhist insights. Importantly, the aim was not to come up with some kind of 'objective' description of the cosmos or the universe, but a description that was both useful and integrated the human being in the cosmos as a meaningful part of it. This particular hermeneutic approach is what Tu Weiming has termed an 'anthropocosmic unity' between the human and the natural.[11] A different formulation of essentially the same feature is what Cheng Chung-ying refers to as the 'onto-hermeneutic' philosophical approach.[12] This ongoing elaboration of the human-cosmic dimension eventually took form as a more or less consistent system with Zhu Xi 朱熹 in the twelfth century. I propose using the neologism 'daology' for this system instead of the usual cosmology, as daology specifies that this constantly evolving whole is operating within a relational yin-yang explanatory framework. For the purposes of this chapter, it suffices to characterize the daological system in the following three main ways:

First of all, reality is a ceaseless process of change, an 'uninterrupted cosmogony' (*ununterbrochene Kosmogonie*) as Gudula Linck has intriguingly put it.[13] The consequences of acknowledging a world in constant flux are wide-ranging. Among the most important is that fixed principles, laws or anything comparable to Platonic forms are excluded from the outset as a logical impossibility. It is only change itself that does not change. Certainly, some level of regularity, continuity and order in terms of repetition of similar occurrences can be discerned in the process, but nothing can be absolutely 100 per cent certain. Hence, the world cannot be conceived as deterministic, not even as one containing necessary natural laws but will at most be explained through tendencies with various degrees of likelihood.

Secondly, everything in this world is relational and all things interpenetrate one another, because there is no unchangeable essence constituting things. Hence, they can only be conceived as what they are by virtue of their relations with other things. Epistemologically speaking, this means that they can only be approached and known from perspectives. There is only perspectival knowledge and understanding. This entails that any understanding of or insight into another thing/phenomenon is a result of the unique relations between knower and known. Daologically, however, relational existence means that everything affects everything else. The world is a web of relations whose understanding excludes reductionism. One change will affect all the others, if in most cases only minimally, but nothing is perfectly isolated and stays intact in the process of changes.

Thirdly, and consequently, the natural and the human are intimately related as a complementary and, in a certain sense, to follow Tu Weiming, moral unity within an anthropocosmic scheme that sees the human dimension as an integral part of cosmic processes. A common portrayal of this union in the Confucian tradition is the tripartite relationship between 'heaven' (*tian* 天), 'earth' (*di* 地) and the 'human' (*ren* 人), indicating some sort of mutual protection or responsibility that secures the preservation of all. A description of the relations as 'intimate' implies a level of emotional attachment modelled on familial relations but extended to the natural realm, other living beings and even phenomena traditionally held to be inanimate. Such a wide extension of intimacy culminates in the personal cultivation of the consummate person (*ren* 仁). In the *Western Inscription* (*Ximing* 西銘), the Neo-Confucian thinker Zhang Zai 張載 (1020–1077) formulated an expression of this inherent relationality and consequent ontological responsibility that could be taken as a kind of Neo-Confucian manifesto:

> Yang is the father; yin is the mother. And I, this tiny thing, dwell enfolded in Them. Hence, what fills Heaven and Earth is my body, and what rules Heaven and Earth is my nature. The people are my siblings, and all living things are my companions. My Ruler is the eldest son of my parents, and his ministers are his retainers. To respect those great in years is the way to 'treat the elderly as elderly should be treated'. To be kind to the orphaned and the weak is the way to 'treat the young as young should be treated'. The sage harmonizes with Their Virtue; the worthy receive what is most excellent from Them. All under Heaven who are tired, crippled, exhausted, sick, brotherless, childless, widows or widowers – all are my siblings who are helpless and have no one else to appeal to. To care for them at such times is the practice of a good son. To be delighted and without care, because trusting Them, is the purest filial piety. … Riches, honor, good fortune, and abundance shall enrich my life. Poverty, humble station, care, and sorrow shall discipline me to fulfillment. Living, I compliantly serve Them; dead, I shall be at peace.[14]

An ontology emanating from quantum physics, the most accurate and up-to-date scientific delineation of how reality functions, is entirely in line with at least the first two of the three characteristics outlined earlier, namely indeterminism and inherent relationality. The physicist and philosopher Karen Barad has convincingly shown how this world view is inevitable if quantum physics were taken seriously and translated into proper ontology.

Quantum physics establishes that wave-particle duality, which implies that things behave differently depending on circumstances, is a universal feature of matter. One implication of this is that a Newtonian kind of causal determinism cannot be sustained. But there is more. Basing her discussion primarily on

Niels Bohr's theories, Barad argues that quantum physics contradicts some fundamental modernist assumptions about our relations with reality: first of all, representationalism, that is, the idea that words and objects, or meaning and matter, have clearly separable spheres of being and that 'objective' reality can be represented with words without difficulties. There are no individually determinate entities to be discovered. All we have, Barad argues, are phenomena continuously arising from the intra-action (as distinct from 'interaction') of 'objects' and 'measuring agencies', and these phenomena are the only available conceptual schemes involving determinate boundaries and properties.[15] Meaning arises when specific 'agential intra-actions' take place, determining the boundaries and properties of the 'components' of phenomena. In this case, 'particular material articulations of the world become meaningful'.[16] In other words, meaning arises necessarily as a co-creation between human and world, but there is no objective reality to be 'discovered' as such.

Secondly, quantum physics undermines metaphysical individualism or individual atomism, that is, the belief that the world is composed of individual and clearly separated units containing certain inner properties or substances with nonrelational properties. In this regard, Barad quotes the physicist N. David Mermin who said: 'Correlations have physical reality; that which they correlate does not.'[17] Quantum physics thus leads to a relational ontology. Barad suggests that 'phenomena' should be taken as the primary unit, but 'phenomena are the ontological inseparability of intra-acting "agencies" … they are the basic units of existence'.[18] This also entails the notion of 'quantum entanglement', giving rise to a profoundly complex relationality between the various phenomena in the world.

Thirdly, and following from the earlier inferences, quantum mechanics reveals that a distinct separation between 'observer' and 'observed', between 'subject' and 'object', is not possible. This leads Barad to work towards a 'posthumanist' approach according to which the human perspective is merely one out of infinite possible interpretations of reality, and not at all a non-natural process. On the contrary, while humanism focuses on the human as something exceptional, Barad's 'posthumanist elaboration of Bohr's account understands the human not as a supplemental system around which the theory revolves but as a natural phenomenon that needs to be accounted for within the terms of this relational ontology'.[19] In other words, this vision requires a breakdown of the classic nature-human, or nature-nurture, dualist dichotomy, understanding human beings and their actions as perfectly natural phenomena.

Certainly, the ontology arising from quantum physics does not involve anything resembling a teleological scheme or 'natural intention', but, strictly speaking, nor does Confucian philosophy. Understanding the human being's role as co-creator of heaven or nature is a further philosophical elaboration of human beings as natural 'products' who have certain capacities that enable them to continue nature's continuous creative process in a constructive manner. To use Barad's formulation, it is therefore an instance of the meaning arising from the intra-action of 'objects' and 'measuring agencies', and thus provides the human being with both a place and a role in the world as a conscious and potentially rational creature whose task it is to cultivate his capacities to become a consummate human being – one that takes both the continuous changes and inherent relationality into account in her decisions and actions.

Education and humanization

Viewed holistically, the Confucian understanding of education is one of life-long learning. It rests upon the assumption that we are born with certain capacities to improve ourselves as human becomings – and that the process by which we endeavour to improve ourselves has no fixed or determinate end goal. Xunzi begins his voluminous work by observing that 'learning can never come to an end'.[20] The *Analects* likewise begins with the well-known rhetorical question, 'Isn't it a joy to learn and then apply what one has learned?'[21] In this section, I shall discuss the basis, or the roots, of such learning and what that learning entails.

The roots of learning in Confucianism are essentially twofold: on the one hand, our natural capacities, and on the other, our cultural tradition or civilization. These are not dualist categories. The cultural tradition is understood as being an outgrowth of, and therefore continuous with, the processes of nature. There is nothing mysterious about such an outlook. Being natural products, we are gifted with certain capacities to excel as human becomings. Among such capacities are reason or understanding, moral judgement, the ability to communicate meaningfully both orally and through physical gestures, affection and love, as well as more specific capacities such as empathy, trustworthiness and loyalty. These are my loose formulations of the core Confucian 'virtues' of *zhi* 知, *yi* 義, *li* 禮, *ren* 仁, *shu* 恕, *xin* 信 and *zhong* 忠, while of course there are many others. Properly nurtured, mutually coordinated and thus reinforced, all these abilities contribute to an individual's successful integration in a community. Such an integration requires first of all the adoption and understanding of the core values, meanings and, indeed, facts (historical and others) pertaining to the cultural tradition. However, in order to be truly successful, the individual, after having matured, also needs to have developed and be able to apply critical and creative powers to facilitate the continuous adaptation of tradition to the circumstances and direction of the incessantly evolving times. Confucius expresses this twofold task with his saying: 'Learning without reflection results in confusion, reflection without learning results in peril.'[22] In other words, if we restrict ourselves to the first task in our life, that of appropriating the tradition, we lose ourselves in some kind of dogmatic preservationism, which is not at all what Confucius recommends. He warns in the *Zhongyong* that those who are 'born into the present age and yet return to the ways of the past will cause themselves misfortune'.[23] In the *Analects* he remarks that 'one who realizes the new by reviewing the old can be called a proper teacher'.[24] In other words, we should above all avoid a dogmatic attitude to tradition. On the other hand, a firm foothold in tradition is nevertheless vital in order to have a clear sense of who we are and where we are heading. Thus, empty ideas that are incapable of being grasped, because they are too far removed from the semantic web in which we are inevitably entangled, will cause us alienation, a weak sense of identity and even lead to a dangerous kind of anomie.

Learning can also be divided into two main phases more or less corresponding to childhood and adulthood. The former is characterized by *xue* 學 and *jiao* 教, learning and teaching (or rather being taught), indicating that we are being guided by others through the process of gaining increased maturity, understanding and social sense. The latter, however, is primarily described as personal cultivation, *xiushen* 修身 or *xiuji* 修己, which refers to the path of personal growth that we need to forge by ourselves, though needless to say in association with others, and is essentially our own responsibility. From a daological point of view, striving to forge that path is indeed our sacred duty as human becomings.

As already mentioned, learning is and should be understood as a never-ending process. This follows logically from the daological scheme that excludes essences and substances, one that demands that things be approached and understood from unique perspectives that are constantly shifting over the course of time. Epistemologically, therefore, instead of formulating absolute universals, one may make use of limited generalities derived from experience and history as helpful but never rigid guidelines for making sense of experience and mastering circumstances. Certainly, there are discernible patterns in reality that can be fathomed, but an openness to novelty must always be kept in mind. Thus, we might say, an inevitable 'gap' between understanding and reality must be accepted, one that can only be bridged through a creative response taking into account both the generalities and the specificities of the situation. Such a response is a cultivated sense, a sophisticated resonance (*xin* 心 or *gan* 感) that is the ripening fruit of thoughtful experience and appreciation of the roots of human association.[25] The notion of 'cultivated sense' as the crux of what education means is intriguingly close to Hans-Georg Gadamer's understanding of the essence of *Bildung* as 'a general and communal sense' (*ein allgemeiner und gemeinschaftlicher Sinn*).[26]

What methods do Confucians propose to appropriate tradition and stimulate a critical and creative attitude? For the former task, the *li*-customs are the primary tools or techniques to absorb and indeed *embody* tradition. *Li* are certainly presented as stylized or ritualized practices to be emulated and learnt, not unlike the complex forms one needs to learn when practising martial arts. In this sense they are certainly formalized. But if they are considered primarily as pedagogical methods, this formalized aspect becomes much less problematic. It is instructive to consult, in this context, Pierre Bourdieu, who speaks of body hexis, individual habits or characteristics, as the embodiment of the habitus, the system of both structured and structuring dispositions within a culture. Habitus 'is constituted in practice [i.e. through hexis] and is always oriented through practical functions'.[27] Furthermore, 'The body believes in what it plays at: it weeps if it mimes grief. It does not represent what it performs, it does not memorize the past, it enacts the past, bringing it back to life. What is "learned by body" is not something that one has, like knowledge that can be brandished, but something that one is.'[28] Thus, body hexis informs deportment, the way and style in which people 'carry themselves' in terms of stance, gait, gesture, etc. This is fully in line with Confucius's remark that 'without studying *li* 禮, one will be unable to take a stance (*li* 立)'.[29] For Bourdieu and Confucius, the body is a mnemonic device that absorbs the basics of culture in a process of learning or socializing. It is through the physical experience of bodily action that the habitus, the socially constituted basis for practices, is inculcated in a way more effective than through oral teaching. Through the performance of (formal) actions, one not only 'learns' the tradition by constructing a framework of meaningful action, but also how to make such actions one's own, to personalize them. The process parallels the above-mentioned forms in martial arts. Initially they are learnt through constant repetition, perhaps even ad nauseam, but eventually they will be appropriated as personalized responses to one's surroundings – as long as one does not give them up somewhere on the way. Generally speaking, then, ritualistic behaviour is a form of learning in much the same way as certain technical training must take place before one acquires a truly profound sense for the task at hand, and can strictly speaking let go of the technical training. With regard to *li*, a person who has successfully internalized the spirit of a certain ritualistic practice is capable of applying it spontaneously when responding to new circumstances by adapting its primary or initially 'stylized' movements to these very circumstances.

It should be noted that the universalist model I am proposing does not suggest a transportation of the *li*-customs specific to ancient China to a different culture. Some of them certainly can be adopted, but the point is not to bring in the Chinese *li* in their cultural specificity – for example, those described throughout the *Book of Rites* (*Liji* 禮記), the *Book of Etiquette and Rites* (*Yili* 儀禮) and others. Rather, it is the formal understanding of the customs, their function and their pedagogical impact in one's own cultural milieu that matters. *Li* represent the cultural tradition as adopted formal or semi-formal behavioural patterns or guidelines that emanate from it and therefore express it. They are the social grammar that enable people to make sense of social situations or the 'footwear' that protects them from spraining themselves when entering the moral and social sphere.[30] As Xunzi puts it: '*Li* is that by which people find footing. When they lose this footing, they are sure to stumble and fall, sink and drown. The negligence of a small matter can result in great disorder. This is what *li* is all about.'[31] There are numerous interpersonal customs in various Western traditions that can be formulated and applied in a manner comparable to *li*. Their increased formalization and explicit 'inculcation' would, I suggest, have a beneficial impact on both individual and society as long as the critical and creative attitude that their mastery requires is not left out of the picture – and to which I shall now turn.

Confucian 'individualism'

While continuity in tradition and culture is important, such continuity entails that they must be constantly revised and reinterpreted in light of the novel circumstances arising in the constant transformation of the world. And this revision and interpretation can only be done by us as individuals, as Confucius himself emphasized: 'Persons are able to broaden the way (*dao* 道); the way does not broaden persons.'[32] It is our task to carry the cultural legacy forward, which is precisely what we do when we interpret and apply our traditional or cultural customs appropriately, critically and creatively.

The 'Great Learning' (*Daxue* 大學) chapter of the *Liji* contains the most succinct formulation found in the ancient classics of the human task. Not only does it describe the ideal way to be travelled by a successfully integrated human being, but it also clearly places the burden on the individual that travels it. The individual person is accountable for cultivating himself or herself, to maintain accord within his or her family and to administer his or her state. 'Things and processes have their roots and branches, affairs have their beginnings and ends; understanding such priorities is to align with world operations (*dao* 道).'[33]

Certainly, the individual is neither alone in this task, nor is he or she somehow exerting influence on the social realm from the outside. Self-cultivation is an integrated part of the process of maintaining accord within family and administering the state. Self-cultivation is therefore largely a social process. But without self-cultivation, attempts to maintain accord within the family and administer the state are likely to be unsuccessful. It would be an instance of trying to change something of which oneself is also an integral part – but without intending to change oneself.

Self-cultivation is simultaneously empowerment. The intended 'product' is a *junzi* 君子, a 'princely' individual or an exemplary person, whose experience and wisdom, communicability and openness, social sense and acquired personal charisma provide him or her with the ability to transform the immediate social environment. This personal power is indeed an important part of what Confucianism is all about, but the individual factor tends to be significantly underplayed. Interestingly, this important aspect is brought to light by a most unlikely interpreter of Confucianism, namely Mao Zedong. In his 'Marginal Notes to Friedrich Paulsen's *A System of Ethics*' from 1917 to 1918, he speaks of 'spiritual individualism' (*jingshen zhi geren zhuyi* 精神之個人注意), which largely rests upon classical Confucianism.[34] 'Spiritual individualism' is described by young Mao as a core of the Chinese nation-building project, whereby individuals should focus on their self-development and fulfilment as a stepping stone in the realization of a successful nation.

Mao was influenced by German Idealism and the Enlightenment in seeing the moral law as residing in the rational self. But in his early thought, he expressed an unmistakable Confucian stance in considering the self to be inherently relational and constructed in a close network with other selves, such that self-interest cannot be meaningfully detached from the interests of others. Mao claims that self-interest is the most powerful motivation for action, but

> It does not stop here. It is also of our nature to extend this to helping others. This is one and the same human nature, so working for the interests of others is in

my own self-interest. ... In all times, there are filial sons, faithful widows, loyal ministers, and devoted friends, those who die for love, for their country, for the world, for their ideals – all to benefit their own spirits.³⁵

Further in the 'Marginal Notes' Mao turns to what he called the 'outstanding scholar' (*haojie zhe shi* 豪杰之士), one who 'develops the original nature with which Nature endowed him, and expands upon the best, the greatest of the capacities of his original nature'. The outstanding scholar has a great 'motive power that is the strongest and truest reality, that is the spring that fulfils his character'.³⁶ Such a person relies upon his own judgements, not unlike Confucius who, at the age of seventy, can give himself free rein without overstepping the limits, as Confucius says about himself in the *Analects* 2.4. Mao further wrote on the scholar-hero:

> The great actions of the hero are his own, are the expressions of his motive power, lofty and cleansing, relying on no precedent. His force is like that of a powerful wind arising from a deep gorge, like the irresistible sexual desire for one's lover, a force that will not stop, that cannot be stopped. All obstacles dissolve before him.³⁷

These words echo the description of *junzi* in the *Mengzi* as those who 'transform where they pass by and work wonders where they abide. They belong to the same stream as heaven above and earth beneath.'³⁸ Indeed, Mao indicates that his depiction of the 'scholar-hero' is inspired by Mengzi's writings, for example, his discussion of 'floodlike *qi*' (浩然之氣 *haoran zhi qi*), the inner power, which, if constantly cultivated and properly nourished with integrity or excellence (*de* 德), 'will fill the space between heaven and earth'.³⁹

It is certainly not my intention to provide anything resembling a Maoist-voluntarist reading of Confucianism. But the sheer fact that Mao took inspiration in this regard from early Confucian writings indicates that they do contain an emphasis on the individual as the only possible matrix of action. To be sure, there is no conception of an atomistic individual, but the final responsibility of evaluating and re-evaluating circumstances, customs and traditions nevertheless rests with the individual. Therefore, I argue, the early Confucians made a point of emphasizing the uniqueness arising in every situation, a uniqueness that involves the particular individual in question along with all the others who take part in and are affected by it. Such uniqueness requires creativity and flexibility, a willingness to engage with the situation without having made principled decisions beforehand. Thus, Confucius remarks, after having praised the steadfastness of some excellent individuals of his time, 'but I am different from these, for I have no "must not" or "must".[40] Ge Rongjin, a contemporary interpreter, comments on this passage that 'not to limit oneself to conventional rules, not to imitate that which is conventionally considered permissible, but to be flexible at all times, and thereby adapt to the variations specific to any situation – this is to "have no 'must not' or 'must'".[41] Such creativity appears most clearly in the performance of the *li*-customs. When sufficiently internalized and personalized, they become a mode of creative expression and interaction that are in effect the manifestation of the individual's contribution to the evolution, indeed the expansion, of the cultural tradition. This is what it means that 'persons are able to broaden the way', but not vice versa. While certainly entailing cultivation of one's person, learning through the practice of *li* cannot be regarded as aim-directed in a simple sense as the relations and all that they engender are changing with time along with all those involved. The configuration of these relations as informed by *li* is therefore subject to a continuous process of re-evaluation. Roger T. Ames understands *li* as 'achieved propriety in one's roles and relations'[42] emphasizing that *li* are first and foremost enacted in the dynamic context of interpersonal relations, especially family relations in which most of us learn to take the first steps in how to function as social individuals.

Furthermore, a critical element is at play that necessarily also includes the acting individual. In a perspectival world, a holistic critical attitude is no less self-reflexively critical than critical of the other elements belonging to each circumstance under consideration. This self-reflexive dimension is one that I have called the Confucian 'transformative self-critical attitude'.[43] It refers to an ongoing and never wholly attainable effort to transform oneself to become fully human, and is therefore an indispensable part of the life-long process of learning. It involves recognizing 'one's moral obligations to both oneself and others, obligations that force one to transcend self-centred activity, that from the Confucian perspective create the basis for the problems we all encounter in the world'.[44] Transcending self-centred activity in this sense is no self-effacement, but a pedagogical process in which our initial and exclusive concern for our own ego is gradually overcome to become a concern for other persons.

Confucianism makes clear demands on individuals to engage themselves in constant critical assessment, appraisal and scrutiny of whatever they are dealing with in every single moment. This critical assessment is not merely an ability to draw strictly logical conclusions as it may not always be the right or the best way to proceed. The parties to any given situation, their position, circumstances and last but not least feelings must also be taken into consideration. As mentioned earlier, one tries to develop a sophisticated 'sense' for situations and the configuration of the elements comprising them. Hence, what comes closest to a universal 'principle' is 'empathy' or 'reciprocity', as expressed in the following conversation between Zigong, Confucius's disciple, and the Master himself: 'Zigong asked: "Is there a single expression that can be applied in one's entire life?" The Master responds: "There is 'reciprocity' (*shu* 恕): do not impose on others what you yourself do not want."'[45]

There is ample evidence of the importance of this sort of self-reflexivity in the early Confucian writings. Xunzi states that a wise person, when in the conduct of official duties, 'when he is adequate, considers situations in which he might be inadequate. When progressing smoothly, he reflects on any rash action he might take.'[46] In other words, a wise person must always be vigilant, prepared for changes and, last but not least, maintain himself or herself in the mode of learning or self-improvement. Similarly, Confucius has no patience for those who are unwilling to examine themselves: 'Oh my! I haven't yet met anyone, who, when identifying his own excesses, is ready to critique himself.'[47] In another passage he remarks: 'When meeting excellent people, think how to become equal to them; when meeting unexceptional people, turn inward and examine yourself.'[48] Any experience, any association with others, is approached as an occasion to improve oneself: 'When in the company of only two others, I am certain to find a teacher. Realizing where they excel, I follow them; realizing where they do not excel, I mend my own ways.'[49]

Concluding remarks

To conclude, I argue in this chapter that there is much in the Confucian philosophy, its outlook on human co-existence, the symbiosis between human and nature, and an elegant kind of human living from which all can learn. Confucianism presents a philosophical framework of humanized cohabitation that can easily be approached as a universal model to be adopted by non-Confucian cultures – by and to which, however, it must certainly also be adapted. One of the main reasons why the Confucian model is approachable in this manner is that it asserts no pre-established principles, dogmas or rules, with the possible exception of the exhortation to endeavour to understand and gain a sense for others' points of view or circumstances. The last point, however, is both relational and circumstantial, and can therefore hardly be conceived as a fixed principle in any usual sense of that notion.

As a universal model, Confucianism presents a form of human co-existence that takes its cue from the continuous processes of the natural realm, the human becoming's natural abilities and propensities and, last but not least, the specific cultural traditions in which it operates.[50] It is therefore by no means paradoxical and most definitely even desirable to have different versions of Confucianisms, in this case Confucianisms that are grounded in and permeated by various cultural traditions. As Confucius says in the *Analects*: 'The natural dispositions of people are similar, but their practices make them different.'[51] By 'practices' one may understand the adaptations, skills and customs of social interaction, *li* 禮, that have been formed by people through the course of time in a given habitat with all its specific advantages and challenges – in short, culture or tradition. An indispensable element of the Confucian philosophy is the reliance on and embeddedness in tradition, which at the same time is an entirely realistic approach to generate its continuous formation and adaptation.

In this sense, the universalism of Confucianism is a kind of 'glocal universalism' – one that starts from the here and now but is at the same time far-sighted in terms of both space and time. And while it can be adopted by any culture without that culture having to lose or undermine itself, the first step it would have to take is to acknowledge its inevitable and continuous transformation from within.

Notes

1 Arthur C. Danto, *Mysticism and Morality: Oriental Thought and Moral Philosophy* (New York et al.: Harper & Row, 1972), vii.
2 Herbert Fingarette, *Confucius – The Secular as Sacred* (New York et al.: Harper & Row, 1972), vii.
3 Gottfried Wilhelm Leibniz, 'Preface to the Novissima Sinica (1697/1699)', *Writings on China*, trans. Daniel J. Cook and Henry Rosemont Jr (Chicago and La Salle: Open Court, 1994), 46–7.
4 See, for example, Henry Rosemont Jr, *Against Individualism: A Confucian Rethinking of the Foundations of Morality, Politics, Family, and Religion* (Lanham et al.: Lexington Books, 2015), 93.
5 It has, for instance, been used by the Taiwanese scholar Huang Chun-chieh in the title of his recent book, *East Asian Confucianisms* (2015). See also my '"Confucianisms" and the Confucian Comeback in China', in *Current Issues in Contemporary Chinese and Oriental Studies*, vol. 1, ed. Alex Alexiev et al. (Sofia: University Press 'St. Kliment Ohridski', 2018), 282–90.

6 See my *Confucian Propriety and Ritual Learning: A Philosophical Interpretation* (Albany: State University of New York Press, 2015), especially Introduction and parts of Chapter One, 1–31.

7 Consider Nietzsche's well-known remarks in this regard in his *On the Genealogy of Morals*:

> Haven't the self-diminution of the human being and his will to self-diminution been in steady progress since Copernicus? Alas, gone is the faith in his dignity, his uniqueness, his irreplaceable position in the chain of being – he has become an *animal*, not a metaphorically speaking, but absolutely and unconditionally – he who in his earlier faith was almost God ('child of God', 'God-man') … Since Copernicus the human being seems to have brought himself onto an inclined plane – he's now rolling always faster away from the mid-point. But where to? Into nothingness? Into the '*penetrating* sense of his own nothingness'?

Friedrich Nietzsche, *Zur Genealogie der Moral. Eine Streitschrift*, Kritische Studienausgabe 5 (Munich, Berlin and New York: dtv/de Gruyter, 1988), §3:25, 404. Similar thoughts can be found with Blaise Pascal and Giacomo Leopardi, for example, the latter's remark that through Copernicus's astronomical discoveries he 'debased the idea of the human being'. Giacomo Leopardi, *Zibaldone di pensieri*, vol. 1 (Milan: Mondadori, 1937), 78 [84]. All translations in this chapter are my own unless otherwise noted.

8 Immanuel Kant, *Kritik der praktischen Vernunft*. Werkausgabe VII (Frankfurt am Main: Suhrkamp, 1974), 300 (A 289).

9 *Zhongyong* 中庸, § 1. All classical Chinese writings referred to in this chapter can be accessed in the Chinese Text Project database: www.ctext.org

10 See, for example, *Mengzi* 公孙丑上, 2A.6.

11 Tu borrows the term 'anthropocosmic' from Mircea Eliade, indicating in his understanding the 'mutuality of Heaven and man. By insisting upon a continuous interaction between them, the human way necessitates a transcendent anchorage for the existence of man and an immanent confirmation for the course of Heaven.' Tu Wei-ming, *Centrality and Commonality: An Essay on Confucian Religiousness* (Albany: State University of New York Press, 1989), 9.

12 Or *benti quanshixue* 本體詮釋學, also more recently appearing as onto-generative hermeneutics, which Cheng defines in one place, as a method 'a philosophy interprets reality and life in light of its understanding of a paradigm based on a tradition of texts or sources from a tradition'. Chung-ying Cheng, 'An Onto-Hermeneutic Interpretation of Twentieth-Century Chinese Philosophy: Identity and Vision', in *Contemporary Chinese Philosophy*, ed. Chung-ying Cheng and Nicholas Bunnin (Malden and Oxford: Blackwell, 2002), 385.

13 Gudula Linck, *Yin und Yang: Die Suche nach Ganzheit im chinesischen Denken* (Munich: C.H. Beck, 2001), 14.

14 Zhang Zai, *Western Inscription* 西銘, trans. Bryan van Norden, quoted in Geir Sigurðsson, 'Anthropocosmic Processes in the Anthropocene', *The Bright Dark Ages: Comparative and Connective Perspectives*, ed. Arun Bala and Prasenjit Duara (Leiden and Boston: Brill, 2016), 87–8. The quoted sentences are from the *Mengzi*.
15 Karen Barad, *Meeting the Universe Halfway: Quantum Physics and the Entanglement of Matter and Meaning* (Durham and London: Duke University Press, 2007), 127–8.
16 Ibid., 333.
17 Ibid., 332.
18 Ibid., 333.
19 Ibid., 352.
20 *Xunzi*, 1.1.
21 *Analects*, 1.1.
22 Ibid., 2.15.
23 *Zhongyong*, § 28.
24 *Analects*, 2.11.
25 The classical Chinese *xin* 心 is nowadays usually translated as 'heart-mind', but Mengzi's use of it seems to indicate a certain sense, for example, in his discussion of the four sprouts (*si duan* 四端) in 2A.6. *Gan* 感 is perhaps a clearer expression of such a cultivated sense or resonance, for example, in the *Classic of Changes*: 聖人感人心而天下和平, 'It is by the sage's resonance with people's minds that the entire empire finds peace.' Zhang Zai also summarized his philosophy of cultivation as the *gan zhi dao* 感之道, or way of sense or resonance. See on this Jinhua Jia, 'From Human-Spirit Resonance to Correlative Modes: The Shaping of Chinese Correlative Thinking', *Philosophy East and West* 66, no. 2 (2016): 457.
26 Compare Hans-Georg Gadamer, *Wahrheit und Methode. Grundzüge einer philosophischen Hermeneutik*, 6th edn (Tübingen: J.C.B. Mohr (Paul Siebeck), 1990), 30. See also my discussion in *Confucian Propriety and Ritual Learning*, 84ff.
27 Pierre Bourdieu, *The Logic of Practice*, trans. Richard Nice (Stanford: Stanford University Press, 1990), 52.
28 Ibid., 73.
29 *Analects*, 16.13.
30 On the metaphor of 'social grammar', see Henry Rosemont Jr and Roger T. Ames, *The Chinese Classic of Family Reverence: A Philosophical Translation of the* Xiaojing (Honolulu: University of Hawaii Press, 2009), 77. On the metaphor of 'footwear', see Léon Vandermeersch, *Etudes sinologiques* (Paris: Presses Universitaires de France, 1994), 144.
31 *Xunzi*, 27.40.
32 *Analects*, 15.29.
33 *Liji*, 'Daxue', 1.

34 Mao Zedong, 'Marginal Notes To: Friedrich Paulsen, *A System of Ethics*', in *Mao's Road to Power. Revolutionary Writings. Vol. 1. The Pre-Marxist Period, 1912-1920*, ed. Stuart R. Schram (Armonk and London: M.E. Sharpe, 1992), 208.
35 Ibid., 205.
36 Ibid., 263.
37 Ibid., 263–4.
38 *Mengzi*, 7A.14.
39 Mao, 'Marginal Notes', 264. *Mengzi*, 2A.2.
40 *Analects*, 18.8.
41 Ge Rongjin 葛榮晉, *Zhongguo zhexue fanchou tonglun* 中國哲學範疇通論 (Beijing: Shoudu shifan daxue chubanshe, 2001), 559.
42 Roger T. Ames, *Confucian Role Ethics: A Vocabulary* (Hong Kong: The Chinese University Press, 2011), 109.
43 See my 'Transformative Critique: What Confucianism Can Contribute to Contemporary Education', *Studies in Philosophy and Education* 36, no. 2 (2017): 131–46.
44 Rodney L. Taylor, 'The Religious Character of the Confucian Tradition', *Philosophy East and West* 48, no. 1 (1998): 95.
45 *Analects*, 15.24.
46 *Xunzi*, 7.3.
47 *Analects*, 5.27.
48 Ibid., 4.17.
49 Ibid., 7.22.
50 For which reason it may be more appropriate to use Henry Rosemont's neologism 'homoversalism' instead of 'universalism' to emphasize its exclusive and specific reference to the human realm. See his *Against Individualism*, 24–5.
51 *Analects*, 17.2.

Bibliography

Ames, Roger T. *Confucian Role Ethics: A Vocabulary*. Hong Kong: The Chinese University Press, 2011.
Barad, Karen. *Meeting the Universe Halfway: Quantum Physics and the Entanglement of Matter and Meaning*. Durham and London: Duke University Press, 2007.
Bourdieu, Pierre. *The Logic of Practice*. Translated by Richard Nice. Stanford: Stanford University Press, 1990.
Cheng, Chung-ying. 'An Onto-Hermeneutic Interpretation of Twentieth-Century Chinese Philosophy: Identity and Vision'. In *Contemporary Chinese Philosophy*. Edited by Chung-ying Cheng and Nicholas Bunnin, 365–404. Malden and Oxford: Blackwell, 2002.

Chinese Text Project: www.ctext.org, 2006–2018.

Danto, Arthur C. *Mysticism and Morality: Oriental Thought and Moral Philosophy.* New York et al.: Harper & Row, 1972.

Fingarette, Herbert. *Confucius – The Secular as Sacred.* New York et al.: Harper & Row, 1972.

Gadamer, Hans-Georg. *Wahrheit und Methode. Grundzüge einer philosophischen Hermeneutik*, 6th edn. Tübingen: J.C.B. Mohr (Paul Siebeck), 1990.

Ge Rongjin 葛榮晉. *Zhongguo zhexue fanchou tonglun* 中國哲學範疇通論. Beijing: Shoudu shifan daxue chubanshe, 2001.

Jia, Jinhua. 'From Human-Spirit Resonance to Correlative Modes: The Shaping of Chinese Correlative Thinking'. *Philosophy East and West* 66, no. 2 (2016): 449–74.

Kant, Immanuel. *Kritik der praktischen Vernunft.* Werkausgabe VII. Frankfurt am Main: Suhrkamp, 1974.

Leibniz, Gottfried Wilhelm. *Writings on China.* Translated by Daniel J. Cook and Henry Rosemont Jr. Chicago and La Salle: Open Court, 1994.

Leopardi, Giacomo. *Zibaldone di pensieri.* Milan: Mondadori, 1937.

Linck, Gudula. *Yin und Yang. Die Suche nach Ganzheit im chinesischen Denken.* Munich: C. H. Beck, 2001.

Mao Zedong. 'Marginal Notes to: Friedrich Paulsen, A System of Ethics'. In *Mao's Road to Power. Revolutionary Writings. Vol. 1. The Pre-Marxist Period, 1912–1920.* Edited by Stuart R. Schram, 175–316. Armonk and London: M. E. Sharpe, 1992.

Nietzsche, Friedrich. *Zur Genealogie der Moral. Eine Streitschrift.* Kritische Studienausgabe 5. Munich, Berlin and New York: dtv/de Gruyter, 1988.

Rosemont Jr, Henry. *Against Individualism. A Confucian Rethinking of the Foundations of Morality, Politics, Family and Religion.* Lanham et al.: Lexington Books, 2015.

Rosemont Jr, Henry and Roger T. Ames. *The Chinese Classic of Family Reverence. A Philosophical Translation of the Xiaojing.* Honolulu: University of Hawaii Press, 2009.

Sigurðsson, Geir. 'Anthropocosmic Processes in the Anthropocene'. In *The Bright Dark Ages: Comparative and Connective Perspectives.* Edited by Arun Bala and Prasenjit Duara, 76–92. Leiden and Boston: Brill, 2016.

Sigurðsson, Geir. *Confucian Propriety and Ritual Learning: A Philosophical Interpretation.* Albany: State University of New York Press, 2015.

Sigurðsson, Geir. '"Confucianisms" and the Confucian Comeback in China'. In *Current Issues in Contemporary Chinese and Oriental Studies*, vol. 1. Edited by Alex Alexiev et al., 282–90. Sofia: University Press 'St. Kliment Ohridski', 2018.

Sigurðsson, Geir. 'Transformative Critique: What Confucianism Can Contribute to Contemporary Education'. *Studies in Philosophy and Education* 36, no. 2 (2017): 131–46.

Taylor, Rodney L. 'The Religious Character of the Confucian Tradition'. *Philosophy East and West* 48, no. 1 (1998): 80–107.

Tu Wei-ming. *Centrality and Commonality: An Essay on Confucian Religiousness.* Albany: State University of New York Press, 1989.

Vandermeersch, Léon. *Etudes sinologiques.* Paris: Presses Universitaires de France, 1994.

3

Realizing virtues: Plato and Buddhism

Chiara Robbiano and Shalini Sinha

Introduction

Plato and Buddhist thinkers are well known for having opposing metaphysical conceptions: while Plato assumes that reality is permanently structured along the lines of eternal forms that are temporally manifested in impermanent phenomena, for the Buddhist there is no reality other than impermanent phenomena.[1] Yet their conceptions of everyday reality, identity and its transformation have significant commonalities that help us to rethink the very idea of identity. For both, persons and their everyday world are composed of interlinked 'qualities': the interweaving of forms in Plato, and causally connected continua of mental and physical qualities in Buddhism. Further, it is the impermanent and changing character of everyday reality and its ethical and normative features, qua 'qualities', that is the ground of personal identity and its transformation in both perspectives. In this chapter, we attempt to rethink the idea of identity, in view of these features, by recognizing that continuous change is not only our very nature but also the condition of possibility of transformation of self and world; by realizing that we lack reality as separate, independent individuals, but our qualities, in particular our desires, have a reality which can draw us towards the good; and that investigating the good, and its realization as self- and world-transformation, is the very task of philosophy. These three themes help us to reconsider the nature of identity in a way that radically alters the boundaries of what we take to be self and world and allows us to see self-transformation *as* world-transformation. We show that these themes are discussed by both Plato and the Buddhists, and discuss, first, how each approach conceives of change or impermanence as characteristic of the everyday reality of individuals and their world, and as the source of opportunities for transformation. Secondly, we show that each, while denying the ultimate reality of the individual,² recognizes that we are always directed by our desires towards what we ordinarily deem good. And that transformation requires the reorientation of desire, as *erôs* and *upādāna*,³ respectively, towards the good, which is to be realized as ever-continuing virtuous activity – at least at the level of worldly or conventional life. Finally, we see that both approaches concur that the transformation of self and world, or of self *as* world, is the goal of philosophy as a way of life.

We examine how these three claims are developed and the tools for identity construction and transformation that underwrite them, and demonstrate that metaphysics and ethics as well as epistemology and ethics are closely linked in both perspectives, and this has its foundations in the constitutive role of the virtues in the very construction of identity – as self *and* world. We show that transformation requires, in each approach, a reorientation of desires and intentionalities, which demands that we move beyond our conventional understanding of ourselves as separate individuals. This requires not only that we recognize the nature of reality and the virtues, and realize the virtues in our actions, but that we recognize that ceaseless virtuous activity is what we *are*. We first discuss Plato's conception of identity and identity-transformation as developed in the *Symposium*. This is based on an interpretation of his metaphysics of individuals which sees the individual as consisting of an interweaving of forms, as suggested in the *Sophist*, and on his ethical intellectualism, which is expressed in various dialogues, such as the *Protagoras* (Sections 1–4). This is followed by a discussion of identity and identity-formation in early and Mahāyāna Buddhism that is based on a metaphysics of persons as causally connected – or 'interwoven' – streams of qualities. As in Plato, transformation of these qualities (*dharma*) or 'virtues' requires cognitive insight which is inalienably linked to affective and ethical transformation (Sections 5–9).

Plato's *erôs* – How can we extend ourselves, and what we deem good, forever?

Socrates, the teacher of Ancient Greek philosopher Plato, investigated what he considered to be the most important virtues (courage, beauty, justice, goodness, self-restraint etc.) by trying to find a definition of virtue that would apply in all cases. Later Plato became interested in the metaphysical *status* of the objects of the definitions Socrates was looking for. These could not be sensible objects, because such objects are subject to change and therefore cannot be the proper objects of knowledge. In dialogues such as the *Symposium, Phaedo, Republic*, Plato sketches the outline of a different order of reality: what are known as Plato's forms or ideas. The encounter with these forms is transformative: by becoming acquainted with Beauty or Goodness itself, we become closer to what is godlike (immortal, not subject to time and space). This is what our well-being consists of: the acquisition of wisdom, which is acquaintance with, and assimilation to, the unchanging forms.[4]

Plato offers us a vision of ourselves that, being grounded in the recognition of our constant change, portrays us as potential makers of meaningful transformation in our communities and the world at large. Plato's vision enables us to identify with something greater than our individual mortal body, without neglecting traits we might regard as core to our humanity – such as striving or desire. The role of change in Plato's philosophy is introduced in this section, which discusses the role of desire in achieving the human goal of possessing the good forever. The second section discusses Plato's metaphysics of forms and its relation to personal identity and ethics and in the final section the role played by the reorientation of *erôs* in achieving transformation. This first part of the chapter aims to show the relationship between self-transformation and world-transformation in Plato by interpreting a crucial passage in the *Symposium* (211e–212a), to which the third section is devoted. This interpretation, we claim, is more persuasive than alternative interpretations of Plato's project, which we will explore later.[5] One of the benefits of our interpretation, we see section 'Knowledge of forms results in deeds: Plato, *Symposium* 211e–212a', is that it stays true to Plato's ethical intellectualism – the idea that as soon as one truly knows what is good or virtuous one will behave accordingly.

In a very clear – and quite Buddhist sounding – passage in the *Symposium*, Plato affirms that what we conventionally call a person and regard as being the same throughout the years is actually an impermanent arrangement of psychophysical phenomena that decays and is constantly replaced:

> Think of what we call the life-span and identity of an individual creature. For example, a man is said to be the same individual from childhood until old age. The cells in his body are always changing, yet he is still called the same person, despite being perpetually reconstituted [*neos aei gignomenos*] as parts of him decay – hair, flesh, bones, blood, his whole body, in fact. And not just his body, either. Precisely the same happens with mental attributes. Habits, dispositions, beliefs, opinions, desires, pleasures, pains and fears are all varying all the time for everyone. Some disappear, others take their place … All continuous mortal existence is of this kind. It is not the case that creatures remain always, in every

detail, precisely the same – only the divine does that. It is rather that what is lost, and what decays, always leaves behind a fresh copy of itself. (207d–208b)[6]

For Plato, this is no reason for dismay, but an opportunity; if we constantly change, then education, self-cultivation and world-transformation are possible.

These transformative possibilities – self-cultivation, education and world-transformation – are grounded in our *erôs*, that is, in our constant striving towards what we lack and want, which intentionally directs us towards objects that we regard as good. This human trait must be cherished, yet reoriented through dialogues that enable the young to discover what is really worth striving for, namely, the real good that we want to possess forever. The reorientation of *erôs* has a clear parallel in the reorientation of *upādāna* (grasping instigated by desire and will) in Buddhism.[7]

But why should we want to reorient our striving towards the real good and engage in deeds that will change our world? This project appears too selfless to be acceptable and far too much in conflict with our individual interests. However, Plato explains that it is only by reorienting our striving towards the real good that we can achieve what the Greeks agree is the default human goal, namely, *eudaimonia*: 'flourishing', 'the good life', 'well-being' or 'happiness', seen not as a fleeting mood but as a stable achievement. In the *Symposium*, Socrates – usually regarded as Plato's mouthpiece – argues that our goal is not only achieving *eudaimonia*, or 'possessing what is good & beautiful' (202c; 205a) but possessing it *forever*. 'Forever' needs to be qualified: forever for impermanent humans means shedding what is old, replacing it with something new (207d, see previous quotation). Socrates refers to Diotima, a wise woman who explains that it is thanks to *erôs* that human beings can possess the good life forever. *Erôs* is the desire (*epithumia*) that drives us all (including other animals) to fill a lack (200a, 204a). *Erôs* is always intentionally directed: it is *of* something (199e; 200e) that we lack and we think is good and beautiful (201a) and want to possess forever (200d, 206a). As we will see, the possession of what is good and beautiful forever is only an achievable goal for those who reassess who or what 'they' are and what they want to possess or achieve forever. If there is something we turn out to 'be', which is good and can be extended forever, our life-project can be regarded as successful.

Nobody can attempt to achieve the good forever *as an individual*, neither those who have reassessed who they are after philosophical dialogues, nor those who, with no reflection on personal identity, try to possess forever simply the life they deem good by giving birth to new individuals and by caring for them. At 206e *erôs* for the good life forever is reformulated as '*erôs 'tês gennêseôs kai tou tokou en tôi kalôi*': 'of engendering and begetting upon the beautiful' (trans.

Fowler) or 'the desire to use beauty to beget and bear offspring' (trans. Griffith). What we translate as 'beautiful' – *kalon* – also means 'noble'; this is how the good appears, and it is this that makes the good attractive and valuable: something anyone would want to possess forever. Since we, and all other things, are constantly changing, we cannot possess anything permanently. We can, however, try to actively replace that which we value and wish to keep for a long time with something similar to it. This is also the natural process described at 207d-208b quoted above: our body continues to exist because our decaying cells leave fresh copies of themselves behind. The human way of possessing anything for a long time is thus to replace the old with the new; which can be reformulated as giving birth to something new (207d–208b). Seen in this way, *erôs* – the desire to possess the good forever – consists in being attracted to what is beautiful and noble, which we regard as good, and in continuously giving birth to more goodness. *Erôs* is ordinarily directed at attractive bodies and results in people giving birth to children: this makes reproduction the germ of immortality (206c-e).

However Plato's suggestion is that *erôs* can be redirected in such a way that it results in the production of real virtue or goodness that grants true immortality – rather than merely the creation of children. This requires us to consider what the production of real virtue means and the relationship it bears to Plato's conception of philosophy as a way of life – a conception which stimulates us towards bringing about profound changes in our community. We might think here of Plato's many descriptions of Socrates's effort to transform Athens for the better by asking people to examine their beliefs (e.g. *Charmides, Euthyphro, Laches*), and the description of the just city-state in the *Republic*, which is Plato's design of a community, based on understanding the good and the forms, especially of the virtues, in which people could flourish. But how should we understand ourselves, if not as stable individuals? And how should we, according to Plato, extend what we deem good in this life? Furthermore, in what way, by constant effort to produce new manifestations of what we deem good, might we transcend our individuality, in space and time, and impact our community and the world we live in?

Plato's metaphysics: We and the rest of reality are 'interweavings' of forms

We need to consider what allows Plato to say that we can transcend our individuality and continue spatially, beyond the boundaries of our skin, and temporally, beyond death. According to Plato, we are individuals only conventionally.[8] In the *Sophist*, Plato shows that everything can be understood as an 'interweaving of forms'[9] ('*sumplokê eidôn*', *Sophist* 259e), including humans. When referring to an individual, for example, Chloe, we might say, 'Chloe is beautiful and friendly'. In this case, we are expressing the relation between what we recognize as Chloe and the forms, that is, the qualities or features – beauty and friendliness – that Chloe manifests for a certain time span. Ordinary predications, like the above, express some of the forms that constitute and explain what we take to be an individual.[10] In other words, Chloe is nothing above and beyond the temporal manifestation of a plurality of forms.

We need to ask, however, what the consequences are of conceiving of our identity as a display of features or an interweaving of forms; that is, what ethical potential is disclosed in the realization that *we*, who might seem independent individuals, are ultimately manifestations of forms. In other words, what do we gain if we accept the suggestion that our being brave, beautiful or friendly can only be understood as a manifestation of the forms of courage, beauty or friendliness, braided together? If we accept that we are impermanent manifestations of *many* different forms, we might realize that it is precisely by being impermanent manifestations of *many* different forms that we can steer the changing display of our plurality of forms. We may display a different array of forms at different moments in our life and the forms we display may well be a consequence of education and self-cultivation.

Knowledge of forms results in deeds: Plato, *Symposium* 211e–212a

What if, while being a changing manifestation of a plurality of forms, we are not manifesting forms of virtues, such as courage or temperance, but we manifest rather cowardice and greed? *Knowledge* of forms of virtues or excellences, the manifestation of which constitute the good life, is the necessary and only step that can reorient us towards the good. The *Symposium* explains how someone who is attracted to one beautiful person and engages with him in conversation (209b; 210a; 210c; 210d) can gradually ascend the ladder of *erôs* (211b–212b). Having reached the top, he will look at beauty in itself (*auto to kalon*), which is how the good appears. Thus, at the culmination of what Diotima refers to as the 'higher mysteries' of her revelation, she speaks of how the lover who has contemplated beauty will give birth not to images of virtues, excellences or goodness (*tiktein ouk eidola aretês*; for example, in love poems or laws) but to true virtue (*aretên alêthê*) (212a):

> [I]magine he were able to see divine beauty itself in its unique essence. Don't you think he would find it a wonderful way to live, looking at it, contemplating it as it should be contemplated, and spending his time in its company? It cannot fail to strike you that only then will it be possible for him, seeing beauty as it should be seen, *to produce not likenesses of goodness (since it is not likeness that he has before him), but the real thing (since he has the real thing before him); and that this producing, and caring for, real goodness*[11] earns him the friendship of the gods and makes him, if anyone, immortal. (211e–212a, italics added)

The question this raises is: What is 'true virtue'? And why do these offspring grant their parents immortality and the friendship of the gods? I argue that giving birth to true virtue means manifesting the virtues we consist of, by carrying out virtuous *deeds* which will result in community and world-transformation. On some interpretations of this passage (see below), the knower of the good will produce only beautiful discourses or accounts. These interpretations are mistaken in two ways: (1) they neglect Platonic ethical intellectualism which entails that once one knows virtue, one will unfailingly act on it; (2) they are mistakenly preoccupied with the lack of individual immortality for the lover who gives birth to true virtue. These interpretations forget that, for Plato, the lovers can be seen as interweavings of forms, rather than as individuals, and so, the immortality they enjoy need not be individual immortality.

A number of interpretations concentrate on the moment of knowledge of the form of beauty, rather than on what happens after contemplating this form, because the latter is considered less important that contemplation itself. Rosen,[12] for example, considers 'true instances' of virtue or goodness to be speeches and accounts that are representations of the contemplated form. Rosen displays what I call the epistemological assumption. This holds that the relation humans have with beauty, or with any other form, is fundamentally *epistemological*: to enter in relation with forms means that our mind knows forms. Scholars who assume that our relation to forms is fundamentally epistemological see the production of true virtue in terms of good accounts of knowledge.

Much is at stake in understanding what this true virtue that is produced once the lover has seen beauty is. In fact, the real virtue produced by the lover is what earns him the friendship of the gods – not the vision itself. The gods love the production of virtue more than the knowledge that necessarily precedes it because, I maintain, achieving knowledge is fundamental in the Platonic project in virtue of its transformative aims. Once one knows courage, for example, one cannot fail to be courageous and perform courageous deeds. This follows from Plato's ethical intellectualism: someone who knows what is right will always act on that knowledge. As Socrates, in the *Protagoras* (352b-c) says:

> The opinion generally held of knowledge is something of this sort – that it is no strong or guiding or governing thing; it is not regarded as anything of that kind, but people think that, while a man often has knowledge in him, he is not governed by it, but by something else – now by passion, now by pleasure, now by pain, at times by love, and often by fear; their feeling about knowledge [352c] is just what they have about a slave, that it may be dragged about by any other force. Now do you agree with this view of it, or do you consider that knowledge is something noble and able to govern man, and that whoever learns what is good and what is bad will never be swayed by anything to act otherwise than as knowledge bids, and that intelligence is a sufficient succour for mankind? My view, Socrates, he replied, is precisely that which you express.

If one knows the virtues, one will express this knowledge through deeds that cannot be other than virtuous. By dispelling ignorance, wisdom brings forth virtuous deeds. This is philosophy as a way of life, which has an impact on one's world because epistemology and ethics are closely connected not only to each other but also to metaphysics: reality consists of forms and we manifest the forms of virtues once we have real knowledge of them (cf. *Euthydemus* 281d). Before this, we might express thoughtless boldness, rather than realizing and manifesting the form of the wise virtue of courage (cf. also *Meno* 88a).

Returning to our passage (*Symp.* 211e-212a), the following interpretations of this passage do appreciate that 'real' instances of goodness (or virtue) are not merely items of knowledge confined to the 'private' mental state of the one who contemplates beauty. In these interpretations, however, 'real' instances of virtue are *discourses*, not deeds. Kurihara,[13] for example, argues that 'Plato thinks of the *telos* of the Ladder of Love as living the philosophical life, not merely grasping the Form of Beauty'; and 'The true virtue that the lover delivers must be philosophy itself'[14]. Yet philosophy is seen as composed of *discourses*, by means of which a teacher guides his students. And giving birth to true virtue is seen as 'giving birth to beautiful and magnificent words and thoughts'.[15] White[16] argues that the goal of *erôs* does not consist in knowledge or contemplation of virtue, but 'in the philosopher's bringing forth of true virtue and in the immortality that it bestows'. Promisingly, he says that true virtue begotten by the true lover is not something concerning him alone, but 'something brought forth into the world and continuing to exist when the true lover is dead'[17]. At the same time, this 'something' is philosophical discourses. Kraut emphasizes the effect of these discourses 'that will still be in place after we die'[18] on the world, but refers to the 'real virtues' as 'notional children',[19] that is, beautiful discourses that one begets after seeing the form of beauty.

The suggestion at *Symposium* 211e–212a that, by giving birth to true virtue, the lover becomes immortal helps us to refine our question about personal identity as follows: in what way, by *knowing* eternal forms and by *regarding ourselves* as interweavings of forms, can we achieve our goal of possessing the good forever? Some interpreters fear that by understanding and articulating the structure of reality one is annihilated rather than immortalized, because one's understanding of the form, if correct, need not to be different from anyone else's.[20] It's difficult to see how one could acquire immortality in this way.[21] Meinwald defends the possibility that the creation of new discourses or proofs, after having seen the form, might grant one individual immortality, in the same way as someone's articulation of a mathematical theorem can differ from the proof given by others of the same theorem.[22] But one may ask, can the creation of discourses about virtues, published in peer-reviewed journals, say, in one's name, be what grants one immortality and the friendship of the gods?

Let's notice that when revealing the 'lower mysteries', Diotima refers to poems and laws as the offspring of the psyche (209b-c) that grant the lovers immortality of the kind that is possible for human beings (207d, 208b). Once she proceeds to the 'higher mysteries', she introduces the new offspring that will not be likenesses of virtues but real virtues. It seems plausible that the likenesses of virtue are the poems and laws referred to as the 'lower mysteries'. Yet the question arises, what is the nature of these offspring that they are superior not only to children of flesh but also to poems and laws?

White maintains that the superior offspring, which bestow immortality on the philosopher, are his philosophical discourses and works, in which he lives on and which are aimed at the virtue of others.[23] White does not mention that these offspring might be virtuous deeds. Interestingly, White refers to Alcibiades's characterization of Socrates, as the true lover, whose discourses can turn the beliefs of his addressees upside down (261a) and help them live a noble and good life (22a). However, White does not mention that Alcibiades talks at great length about Socrates's *deeds* that manifest the most important virtues. Socrates is capable of restraint (*sôphrosune*, 216d) and courage (*andreia*, 219d), which he manifested when resisting the advances of Alcibiades himself, one of the most attractive men in Athens (217a–219e). In war, he manifested toughness, endurance, indifference to weather, excellent conduct in action and selfless behaviour – when he saved Alcibiades's life after he was wounded – as well as prudence and composedness (219a–221c). Alcibiades's speech shows that, if Socrates is the true lover, his production of real virtues consists not only in his discourses but in his deeds, which manifest the most important virtues and make a deep impression on everyone who witnesses them. Unfortunately Alcibiades did not manage to reorient his *erôs* properly; he did not manage to ascend the ladder of *erôs*, which would have led him to know the good and manifest it in his deeds.

There are however people who, after spending time with a lover who has known the good and manifests the good in his deeds, manage the ascent and the reorientation of their *erôs*. After this, the lover's *erôs* for the beloved does not consist in the desire to possess him (only) as a body. The beloved is *no more identified with a mortal body, but with the manifestation of forms, especially of virtues, which the beloved can now manifest after having known them.* The lover might tell his beloved: 'I desire the courage that you manifest and that you are.' To desire and to want to possess forever the courage (or another virtue) manifested by one's beloved means to want to give birth to more courage. The lover-knower, who was always an interweaving of various forms, is now a manifestation, among other forms, of the form that he has known at the top of his ascent that culminates in transformative knowledge. By *knowing* eternal forms, we will realize that our immortality and our possession of the good forever depend on our capacity to produce the best kind of spiritual offspring: virtuous deeds, which result from our transformative knowledge of the forms of virtues. For example, the spiritual children of a couple of lovers of courage are manifestations of courage – as deeds, not only discourses – in the community, by which more courage will be born and manifested. These offspring do not grant *personal* immortality. We do not become immortal as individuals because, ultimately, we are not individuals. What is passed on is virtues, not one's name.

Plato: From identification with the forms and continuous realization of the virtues to world-transformation

In order to make the good present in the impermanent reality of our community, we need not only to continue engaging in discourses about eternal virtues – such as courage, restraint and wisdom – but also to continue replacing old deeds with new deeds in an open-ended chain of manifestations of the eternal in time. This, in conclusion, is Plato's suggestion. If the possession of the good forever is the goal of every human being, it cannot be a characteristic or achievement of anyone as an individual. By setting this goal for ourselves, we will not try to hand down what is individual in us, but the virtues or values that are constitutive of us. In order to reach this goal, we need to stop identifying with our idiosyncratic desires and opinions, and with an individuality that terminates at the boundaries of our skin and at the time of our death. Seeing ourselves as interweavings of forms of virtues might urge us to know virtues and freely to choose those virtues we wish to manifest. We might consider regarding a successful life that of the person who – in the face of her own individual mortality – continuously increases both the quantity and the extension in time of the manifestation of virtues in their community. We might see education as exposing the youth to discourses and virtuous deeds, which will reorient their *erôs* towards the good life forever. And they will thus try to achieve immortality by replacing the old with new virtuous deeds, performed either by what one conventionally refers to as 'me' or by other temporary manifestations of virtues. The suggestion is that, by conceptualizing our identity in this way and by untiringly realizing what is good in our discourses and actions, we can transform our world.

From identity to identitylessness: A Buddhist perspective on realizing virtues

Buddhist philosophy denies that persons and objects have identities: substantive cores that may each be called a 'self'.[24] Recognizing that phenomena lack identity transforms what we take to be self (*ātman*), person (*pudgala*) and world (*loka*).[25] This discussion investigates how the metaphysics of dependent co-arising (*pratītyasamutpāda*) in early and Madhyamaka Buddhism embeds the transformative practices of no-identity (*niḥsvabhāva*) or no-self (*anātman*). Dependent co-arising is the claim that the mental and physical phenomena that constitute everyday reality arise in dependence on other such phenomena, which are the causes and conditions of their arising. In what follows, we demonstrate that, for the Buddhist, metaphysics is an ethical practice.[26] And it is the interlinking of metaphysics and ethics that makes it possible that practising no-self or no-identity *is* realizing the normative aims and values that dependent co-arising explicates.

The next section discusses the metaphysical and normative features of dependent co-arising that make Buddhist philosophy a practice of transformation. The following section examines the Madhyamaka notion of self as grasping or appropriation, and how this underpins the construction of person and world. Then we discuss disappropriative practices of the self, in particular, Śāntideva's path of virtuous transformation *as* the practice of no-self or, synonymously, the practice of dependent co-arising. It considers the cognitive, emotional and behavioural virtues cultivated on this path in pursuit of its aim: the unceasing realization of virtuous freedom *as* identitylessness, which is discussed in the final section.[27]

The normative features of early Buddhist and Madhyamaka metaphysics

It is no exaggeration to say that Buddhist metaphysics *is* a metaphysics of suffering (*duḥkha*). The Four Noble Truths (*satya*) of Buddhism, which also designate the four realities (*satya*) of existence, declare the pervasiveness of suffering, its arising from causes and conditions, its cessation, and the path to its cessation by the elimination of its causes and conditions. The four truths explicate two normative constraints, namely suffering and freedom from suffering. If the human condition is diagnosed as one of suffering by the Buddhist, it is the primary, if not the sole aim of philosophy, to cure the 'dis-ease' of suffering by a programme of eight-fold virtuous cultivation set out in the fourth truth.

The central assumption here is that the metaphysical and the normative, what 'is' and what 'ought' to be, are not separable, and insight into the nature of reality is transformative, cognitively, affectively and ethically.[28] This is reminiscent of Plato's assumption that the reality of the forms of virtues, once known, transforms the knower's behaviour so that it cannot but be virtuous. Moreover, Plato's reality consists of forms that, because they are firmly grounded in the form of the good, constitute a good reality – one which can be understood by whosoever understands the good of every aspect of it. In a not dissimilar vein, the Buddha claims that 'He who sees dependent arising (*pratītyasamutpāda*) [of the psychophysical qualities (*dharmas*) that constitute persons and objects] sees *dhamma* (Skt. *dharma*, the truth about how things really are); he who sees *dhamma* (the truth about how things are) sees dependent arising [of the *dharmas*].'[29] This says that we come to understand the truth of the Buddha's teachings, or *dharma*, by recognizing the dependent co-arising and passing of the mental and physical qualities or characteristics (*dharmas*) that are constitutive of persons and objects.[30] We do so by observing *dharmas as dharmas*, that is, by seeing their causal arising and passing as that of impersonal characteristics, rather than of personal attributes.

It is then possible to observe how *dharmas* arise and pass away, and to recognize how those *dharmas* or (virtuous) qualities (cognitive, emotional, dispositional etc.) that one wishes to develop might be cultivated and those (nonvirtuous) qualities one wishes to abandon may be abandoned.[31] Observing the dependent co-arising of *dharmas*, one comes to understand the four truths they manifest as causally arisen, impermanent (*anitya*) phenomena. Namely, their nature as suffering; the causes of suffering (delusion, attachment and aversion, especially the delusion of a self which leads to identification with the *dharmas* as 'I' or 'mine' and instigates the other two causes of suffering, attachment and aversion to transient phenomena); the cessation of suffering (when delusion and, with it, attachment and aversion cease); and the path to the cessation of suffering (which cultivates the extinguishment of delusion, attachment and aversion). By 'seeing these four truths one *realizes* the ultimate truth', or *dharma*, namely the extinguishing (*nirvāṇa*) of suffering.[32] This mode of metaphysical analysis of the *dharmas* – or of collections of *dharmas* called the aggregates (*skandhas*) – to achieve normative aims (freedom from suffering) underwrites the path of virtuous cultivation, whether in the eight-fold path of early Buddhism or the path of perfections in Madhyamaka Buddhism.

The Madhyamaka ('Middle-Way') philosopher, Nāgārjuna (second century CE) agrees that all phenomena co-arise dependently and that this entails suffering. But dependent co-arising means, he claims, that all phenomena are empty (*śūnya*) of intrinsic nature, that is, of inherent or independent existence (*svabhāva*) – a claim which accords with the Buddha's view that all phenomena, in virtue of being dependently arisen, lack a substantial core, a 'self' (see *MN* 22, for example).[33] Moreover, recognizing that conventional, everyday phenomena, including dependent arising itself, are empty of inherent or substantive existence is recognizing their 'ultimate reality' as unproduced, non-conceptual, peaceful and beyond all suffering: 'Not known through anyone else, peaceful, not expressed by discursive ideas, non-conceptual, not diverse – this is the definition of reality' (*MMK* 18.9). Nāgārjuna's commentator Candrakīrti (seventh century CE) reiterates this claim, 'from the outset, all phenomena are peace, are unproduced, transcending by their nature every pain' (*MA* VI.112b-c).

Madhyamaka philosophers claim that peace ensues with the 'realization' of emptiness, the 'nonconceptual' insight that dependently co-arising phenomena, and dependent co-arising itself, are empty of inherent existence (*svabhāva*). Non-conceptual insight sees phenomena as unproduced (not-arisen) and peaceful (because non-arising leaves no basis for craving or suffering).[34] The tranquillity and peace of 'ultimate' reality is the normative aspect of metaphysical insight which is explained by Śāntideva in the following way: '[w]hen neither entity nor nonentity remains before the mind, since there is no other mode of operation, grasping no objects, it (the mind) becomes tranquil' (*BCA* IX.34). That is to say, when conceptual grasping of objects ceases, the mind becomes tranquil. How this happens is explained next.

Self *as* appropriation: The construction of self, person and world

Two interrelated terms in the above set of claims need to be unpacked – 'grasping' and 'conceptuality' – which are interlinked with the concept of 'I'. Nāgārjuna claims:

> [A]ll beings have arisen from the conception of *I* (*aham*)
> And are enveloped with the conception of *mine* (*mama*). (*Ratnāvalī*, I. 27)
>
> As long as the aggregates are conceived [as having intrinsic nature or existence (*svabhāva*)],
> So long thereby does the conception of I exist.
> Further, when the conception of I exists,
> There is action, and from it there also is birth. (*Ratnāvalī*, I. 35)

Nāgārjuna says that conceiving the aggregates as really existent is tied to the conception of 'I' as really existent. And the concept of 'I' is, in some way, the basis from which living beings arise. The notion of 'I' or self is elucidated by Candrakīrti. Self, he claims, is simply the sense of ownership we have of our experiences, emotions, bodies and so on. It is simply the sense of personal existence that we refer to when we say, 'I am.'[35] The sense of self *is* the I-concept or I-object (*ahaṃkāra*) that is constructed *in* and *by* the activity of conceptually appropriating (*upādāna*) to oneself the stream of psychophysical aggregates: 'That which is constructed in the appropriating of them [the psychophysical aggregates] is said to be the appropriator, the thinker, the performing self. In this is generated [the activity of] "I-ing", that is, the activity of appropriating, or laying to claim to, the aggregates which *is* conceptually constructing a sense of self.'[36] Appropriating, then, *is* positing a conceptually constructed subjective object, the I-object or self.

'Self' is an appropriative term here; it is the appropriative activity of 'I-ing', that is, of appropriating or grasping that *is* conceiving psychophysical objects as 'I' and 'mine'. It is this 'I-ing' that binds the person-bundle of psychophysical aggregates together as a dependently co-arising continuum (Candrakīrti, *PP B* 350[37]; *Ratnāvalī* I. 35). What Candrakīrti is pointing to is that the sense of 'I', or ownership, as the subject (or self) and its object, arise in the very activity of grasping as the *feeling* or *sense* that the subject and its object *really* exist. The creation of a subjective sense of 'I' is the creation of a subjective object, the subject of experience who Candrakīrti describes as 'the illusion of the "I" [that] is conceived as in and of [the nature of] personal existence'.[38]

The creation of the subject and object of experience is explicitly theorized in Yogācāra Buddhism (third century CE), in which appropriation (*upādāna*) is the key aggregate, and it is through *appropriative movement* that the appropriated is constructed in the manner of, or as, *grāhaka* (appropriator) and *grāhya* (appropriated) or subject and object.[39] The subject, as grasper or appropriator (*grāhaka*), and its object, as the grasped or appropriated (*grāhya*), describe the structure of intentional consciousness in ordinary, appropriative cognitions, and more generally in actions. It is this dualistic subject–object structure of intentional consciousness that motivates intentional actions (*karman*), which bring into existence appropriated objects, subjective and objective, as a karmic result.

The subject–object structure of intentional consciousness, as appropriator and appropriated, grants the directedness and content of 'I-ing' which informs intentional actions. This karmically consequential grasping (*upādāna*) – as self or ownership – both generates and 'binds together' appropriated *dharmas* in a unified person-continuum. Note that appropriation or grasping mental and physical qualities, as a self, arises in dependence on craving (*tṛṣṇa*) and feeling (*vedanā*); in turn, dependent on appropriation, the aggregates come together as 'becoming' which leads to birth, the coming into existence of a living being and its world of embodied experience (see *MN* 115.11).[40] Given the integrative effect on the stream of person-*dharmas* of the sense of ownership or self, it is not surprising that the Buddha proclaims, 'beings are owners of their actions, heirs of their actions; they originate from their actions, are bound to their actions' (*MN* 135.3).

Disappropriative practices of the self: Attenuating ownership

If grasping or appropriation is the conceptual construction of 'I' and 'mine', we might surmise that non-grasping or non-appropriation eliminates the notion of 'I' because it is 'nonconceptual' in some way. Nāgārjuna explains that when the conceptual appropriation of mental and physical phenomena as 'I' and 'mine' is 'destroyed both Merleau-Ponty within and without appropriation comes to an end; [and] with its demise, rebirth [i.e. the dependent co-arising of a person-continuum of aggregates] ends' (*MMK* 18.4). Appropriation ends by recognizing 'the aggregates as [ultimately] untrue' (*Ratnāvalī* I. 30), that is, as 'empty' of inherent or ultimate existence.[41] The practices which make conceptual disappropriation of the aggregates possible are explicated in Śāntideva's path of the six perfections.

The path of perfections

Śāntideva outlines a path of cultivation of six virtuous perfections (*paramitā*). This is founded on the core commitment of the Buddha-to-be, the *bodhisattva* (awakening-being), to the development of *bodhicitta* (awakening mind) which seeks to alleviate the suffering of all beings – consistent with the four truths of the Buddha. The perfections are giving or generosity (*dāna*), moral discipline (*śīla*) which includes restraint from appropriative activities, patience or forbearance (*kṣānti*), zeal (*vīrya*), meditation (*dhyāna*) and wisdom (*prajña*). These virtues initiate a series of conceptually disappropriative *movements* of the aggregates that transform the subject–object structure of intentionality from a grasper–grasped relationship of ownership, or 'self-appropriation', to one of disowning or 'other-appropriation', and, finally, non-ownership or 'non-appropriation'.

Behavioural practices at the beginning of the path include generosity towards others, moral conduct and patience which attenuate the sense of ownership by cultivating 'giving away' (see *BCA* III, V.10), or practising mental and moral introspection, and restraint and forbearance in the face of pleasant and unpleasant circumstances (*BCA* V-VI). These practices cultivate 'other-appropriation' which favours other sentient beings over oneself, or otherwise mitigate self-clinging.

Behavioural practices of disowning prepare the ground for meditative practices (*dhyāna*) that cultivate non-appropriation of objects by the senses and mind. Thus, *bodhisattvas* 'do not grasp at signs and do not grasp at characteristics' with the senses, nor do they grasp conscious experiences with the mind (*manas*) (*ŚS* 199-200). Meditative training, however, also involves more direct practices of 'other-appropriation' or 'other-ing', as opposed to 'I-ing', using metaphysical analysis to develop a wholly non-appropriative stance.

Metaphysical analysis as ethical practice

Metaphysical analysis, Śāntideva claims, is transformative because 'seeing things as they really are' extirpates the notion of 'I'.[42] As in early Buddhism, '[a]nalysis is created as an antidote to that false notion [of "I" created by conceptual appropriation]' (*BCA* IX.92). It is by analysis that we come to see sentient and non-sentient objects as impersonal bundles of qualities (*dharmas*). For example, by analysing the body into its constituent parts, we come to see the body as simply a mechanical construction of bones and muscles constituted of dependently arising *dharmas* (*ŚS* 231). Similarly, by analysing a corpse, we come to recognize its putrefied attributes as no different, in reality, from the attributes of our own body (*ŚS* 206-8). Analysis of this sort is an ethical practice that cultivates an impersonal view of the body to eliminate the attachments and aversions that are associated with it and the afflictive emotions that follow from this. Thus, coming to see the body as an arrangement of dependently arising *dharmas* can help overcome afflictive emotions, such as anger and fear, by realizing that these emotions are not attributable to *someone* (*BCA* IV.47, VI.31-33, VIII.48).

Self as 'other': Cultivating equality and exchange

The most concerted metaphysical practices of conceptual disappropriation are perhaps the equality and exchange of self and other. As before, metaphysical analysis prompts the realization that persons are merely composites of impersonal mental and physical *dharmas*, which qua *dharmas* are 'equal' or the 'same' (*sama*). With this recognition of the sameness of person-bundles comes its normative aspect, namely that the suffering associated with each bundle of *dharmas* is the 'same' and equally worthy of alleviation (*BCA* VIII.90, 94-96). Analysis of this sort seeks to overturn the 'habit' of identifying the suffering associated with *this* psychophysical bundle of *dharmas* as my *own*, and of *that* psychophysical bundle as *other*, and so less worthy of concern (*BCA* VIII.115). It attempts to foster practices that move from appropriating *this* bundle of *dharmas as* self to appropriating *other* person-bundles *as* self, and finally to appropriating all person-bundles, that is, the social community as a whole *as* self – to assure its well-being. Epistemic practices are transformative here and have direct ethical and emotional consequences.

But how exactly do epistemic practices transform our emotional and ethical life? The argument appears to run as follows. Recognizing the impersonality of *dharmas* is recognizing their ownerlessness and so, the ownerlessness of the person-bundles they constitute. It is 'seeing *dharmas* as *dharmas*' and therefore, bundles of *dharmas* as impersonal bundles that (ultimately) do not constitute *someone* nor belong to *someone*. This is also a recognition of the ownerlessness of the suffering that is associated with each bundle of *dharmas* (BCA VIII.101-102) – which is possible on the core assumption that the arising and passing of *dharmas is* suffering. The question remains, How *can* 'ownerless suffering' elicit compassion or lovingkindness?[43]

The relationship between ownerlessness and compassion, or benevolence, may be unpacked in the following way. Self or 'I' is the sense of personal existence and ownership that comes from appropriating the aggregates. However, when 'I' is extended to others, becoming other, at least perspectively, it is a disappropriative movement of 'other-ing'. 'I' can extend itself *as* other only if it sees no difference between *this* bundle and *that* bundle, that is, if it sees aggregate-bundles as impersonal and ownerless. If the movement of grasping is owning, the movement of extending is *disowning*. What appears, however, to tie the recognition of ownerlessness and the movement of disowning with a compassionate attitude rather than one of mere indifference, say, is the assumption that ownerlessness arises *as* the expansion or universalization of appropriating or 'I-ing', *and* the 'caring for oneself' that ordinarily goes with this. This says that 'I' can extend itself to any and all person-aggregates and still remain 'I'. And whereas the sense of 'I' as grasping invokes attachment and aversion, the extension and expansion of 'I' to others, its reorientation, invokes benevolence and wholesomeness in the forms of giving, compassion and so on.

So, reorienting the sense of 'I' as 'other-ing', by binding oneself to other ownerless, yet suffering, person-bundles promotes *compassionately* appropriating evermore bundles of *dharmas* as 'I', until one comes to appropriate the social community as a whole as 'I' (see *BCA* VIII.114-117, 137). The core assumption here is that 'emotional expansiveness' is a constitutive aspect of the expansiveness of 'I' as the *movement* of 'other-ing'. This might arguably follow from the view that if emotional constriction, qua greed and aversion, is a constitutive feature of 'I-ing' as owning, emotional expansiveness as lovingkindness and compassion is a constitutive feature of the *movement* of disowning *as* 'other-ing'. This appears, plausibly, to be the basis of Śāntideva's view that just as bodily parts function as a unity in ways that contribute to the proper functioning and well-being of each part, presumably because these parts are integrated in the same stream of 'I-ing'; so might persons act 'functionally' for the well-being of the whole – *as* oneself – by subsuming all *dharma*-streams under the umbrella of 'I' (see *BCA* VIII.91, 114-117).

At the heart of this view is a claim about intentionality. It says that when 'I' expands and binds itself to other aggregate-bundles, its expansive scope as 'other' transforms its contents and its quality to one of spaciousness or emptiness that has the nature of benevolence and happiness (see *BCA* VIII.129). The structure and contents of intentionality and intention are reoriented, in this case, as the subject-grasper recedes in favour of the world which is grasped. This appears to be implicit in Śāntideva's assertion that aggregates which are appropriated *to* oneself, as one's *own*, in a stream of *dharmas* that is associated with a limited or narrow sense of self, generate, by dependent arising, an experientially 'limited' conscious embodiment and world: an embodiment that presents a phenomenology of suffering (*BCA* VIII.127). Where aggregate-bundles are constituted by a stream of 'I-ing', as 'other-ing', which recognizes the ownerless nature of person-bundles and their suffering, the aggregates act disappropriatively, with compassion. This generates a world of embodied experience that presents, in relevant ways, a phenomenology of happiness (*BCA* VIII.129).

The unceasing virtues of emptiness: Lovingkindness and the other immeasurables

Practices of 'other-ing', by their expansiveness, attenuate the sense of substantial or objective existence of subject and object that grasping begets. Phenomenologically, this is the experience of de-substantialization or emptiness. Objects now arise as 'bundles or interweavings of qualities' that appear insubstantial; for example, physical forms that arise may have colour, shape, size, taste, smell and so on, but these qualities and the bundle they constitute appear to lack substantial existence, an identity of their own. They appear 'illusory' or 'dream-like', empty of inherent or substantive existence (*svabhāva*).

Once *dharmas* are no longer reified as objective existents, they arise simply as 'doings' that too are empty of inherent existence.[44] Mental *dharmas*, whether perception and cognition, sensation and feeling, emotion or disposition 'embody' the realization that all *dharmas*, all phenomena lack substantial, objective existence, an identity of their *own*, and are, in this sense, empty. Cognitions, feelings, emotions and behaviour can then arise unobstructed by conceptually constructed substantializations and biases of self and other, subject and object: they can arise as virtuous *dharmas* that are oriented 'equally' towards all (*BCA* VIII.103, 107-110, 114, 117).

Virtuous activities 'embody', as 'doings', the emptiness or identitylessness, of all *dharmas* because they recognize 'the nonarising' of substantial or reified objectivity, including dependent co-arising itself (*ŚS* 209).[45] As such, virtuous doings, such as lovingkindness, are not-dependent on reified objectivity, as either causes or conditions, for their arising or ceasing. We might say that unobstructed by 'substantial objectivity', they are 'self-arising'.[46] Virtuous activities or qualities, such as lovingkindness, compassionate caring, sympathetic joy and equanimity, insofar as they do not recognize substantial objectivity or limitations are 'objectless'. They are, for this reason, also 'immeasurable' (*apramāṇa*), that is, unobstructed by the conceptual limitations of substantial objectivity that grasping imposes.[47]

Meditative analysis qua metaphysical analysis brings deepening insight into the emptiness of all phenomena – into 'how things really are' (*yathābhūtam*). It is the basis of wisdom (*prajñā*), the understanding that all phenomena lack inherent existence, because they co-arise dependently. Yet meditative insight itself comes only with the cultivation of virtues such as giving, moral restraint and patience and, in turn, perfects them. The six perfections of generosity and moral discipline, patience and zeal, meditative concentration and wisdom then arise not only sequentially, as presented earlier, they also reinforce each other, and 'bring to completion all the qualities of a Buddha, and ... Awakening' (*ŚS* 290; 316–317). That this should be so is unsurprising because virtuous *dharmas*, behavioural, emotional, dispositional, cognitive and so on co-arise in dependence on each other, so that they are 'mutually cooperative and linked' (*sahitāny-anuprbaddhānī*) (*ŚS* 316-317).[48] Note, however, that the perfection of virtues and their ceaseless arising continue only as long as dependent co-arising continues and this continues only so long as the aspirations of 'I' *as* other of the *bodhisattva*, that marks a commitment to the welfare of all sentient beings, continues.

Conclusion

Plato suggests that our everyday world is characterized by change, which he describes in terms of the constant replacement of the old with the new. The individual is a constantly changing manifestation of different forms, at different times, so that ultimately there are only forms, which are temporally manifested in our actions. Transformation is possible because, after dialogue leading to knowledge of the forms of virtues, we can start manifesting those forms we did not possess earlier.

In the Buddhist view, there is no self or agent who owns her actions. Instead, there are only 'doings' that are simply qualities (*dharmas*). Transformation of self and world is possible only through knowledge of 'things as they really are', as ever-changing, interdependent qualities (*dharmas*), which in virtue of their dependent co-arising are empty of inherent nature or of independent existence (*svabhāva*). It is insight into the dependent co-arising of phenomena – which is synonymous with this notion of emptiness – that underwrites the path of transformation. It is also on account of the dependent co-arising of phenomena that cultivating one's qualities *is* transforming the world.

In both Plato and Buddhism, transformation is possible through a reorientation of intentionality, from the individual we conventionally identify with, towards the world, which is a reorientation towards the good. In Buddhism the highest good (*niḥśreyasa*) is neither an object nor a goal. It is rather a reorientation that moves from the habitual appropriation (*upādāna*) of 'self' to the appropriation of 'others' and seeks, in Madhyamaka Buddhism, to remove the suffering of all living beings. Beginning with removing the suffering of the conventional 'other', it moves in ever-widening circles towards sheer virtuous activity that has neither a subject nor an object. In Plato, on the other hand, transformation is fuelled by *erôs*. This is a powerful desire that always orients us towards what we lack but deem good and beautiful and wish to have and possess forever. *Erôs* begins as an attraction to the beautiful other, which allows us to continue forever what we deem good, by creating offspring that replace the old with the new. But *erôs* can be reoriented from desire for the body of the other, which results in physical progeny, to desire for the virtuous qualities the other ultimately consists of. Thanks to a dialogue with the other, we may acquire knowledge of the virtues we are attracted to in the other. If we reach this knowledge we will unfailingly begin to realize these virtues in virtuous behaviour, extending thereby their presence in the everyday life of the community. In both Plato and Mahāyāna Buddhism, this realization is not an end goal to be achieved once and for all. Rather, the reorientation of *erôs* and *upādāna*, respectively, leads to continuous virtuous doing.

Knowledge, or wisdom, is not only insight into reality but also realization of the virtues in both traditions. For Plato, realization consists in knowledge of the forms of the virtues that compose reality, which then results in virtuous deeds. For the Mahāyāna Buddhist, knowledge is understanding the emptiness of all phenomena, which comes through the cultivation of virtues and is realized in ceaseless virtuous doings. In the Buddhist view, a virtuous quality, such as compassion, is simply a conventional reification of virtuous doings, which co-arise dependently and so are empty of inherent existence. For Plato, on the other hand, every virtuous action is a manifestation of the form of that particular virtue, say courage, which exists in relation to all the other forms that structure a reality ultimately grounded in the form of the good.

In both cases, the impermanence of everyday reality and the human capacity for knowledge provide opportunities for self-transformation. This immediately results in world-transformation, because reality does not consist of separate individuals but of qualities: forms, ultimately grounded in the form of the good for Plato and doings, which can be re-oriented towards the good, as the removal of suffering, for the Buddhist.

Notes

1 The impermanence of phenomena is the core metaphysical postulate on which all metaphysical and ethical claims of early Buddhism and Mahāyāna Buddhism rest. However, *nirvāṇa*, in early Buddhism, is a reality that is not one of impermanence; and ultimate reality in Mahāyāna Buddhism is simply conventional (impermanent) reality understood as being empty of inherent nature. Nevertheless, given the lengths to which both early and Mahāyāna Buddhism avoid presenting *nirvāṇa* and 'emptiness' as 'ultimate' metaphysical existents, impermanence may rightly be considered to be the only reality that Buddhists emphasize and advocate, if only 'conventionally' or pragmatically.

2 This appears to be a controversial claim regarding Plato, especially if we think of the *Phaedo*, where the human soul is described as the stable, self-identical entity, opposed to the body, that we really are. However, Plato argues in various other dialogues that everything consists of forms. We show that, according to Plato, human beings also consist of forms, and this helps to make sense of a crucial passage in the *Symposium*.

3 *Upādāna*, is grasping or appropriation instigated by desire and will.

4 For an excellent introduction to Plato, see Constance C. Meinwald, *Plato* (New York: Routledge, 2016).

5 For example, Stanley Rosen, *Plato's Symposium* (New Haven and London: Yale University Press, 1968); Richard Kraut, 'Plato on Love', in *The Oxford Handbook of Plato*, ed. Gail Fine (Oxford: Oxford University Press, 2008).

6 Plato, *Symposium*, trans. Tom Griffith (Berkeley and Los Angeles: University of California Press, 1993). We use Griffith's translation unless otherwise specified, when Fowler's translation is offered as a comparison.

7 We would like to thank Stephen Harris for suggesting this connection during a lecture on this topic at the 13th Annual Meeting of The Comparative & Continental Philosophy Circle, April 2018, Bath, UK.

8   This might seem a bold claim to make about Plato, especially if one thinks of the 'soul *versus* body' opposition as presented in the *Phaedo*. However, we should keep in mind that Plato has various models of the soul in different dialogues that can be explained as ways to adapt to Socrates's changing interlocutors and the specific topic at hand – rather than as definitive metaphysical accounts. Michael Griffin, 'The Ethics of Self-Knowledge in Platonic and Buddhist Philosophy', in *Ethics without Self, Dharma without Atman*, ed. Gordon F. Davis (Cham: Springer, 2018), 48 refers to the tension between the unified soul of the *Phaedo* and the complex soul of the *Republic*. In the *Republic*, the soul consists of strands or parts (reason, temper, desire) and different motivations and functions, each of which may pull in different directions. Griffin convincingly argues (38–9) that, for Plato, the soul's unity is the goal of *cultivation* rather than a metaphysical given: unity and harmony happen when each of the different principles of the soul engage in their own function and not interfere with each another (*Rep.* 4. 443D-E). In *Rep.* 9. 588C ff. Plato compares the default state of human beings to a manifold: a many-headed beast, which looks like one man from without but like many from within. Whereas the cultivation of justice makes the different parts allies of each other, injustice results in the parts pulling in different directions: 'our ordinary (descriptive) experience of selfhood really is plural, but we can strive (prescriptively) to constitute ourselves as a unity by identifying with our capacity for pure and practical reason' (38).

9   Seth Benardete, *The Being of the Beautiful: Plato's Theaetetus, Sophist, and Statesman* (Chicago: Chicago University Press, 2008), II:57 translates: 'It's on account of the weaving together of the species with one another that (the) speech has come to be for us.' Even if Plato uses this phrase to explain that no *discourse* is possible without the weaving together of forms, he seems to regard the interweaving of forms as reflecting what something ultimately is. When in the *Sophist*, they define what a sophist is, their account includes a range of 'interwoven' forms, including, among others, 'producing', 'imitating' and 'being human'.

10 Meinwald, *Plato*, 262.

11 The original Greek of the passage I have italicized is: '*tiktein ouk eidola arêtes, ate ouk eidôlou ephaptomenôi, alla alêthê, ate tou alêthous ephaptomenôi: tekonti de aretên alêthê …*' Harold N. Fowler, *Plato in Twelve Volumes*, vol. 9 (London: William Heinemann, 1925) translates as follows: 'to breed not illusions but true examples of virtue, since his contact is not with illusion but with truth. So, when he has begotten a true virtue …'

12 Rosen, *Plato's Symposium*, 276.

13 Yuji Kurihara, 'Telos and Philosophical Knowledge in Plato's Symposium', in *X SYMPOSIUM PLATONICUM-THE SYMPOSIUM* (Pisa: Proceedings, 2013), 15.

14 Ibid., 18–19.

15 Ibid., 17.

16 F. C. White, 'Virtue in Plato's Symposium', *Classical Quarterly* 54 (2004): 366.
17 Ibid., 374.
18 Kraut, 'Plato on Love', 300, 308.
19 Ibid., 298.
20 For example, Gabriel Richardson Lear, 'Permanent Beauty and Becoming Happy in Plato's Symposium', in 'Plato's Symposium'. *Issues in Interpretation and Reception*, ed. James Lesher, Debra Nails and Frisbee Sheffield (Harvard, MA: Harvard University Press, 2006); and Rosen, *Plato's Symposium*.
21 Lear, 'Permanent Beauty and Becoming Happy in Plato's Symposium', 111 n. 20, in Meinwald, *Plato*, 103, finds Plato's suggestion problematic that children of the psyche are better than children of flesh in making 'us' immortal. She refers to the discourses (*logoi*) about virtues, in dialogue with a younger friend, that lead to the generation of offspring of the psyche and comments: 'If the lover's understanding is genuine, then the account he grasps will not differ from the account of anyone else who genuinely understands. But in that case, how will his articulation of the account bring about the quasi-immortality of him rather than of anyone else who understands?' Rosen, *Plato's Symposium*, 228–9, interprets the Socratic remark that philosophy is preparation for dying as implying that noetic unity with the forms involves loss of one's individuality and concludes: 'Man is perpetually intermediate between two species of nothingness: the death of the body and the perfection of the psyche ... perfection of the psyche is a progressive loss of personality, and so a falling away from personal immortality.'
22 Meinwald, *Plato*, 104.
23 White, 'Virtue in Plato's Symposium', 374–5.
24 Buddhists reject the claim that there is such a thing as identity, including personal identity and existence, if this refers to the numerical identity of persons or objects over time (*SN* I.134-135; *MN* 22, 72; *Milindapañha* 25–8, 40–1), or the existence of a substantive self or substantial objects (*MN* 22; *Ratnāvalī* I.27–8, 30).
25 See *MN* 22. It is because the practices of no-self attenuate the sense of self and lead to the realization that the idea of self is, in some way, illusory that they prove transformative.
26 See, for example, Amber Carpenter, *Indian Buddhist Philosophy* (Abingdon, Oxon and New York: Routledge, 2014).
27 In early Buddhism (third to fourth century BCE), what might be called 'virtues' include in their scope moral conduct (*śīla*), which includes the cultivation of non-afflictive emotions (*akleśa*), good or meritorious (*puṇya*) actions, skilful or wholesome (*kuśala*) actions; insight or wisdom (*prajñā*) which recognizes the 'truth' of the Buddha's teachings; and meditative cultivation (*samādhi*). In Mahāyāna Buddhism (from the first century CE onwards), the virtuous perfections (*pāramitā*) include generosity, moral conduct, patience, energy, meditation and wisdom (see § 2.1).

28 Rupert Gethin, 'He Who Sees Dhammas Sees Dhamma: Dhamma in Early Buddhism', *Journal of Indian Philosophy* 32 (2004): 534–6.
29 Ibid., 536.
30 Note that *dharmas* are the five types of phenomenologically distinct mental and physical qualities that characterize the experience of embodied existence in a world (*loka*), namely the body and senses (*rūpa*); sensations and feelings (*vedanā*); perception and cognition (*saṃjñā*); dispositions, conative impulses and constructive factors (*saṃskāra*); and consciousness (*vijñāna*). Collections of each of the five types of *dharmas* are called the five aggregates (*skandhas*).
31 Gethin, 'He Who Sees Dhammas Sees Dhamma: Dhamma in Early Buddhism', 536.
32 Ibid., 536. The extinguishment of suffering comes from extinguishing its three 'roots', delusion (*moha*), especially the delusion of a self or identity, which leads to desirous attachment (*rāga*) and aversion (*dveṣa*).
33 Whatever is dependently co-arisen / That is explained to be emptiness. / That, being a dependent designation, / Is itself the middle way [of the Buddha] (*MMK* 24.18).
34 This is, of course, akin to the Buddha's description of *nirvāṇa* as 'unborn, unbecome, unmade, unfabricated' (*AN* 4.179) because it is the extinguishment of dependent co-arising. The distinction between early Buddhism and Madhyamaka is that whereas the Buddha's description refers ultimately to *parinirvāṇa* which comes with the death of the aggregates, for Madhyamaka this is a description of ordinary, conventional reality, *saṃsāra*, seen by the enlightened mind. This does not necessarily contradict what the Buddha says, given that the awakened one of course sees the phenomena of ordinary, conventional reality as 'unborn, unbecome, unmade' and so on.
35 See Jonardon Ganeri, *The Concealed Art of the Soul* (Oxford: Oxford University Press, 2007), 201–4.
36 As Candrakīrti says, 'from the beginning it (appropriating) has in its scope a sense of self' (Candrakīrti, *PP B* 212, 1.25–6, quoted in Ganeri, *The Concealed Art of the Soul*, 201).
37 In Ganeri, *The Concealed Art of the Soul*, 204.
38 M. Sprung, trans. *Lucid Exposition of the Middle Way: The Essential Chapters from the Prasannapadā of Candrakīrti* (London and New York: Routledge, 2008), v. 213, 141.
39 Dan Lusthaus, *Buddhist Phenomenology: A Philosophical Investigation of Yogācāra Buddhism and the Ch'eng Wei-Shih Lun* (London and New York: Routledge, 2002), 66, 162.
40 We might say that the stream of qualities (*dharmas*) is unified by what Maurice Merleau-Ponty, *The Phenomenology of Perception*, trans. Colin Smith (London and New York: Routledge, 1962), 157 terms an 'intentional arc' (Matthew MacKenzie, 'Enacting Selves, Enacting Worlds: On the Buddhist Theory of Karma', *Philosophy East and West* 63, no. 2 (2013): 205).

41 Candrakīrti, similarly, suggests that abandoning 'all activity of self-appropriation of the psycho-physical ... is the end of the individual self', (*PP B* 350 in Ganeri, *The Concealed Art of the Soul*, 201–3).
42 See similar claims by the Buddha in *MN* 22. Note that metaphysical analysis is an aspect of meditative practice in the *BCA*.
43 See Jay L. Garfield, Stephen Jenkins and Graham Priest, 'The Śāntideva Passage: *Bodhicaryāvatāra* VIII.90-103', in *Moonpaths: Ethics and Emptiness*, ed. the Cowherds (New York: Oxford University Press, 2016).
44 Gethin, 'He Who Sees Dhammas Sees Dhamma: Dhamma in Early Buddhism', 535.
45 We may say of such activities, for example, lovingkindness, that they are 'self-arising', because they are 'self-enlightened', insofar as they embody and actualize – and indeed co-arise ceaselessly and unobstructedly with – the understanding of universal emptiness. See *The Holy Teaching of Vimalakīrti. A Mahāyāna Scripture*, trans. Robert Thurman (University Park: The Pennsylvania State University Press, 1976), 56.
46 *The Holy Teaching of Vimalakīrti. A Mahāyāna Scripture*, trans. Thurman, 56.
47 Note that altruistic activities such as lovingkindness (*maitrī*) follow three stages of metaphysical-meditative insight, first taking sentient beings as their object, then the *dharmas*, before becoming 'objectless' (ibid.).
48 As Nāgārjuna (*Ratnāvalī* I.1-I.9, III.30–40, IV.63, 98); see Amber Carpenter, 'Aiming at Happiness, Aiming at Ultimate Truth – in Practice', in *Moonpaths: Ethics and Emptiness*, ed. the Cowherds (New York: Oxford University Press, 2016) points out, moral discipline leads to the cultivation of wholesome (*kuśala*) mental states that are conducive to stability of mind. They promote happiness (*sukha*) or flourishing (*abhudaya*) that can function as a motivating factor at the beginning of the path of virtuous cultivation. Mental stability is necessary for mindfulness and meditative concentration that, in turn, foster evermore enduring states of happiness. Progression on the path invites a revision of aims towards evermore enduring states of happiness and goodness that lead to the highest good (*niḥśreyasa*), liberation (*mokṣa*).

Bibliography

Benardete, Seth. *The Being of the Beautiful: Plato's Theaetetus, Sophist, and Statesman*. Chicago: Chicago University Press, 2008.

Bodhi, Bhikkhu, trans. *The Connected Discourses of the Buddha: A New Translation of the Saṃyutta Nikāya*, vol. II. Boston: Wisdom Publications, 2000. [SN]

Bodhi, Bhikkhu, trans. *The Numerical Discourse of the Buddha: A New Translation of the Aṅguttara Nikāya*. Boston: Wisdom Publications, 2012. [AN]

Candrakīrti. *Introduction to the Middle Way. Chandrakirti's Madhyamakavatara with commentary by Jamgon Mipham*. Edited and translated by Padmakara Translation Group. Boston and London: Shambhala, 2012. [*MA*]

Carpenter, Amber. 'Aiming at Happiness, Aiming at Ultimate Truth –in Practice'. In *Moonpaths: Ethics and Emptiness*. Edited by The Cowherds, 21–42. New York: Oxford University Press, 2016.

Carpenter, Amber. *Indian Buddhist Philosophy*. Abingdon, Oxon and New York: Routledge, 2014.

Dennett, Daniel C. 'The Self as a Center of Narrative Gravity'. In *Self and Consciousness: Multiple Perspectives*. Edited by F. Kessel, P. Cole and D. Johnson. Hillsdale: Erlbaum, 1992. Available online: http://cogprints.org/266/1/selfctr.htm (accessed 17 July 2018).

Ganeri, Jonardon. *The Concealed Art of the Soul*. Oxford: Oxford University Press, 2007.

Garfield, Jay L., trans. *The Fundamental Wisdom of the Middle Way: Nāgārjuna's Mūlamadhyamakakārikā*. Oxford and New York: Oxford University Press, 1995. [*MMK*]

Garfield, Jay L., Stephen Jenkins and Graham Priest. 'The Śāntideva Passage: *Bodhicaryāvatāra* VIII.90-103'. In *Moonpaths: Ethics and Emptiness*. Edited by The Cowherds, 55–76. New York: Oxford University Press, 2016.

Gethin, Rupert. *The Foundations of Buddhism*. Oxford: Oxford University Press, 1998.

Gethin, Rupert. 'He Who Sees Dhammas Sees Dhamma: Dhamma in Early Buddhism'. *Journal of Indian Philosophy* 32 (2004): 513–42.

Griffin, M. 'The Ethics of Self-Knowledge in Platonic and Buddhist Philosophy'. In *Ethics without Self, Dharma without Atman*. Edited by Gordon F. Davis, 21–72. Cham: Springer, 2018.

Goodman, C., trans. *The Training Anthology of Śāntideva: A Translation of the Śikṣā-samuccaya*. Oxford: Oxford University Press, 2016. [*ŚS*]

Hershock, Peter D. *Valuing Diversity: Buddhist Reflection on Realizing a More Equitable Global Future*. Albany: SUNY Press, 2012.

Hopkins, Jeffrey., trans. *Nāgārjuna's Precious Garland: Buddhist Advice for Living and Liberation*. Boston and London: Snow Lion Publications, 2007.

Kraut, Richard. 'Plato on Love'. In *The Oxford Handbook of Plato*. Edited by Gail Fine, 286–310. Oxford: Oxford University Press, 2008. Available online: https://www.scholars.northwestern.edu/en/publications/plato-on-love-2 (accessed 17 July 2018).

Kurihara, Yuji. 'Telos and Philosophical Knowledge in Plato's Symposium'. In X SYMPOSIUM PLATONICUM–THE SYMPOSIUM. Pisa: Proceedings, 2013. Available online: https://www.aicgroup.it/wp-content/uploads/X-SYMPOSIUM-PLATONICUM_proceedings_1.pdf (accessed 17 July 2018).

Lear, Gabriel Richardson. 'Permanent Beauty and Becoming Happy in Plato's Symposium'. In 'Plato's Symposium'. *Issues in Interpretation and Reception*. Edited by James Lesher, Debra Nails and Frisbee Sheffield, 96–123. Harvard: Harvard University Press, 2006.

Lusthaus, Dan. *Buddhist Phenomenology: A Philosophical Investigation of Yogācāra Buddhism and the Ch'eng Wei-Shih Lun*. London and New York: Routledge, 2002.

MacKenzie, Matthew. 'Enacting Selves, Enacting Worlds: On the Buddhist Theory of Karma'. *Philosophy East and West* 63, no. 2 (2013): 194–212.

Meinwald, Constance C. 'Goodbye to the Third Man'. In *The Cambridge Companion to Plato*. Edited by R. Kraut, 365–96. Cambridge: Cambridge University Press, 1992.

Meinwald, Constance C. 'How Does Plato's Exercise Work?' *Dialogue* 53 (2014): 465–94.

Meinwald, Constance C. *Plato*. Abingdon, Oxford: Routledge, 2016.

Merleau-Ponty, Maurice. *The Phenomenology of Perception*. Translated by Colin Smith. London and New York: Routledge, 1962.

Ñāṇamoli, Bhikkhu and Bhikkhu Bodhi, trans. *The Middle Length Discourses of the Buddha: A New Translation of the Majjhima Nikāya*. Boston: Wisdom Publications, 1992. [MN]

Ophuijsen, Johannes M. Van. 'The Continuity of Plato's dialectic: An Afterword'. In *Plato and Platonism* Edited by Johannes M. Van Ophuijsen, 292–314. Washington DC: Catholic University of America Press, 1999.

Plato. *Plato in Twelve Volumes*, vol. 3. Translated by W. R. M. Lamb. Cambridge, MA: Harvard University Press; London: William Heinemann Ltd., 1967. Available online: http://www.perseus.tufts.edu/ (accessed 17 July 2018).

Plato. *Plato in Twelve Volumes*, vol. 9. Translated by Harold N. Fowler. Cambridge, MA: Harvard University Press; London: William Heinemann Ltd., 1925. Available online: http://www.perseus.tufts.edu/ (accessed 17 July 2018).

Plato. *Symposium*. Translated by Tom Griffith. Berkeley and Los Angeles: University of California Press, 1993.

Rhys Davids, T. W., trans. *The Questions of King Milinda*, 2 vols. Oxford: Clarendon Press, 1890, 1894.

Ricoeur, Paul. 'Narrative Identity'. *Philosophy Today* 35 (1991): 73–81.

Rosen, Stanley. *Plato's Symposium*. New Haven and London: Yale University Press, 1968.

Sprung, M., trans. *Lucid Exposition of the Middle Way: The Essential Chapters from the Prasannapadā of Candrakīrti*. London and New York: Routledge, 2008. [PP]

Thurman, Robert, trans. *The Holy Teaching of Vimalakīrti: A Mahāyāna Scripture*. University Park: The Pennsylvania State University Press, 1976.

Wallace, Vesna A. and B. Alan Wallace, trans. *A Guide to the Bodhisattva Way of Life (Bodhicaryavatara) by Santideva*. Ithaca: Snow Lion Publications, 1997. [BCA]

White, F. C. 'Virtue in Plato's Symposium'. *Classical Quarterly* 54 (2004): 366–78.

4

Application of tradition in Gadamer and the sameness-otherness of Islamic philosophy

Selami Varlik

Introduction

One of the criticisms that is addressed today to the study of Islamic philosophy is that it is seen as part of a past cut off from the contemporary world. According to Nader El-Bizri, this archival approach to the intellectual history of Islam is an antiquarian compiler of knowledge and is not strictly philosophical since it uses the methods of historiography and philology to establish primarily textual documents.[1] El-Bizri believes that this way of approaching the Islamic corpus lies in continuity with classical and medievalist methods of the study of Greek and Latin texts, in the context of which Islamic philosophy is identified. This approach is of course necessary; but it leaves little room for the question of the meaning and value of the concepts involved from the point of view of contemporary thought.[2] In contrast to this approach is the desire to revive Islamic philosophy in a close correlation with contemporary thought.[3]

Comparative or intercultural philosophy responds to a certain extent to this concern for an application of Islamic philosophy to the present.[4] On the one hand, it does this directly by bringing together a former author of the Islamic tradition (such as Mulla Sadra, Avicenna, Ibn Arabi) and a Western contemporary author (such as Heidegger, Derrida).[5] The works of Henry Corbin, who was a reader and translator of Heidegger, played an important role in the development of this comparatist approach as a rapprochement between the transformative scope of Islamic philosophy and the phenomenology of the subject.[6]

On the other hand, the method of comparative studies indirectly affects the issue of the application to the present, when two ancient authors, such as Avicenna and Leibniz or Mulla Sadra and Master Eckhart, are compared.[7]

These new readings are more generally part of a constant reconstruction of their representation of the past and are engaged in a re-evaluation in contemporary contexts, to achieve new goals specific to new situations.[8] This process is therefore never merely descriptive and neutral; it is anchored in the present of the very subject who makes the comparison. In this sense, the comparison is always based on some form of reinterpretation, or at least a reformulation of philosophical traditions.

While the comparisons focus the content of these philosophies through a conceptual encounter, this chapter aims to approach the question from a formal angle by discussing via Gadamer the very question of the application of tradition to the present as a philosophical problem. For Gadamer, since the application is not a second phase independent of understanding, we have to apply 'the text to be understood to the interpreter's present situation'.[9] The poetic and philosophical texts are thus inexhaustible because in both cases, the course of events brings out new aspects of the meaning of historical documents.[10]

This raises the question: Could the Gadamerian notion of application, particularly developed in *Truth and Method*, be used to defend a similar process in the field of Islamic philosophy? The challenge would be to ask the question of the conditions of contemporary reinterpretation of the past in the specific case of the texts of the Islamic tradition that have to do with both the figure of the same and the other. This is because behind the question of the synchronic otherness between two traditions lies a deeper question of how to cross the historical distance with the past. For Gadamer, to understand a text requires an application to oneself through a reappropriation of tradition. So, we will see first how the application of philosophical texts requires a reciprocal questioning between the past and the present; secondly, to what extent this questioning implies the sharing of a common but plural tradition; thirdly, why Islamic philosophy represents a historical figure of sameness-otherness, both within Western tradition and outside; and finally, how in this way a cross is formed between two hermeneutic circles, by which the application of the other tradition becomes also an opportunity of self-transformation.

Application and mutual questioning

Romantic hermeneutics was been wrong to conceive the interpretation according to the philological model which suggests that the stage of application to a new situation is a second step, independent of understanding itself. This model has resulted in a generalization of the historical distancing of the text thus objectified. Whereas instead, it seems that understanding occurs simultaneously with the application. Understanding is based on the tension between the text, which is always identical, and its application at the concrete moment of interpretation.

The application of the text to the present is in fact both application to oneself and appropriation of a tradition. Firstly, the application is not only an application to a new situation but also and especially an application to the self at stake in this situation. The actualization of the meaning of the text requires applying something universal to oneself.[11] We must specify what the requirement implies here. Gadamer's position is incontestably above all descriptive. He does not propose a certain method to ensure good understanding, but elaborates a phenomenology of the experience of understanding. He does not therefore claim that the meaning originally acquired *must* be applied. This 'naive application of tradition' is still part of the duality between the understanding phase and the application phase.[12] But he does say that a good understanding *must* include the question of application. The difference between the two requirements is that only the latter affects the very understanding of the text. He thus advocates a certain way of reading by stating that 'understanding philosophical texts always *requires* re-cognizing what is cognized in them', without departing from the historical conditions in which the reader is situated.[13] If application, as concretization of a universal sense, is thus presented as a 'task', it means that understanding must involve the application and not that what has been understood must be applied.[14] So, his philosophical hermeneutics 'is "normative" to the degree that it aims to replace a bad philosophy with a better one'.[15]

Legal and theological hermeneutics, namely the application of the law and the preaching of the Word, represent here a model. The text of the law and the religious text are not historical documents that exist independently of their application. The first must have legal authority and the second must have a saving effect affecting the very being of the reader. Theological hermeneutics presupposes that 'the word of Scripture addresses us and that only the person who allows himself to be addressed – whether he believes or doubts – understands'.[16] From then on, the application of any philosophical text passes by the possibility of considering it according to a theological, religious model turned towards the personal application. Given the close relations of Islamic philosophy with Islamic theology and law, it seems to us to be fully integrated into Gadamer's schema of the self-application of philosophical discourse, especially since, as we indicated earlier, Islamic philosophy is itself inscribed to a certain extent in this paradigm of salvation of the soul.

But by writing 'whether he believes or doubts', Gadamer reminds us that he offers the possibility of seeing how the contemporary application operates in the very form of the process independently of the – religious – content of the message. Just as Gadamer does not propose a method of comprehension but describes the experience of the subject who understands, so the phenomenological description of the application process is independent of the content to be applied. It is also in this sense that his hermeneutics is universal and goes beyond the framework of theological, poetic or philosophical texts. It is less a question of how to apply – as with the legal or religious texts – than the formal question of application to the reader's life of the idea of application that the text carries in its content.[17]

The crucial question, then, is how to apply a philosophical text which has no normative or prescriptive scope. Here it is not a question of playing a score, of obeying a law or of answering a religious call, but of the application to one's particular life of a philosophical text which claims to contain a universal truth, and which, even if it is influenced by religious patterns – in the case of Islamic philosophy – is not a religious text. Gadamer answers the question with the logic of question and answer that operates within a tradition of thought animated by the dynamism of the work of history. The application of the philosophical text takes place through a question-and-answer game between the text and the reader, where each is the questioner and the questioned. The necessity defended here is not that of the application of a philosophical text already understood but that of an understanding including the moment of application through questioning, because 'a person who wants to understand must question what lies behind what is said'.[18] Gadamer uses Collingwood here to defend the necessity of asking the question that the text answers, but he thinks of this answer itself in its relation to the questions posed by the reader and the questions put to her by the text. And it is this reciprocity of questioning that prevents the application from sliding into a domineering possession of meaning.

At the very moment of interpretation application is in fact doubly transformative of both the object applied and the *locus* of application. And this double transformation is the counterpart of the tension created by a double fidelity. On the one hand, as an application *to someone*, any application is loyal to a particular context. It is here that the applied text that is pushed towards new horizons of meaning. For a reader to think about a text is always for her to ask questions from her particular horizon of interrogation. But on the other hand, as an application *of something*, the application is also a fidelity to the text being applied. In this sense, it is the very *locus* of the application of the text that is transformed. The text itself does not just provide new answers to new questions, because its questions themselves question the reader, so that 'the questioner becomes the one who is questioned'.[19] Gadamer sums up this ambivalence through the notion of 'tension' between the text (art, theology, law) and the new situation. Between these two senses of questioning the relation is circular because the reader questions precisely in order to answer the questions posed by the text. It is to answer the questions of the text that she questions herself. This dialectic makes it possible to maintain the questioning.

A common and plural tradition

The condition for this model of mutual questioning to work is the sharing of a common tradition – at least the belonging of the text and the reader to the same history of effects. It is the *Wirkungsgeschichte*, to which one is always already subjected, which allows the determination of the right new questions.[20] The fact that the reader's questioning lies in the continuity of the effects of meaning of the same text in the long history of its reception is a fundamental 'criterion' for Gadamer.[21] We therefore find a certain criteriological dimension already cited; belonging to a tradition is 'one of the conditions of understanding in the human sciences'.[22]

A common tradition is central because the question-answer dialectic is based on a common language so that the interlocutors can at least understand each other.[23] Since this language is that of the interpreter, the other is obliged to speak the language of the self in order to be part of the questioning play. The mutual questioning operates in both directions through the continuity of a tradition. On the one hand, the tradition that carries the texts of the past answers the questions posed by the contemporary reader; but on the other hand, it's the same tradition that questions the reader, who is 'perplexed by the traditionary word'.[24] The very expectation of the answer given by tradition presupposes that the questioner is part of the tradition and regards herself as addressed by it. It is the continuity of tradition that allows the application of a text to a new situation.

But, as the tradition of the other is then always reduced to the tradition of the self, one could fully question the legitimacy of the application to a text of a completely different culture. For Gadamer, tradition in the singular is mainly the 'Western philosophical tradition'.[25] The multiple breaks and discontinuity do not call into question the fact that this tradition is thought of as a fundamental continuity. This notion of the homogeneity of tradition thus seems quite hermetic to the idea of a cross-cultural understanding, and Gadamer has often been criticized on this point. Waldenfels judges that Gadamer remains in a Hegelian perspective, in which the mind can only know itself. The fusion of horizons is thus an 'act of violence', in which the foreigner always ends up losing his irreducibility in the very act of understanding.[26] According to Waldenfels, the problem lies in the hermeneutic circle itself, which, closed on itself and moved by the immediacy of pre-comprehension, fails to open up to the other. A similar criticism is formulated by Caputo, for whom, the fusion of horizons operates as a negation of strangeness because 'we make the Other our own'.[27]

Yet, if Gadamer can hardly make room for an external otherness, he nevertheless leaves a place for plurality within each tradition itself. The form of otherness that seems most obvious is less that of the totally different tradition than an internal alterity allowing one to hear tradition and the work of history in a plural sense. The Western tradition is itself recognized as multiple since Gadamer evokes 'the traditions in which we stand'.[28] He gives examples of the internal plurality of tradition, citing how St. Augustine or early Protestantism tried to reconcile the Old Testament and the Christian message.[29] We find this same inner plurality when Gadamer explains why he speaks of the fusion of horizons in the plural even though he defends a continuity between these horizons.[30]

One passage of *Truth and Method* is particularly explicit:

> Our historical consciousness is always filled with a variety of voices in which the echo of the past is heard. Only in the multifariousness of such voices does it exist: this constitutes the nature of the tradition in which we want to share and have a part.[31]

These few lines are doubly emblematic. First, they clearly present past tradition as intrinsically plural – the plurality of voices echoing the word of tradition we cannot avoid hearing. Second, they present belonging to tradition as a dual relationship involving both the volunteer and the involuntary, as if the subject were free to feel closer to this or that tradition to which she already belonged.

Later, Gadamer will be much more explicit about this internal diversity of Western culture stating that it may be a particular privilege of Europe that it has learned, more than other regions, to live with others, even when they are different.[32] This co-existence with alterity would be precisely the 'true heritage of the European humanities'. In his interview with Pantham, he presents Europe's legacy as a unity in diversity without any uniformity or hegemony, and he adds that this model must become a global formula and be extended 'to the whole world – to include China, India, and also Muslim cultures'.[33]

Sameness and otherness of Islamic philosophy

However, this need for European openness to Chinese and Islamic cultures confirms precisely the evidence of profound otherness. In another late text Gadamer recalls that philosophy is born entirely in Europe and that East Asia and India really represent other worlds for European philosophy.[34] Furthermore, Fred Dallmayr admits that *Truth and Method* is even more closed to other traditions than later works.[35] We have seen to what extent the primacy of a common tradition makes it difficult to open up to a totally different culture like the Far East. But can Islamic thought be placed in the same category – the category that does not distinguish religious, philosophical and poetic dimensions – as Gadamer indeed does place it a few times?[36] Or, whether in the observation of difference or in the desire for rapprochement, does Islam represent for Gadamer the absolute other of Judaism and Christianity?

To answer the question, one would have to take a closer look at the part of otherness that a tradition contains in itself. Gadamer describes the links that a tradition represents as not self-evident, since the relation with the text is not an unquestioned, unbroken stream of tradition; it thus oscillates between familiarity and strangeness. Yet, here, the strangeness is only that of the historical distance that is overcome through objectifying historical science.[37] But it seems to us that the dual position of sameness and otherness of Islamic philosophy may represent another form of internal tension between familiarity and strangeness. For here the tension is not limited to the relation between the sameness of belonging, on the one hand, and the otherness of historical distance, on the other hand. The sameness is that of certain common notions and pre-comprehensions; and the otherness is that of a different conception of these notions or of a relation with other totally different notions. Islamic thought has indeed a hybrid status because unlike other non-Western traditions studied in comparative philosophy, it has 'both an "Eastern" and a "Western" face'.[38] It is inscribed to a certain extent in the continuity of the Greek philosophy and the Judeo-Christian monotheistic heritage that determine European identity; but it also has its own specificity which is a true theological and legal otherness.

The Islamic intellectual tradition cannot be confused with Greek and medieval notions of reason – given the extent to which uses of reason that in Islam are distinguished from the Greek *logos*. However, there is a crossroads: an intersection that is neither full sameness nor total otherness of tradition. Gadamer thus sheds light on our initial problem of the application of Islamic philosophy to the present, since he shows that it is only on the basis of a common history of effects that the application of the questioning answers of the past may be applied to the present. This approach allows us to question the relationship of otherness still ascribed to Islamic philosophy within Western philosophical circles.[39] This otherness can be religious or cultural when it is seen as Middle Eastern thought[40]; but it can also be chronological when Islamic philosophy is seen as a discipline of the past (not contemporary enough) and is identified with the Middle Ages – an image against which medieval philosophy itself had to struggle in the last century.[41]

Yet Islamic philosophy is only partially the other of European thought. And this can be shown by resorting to the very content of Gadamer's thought and not only the formal framework he proposes. It is thus important to note that he places his theory of belonging to tradition, to history, in continuity with the way that truth belongs to being in classical metaphysics. Ontological belonging serves as a general paradigm for the totality of the work, from aesthetic experience to language.[42] Belonging means that knowledge does not depend on a subject transforming everything into an object; it is rather an element of being itself. Gadamer reminds us that 'in metaphysics *belonging* refers to the transcendental relationship between being and truth'.[43] It is in this sense that Gadamer's approach is phenomenological, as a discovery of the mode of donation of things as they give themselves. The classical metaphysics to which Gadamer proposes to return is essentially the science of the transcendental. What is fundamental here is the fact that the universal predicates – the Beautiful, the Good, the True – are those of the very being and not those of the knowledge of the subject.[44] This is why, according to him, a return to the problems posed by classical metaphysics is necessary.

The formula that perfectly summarizes this belonging is that of the adequacy of knowledge to the known thing, which finds its origin in St. Thomas Aquinas for whom it is the convenience of a thing to the intellect that makes *adaequatio* possible. In Gadamer this link will take the form of a fusion of the thing and of understanding.[45] But when Thomas defines the truth as being in relation to which the truth of our knowledge is second, he appeals to two of his predecessors: 'This is why Augustine writes: "The true is that which is"; and Avicenna: "The truth of each thing is a property of the act of being which has been established for it".'[46]

More generally, the doctrine of the transcendentals that Gadamer evokes is considered to be inherited to a certain extent from Islamic philosophy. The idea goes back at least to Avicenna, who explains that all simple knowledge is based on certain first and indefinable concepts – *ens*, *res* and *necesse* – which are spontaneously and always internally received in the intellect.[47] These concepts originally printed in the soul function as *a priori* forms or conditions of knowledge of all things. Medieval philosophy specialist Jan Aertsen presents Avicenna as the author of the doctrine of transcendentals: 'What is usually credited to medieval philosophy should instead be regarded as an achievement of Arabic philosophy. Avicenna is more than a source of transcendental thought; he is the author.'[48] It is not a question of seeing here any pure or first origin, but of realizing to what extent Gadamerian philosophy is situated in a distant continuity to these debates within which the Islamic philosophy was an undeniable part.

This observation does not pose any real difficulties as Avicenna is also considered part of Western medieval heritage. But Islamic philosophy itself cannot be considered independently of Islamic thought in general, as the other of the Greek tradition. The Avicenna whom Gadamer situated in a distant continuity is not only a Greek figure since, even in the very notions that determined the history of medieval metaphysics, this figure of Avicenna also belongs to an otherness, that is an Islamic usage of reason. In other words, the idea of reason inherited by medieval metaphysics was not only Greek.[49]

Avicenna formulates this definition of truth in a passage on the truth of the Necessary Being, before which possible beings are non-existent, and concludes by quoting the verses 'All that is on earth will perish, but will abide [for ever] the Face of thy Lord, – full of Majesty, Bounty and Honour.'[50] This passage represents a convergence of Avicenna's prior epistemological accounts of truth with his theological identification of this truth with the divine being. For his theory of essence and existence cannot be thought independently of Islamic theology. In his study on the origins of the ontology of Avicenna, Jean Jolivet shows how it has one of its roots in properly Islamic speculation for 'it is in the *kalâm* that has prepared his doctrine of essence, which is undoubtedly the main element of his ontology'.[51] He evokes more precisely the question of the thingness of the non-existent and judges that the term 'thing' does not have a technical meaning in Aristotle, and that to find it in the form of a concept we must go back to the ninth- and tenth-century debates while the *mutakallimûn* were discussing whether God is properly speaking a thing like the others or not. Avicenna transposed their content into the philosophical field, but remained indebted to them in the detail of vocabulary, problematics and analyses.

Once again, it is not a question of reasoning in terms of pure origin, or even debt, but to resort to the idea of the plurality of traditions involved in the work of history in order to question the argument of a radical autonomy of philosophical discourse of the *falâsifa* with regard to theological discourse, or at least of the exclusivity of the Greek source, reducing religious references to non-philosophical popularization.⁵² Thus, de Libera believes that the first confrontation between Hellenism and monotheism, between faith and reason, took place in the Muslim world and that the West inherited this conflict already present in Islam.⁵³ It is therefore a religious rationality, 'put, for the first time and rigorously, in the service of a monotheistic religion' that initiates the medieval West.⁵⁴

Two crossing hermeneutic circles

Gadamer does not seem to be aware of this dimension of sameness-otherness of Islamic philosophy; yet his model of the application of traditional texts to the present can make room for this ambivalence precisely because philosophical dialogue does not imply an agreement on what should be said. For Gadamer, it is talking about the same common subject matter (*sache*) that is important, not saying the same thing. And because the tradition is primarily linguistic, the two interlocutors must speak the same language, in order to be able to understand each other, even if they do not defend the same visions of the thing.⁵⁵ There is therefore agreement on the question, not on the answer. Whether the philosophical dialogue takes place with the other or with the past of the self, in both cases it is rather an 'open "court" of dialogue and mutual questioning'.⁵⁶ And what for Gadamer permits this reciprocal questioning is precisely the fact that – and he says it precisely to refuse the accusation of logocentrism formulated by Derrida:

> Difference exists within identity. Otherwise, identity would not be identity. Thought contains deferral and distance. Otherwise, thought would not be thought.⁵⁷

What thus makes possible the diversity of the future appropriation of tradition is thus its plurality, its internal inadequacy.⁵⁸

Yet, in *Truth and Method*, the tradition that allows the unfolding of this questioning is above all the Western tradition, which can be characterized as a conflict between different visions about the same things. Here difference is mainly difference in the same. Islamic thought can precisely expand this model from the inside, because, thanks to its hybrid status, it crosses the synchronic otherness of the other today and the diachronic otherness of the self yesterday, both the other outside and the other within the self. Just as de Libera states that we cannot 'work on the Middle Ages without letting the Middle Ages work in us', so it seems that the same can be said of Islamic philosophy.[59] To work on Islamic philosophy by going beyond the strict historical approach and by making the effort of applying its concepts to contemporary philosophy requires Western philosophy to accept being worked by this other. We therefore fully subscribe to the wish of de Libera who, using the same logic of questions and answers as Collingwood, invites us to 'repatriate the Arab-Muslim philosophy into the history of philosophy' and thus to propose another history of reason in order to proceed to a cultural and religious opening up.[60]

By taking this approach, the application of the other tradition through the development of a contemporary Islamic philosophy and the emergence of new concepts also becomes a means of the self-transformation of Western philosophy. The encounter with the other, therefore, has a critical dimension for the self. The aim is therefore not to reinforce the centrality of Western philosophy, but on the contrary to give oneself the means to criticize it, and to make sure that this criticism is part of the very potential of the history of its concepts, so that the evolution is real. In other words, the otherness of the other is of truly critical importance only in so far as it relays and radicalizes an alterity already present in itself. It is this internal otherness that can allow a true opening to an external otherness. This is the counterpart in the play of double questioning that we described earlier. The dialectic of reviving can only be undertaken out of a tension between familiarity and strangeness: the familiarity of a tradition, of a partly common history of concepts, and the strangeness of another religious relation to these notions.

Therefore, the hermeneutic circle can evolve from within. If Waldenfels is right and the circle is closed on itself, the only way to open it up is to see the parts it has in common with another circle. In this way, we obtain a crossing of two hermeneutic circles: it is not so much two sets that intersect on a common area as two hermeneutic circles with common philosophical concepts. In this reflection, we take Avicenna as a common element participating in different wholes. In the very name of the history of effects described by Gadamer it is precisely because theological and religious references are present in the origins of his metaphysics that downstream he will be so decisive for the theology and sufism of post-classical period. From the point of view of the conceptual language that he instituted, Avicenna will therefore be unavoidable for Ghazali or Mulla Sadra, to whom Heidegger is often compared.[61] But his metaphysics, and especially the essence-existence duality, also had a major influence on medieval thought, especially on Master Eckhart.[62] We cannot think of this influence independently of his relation to religious language; prophecy, for example, is one of the Avicennian elements whose impact in Master Eckhart is the 'most evident'.[63] And it is some of the key ideas of this same Master Eckhart that we will find in Heidegger.[64]

Conclusion

For Gadamer, tradition is movable, expandable and can open up to new horizons. So, we ourselves participate in its evolution because 'we produce it ourselves inasmuch as we understand, participate in this evolution of tradition, and hence further determine it ourselves'.[65] The circle of understanding is not a methodological tool in the hand of the subject who dominates the meaning but an ontological circle in which she is always taken up. To join a tradition is at the same time an alteration and not simply a defence of existing conditions.[66] But this evolution itself is possible only from the movement of a common basis, which we precisely have in the case of Islamic philosophy. Like the ship of Theseus, tradition evolves only gradually, through a dialectic of sameness and otherness. Like the horizon of the gaze, which, when it moves, never changes suddenly, but abandons and integrates certain elements from a common base, 'horizons change for a person who is moving'.[67] It is the refusal of this change that exposes us to the risk of a Western hegemony.

It is undeniable that we are talking here of two different intellectual and religious traditions with many theological divergences, which are sometimes even of the order of the incommensurable. For, participation in Gadamer is also participation in exclusively Christian doctrines, such as incarnation in St. Augustine. This model does not exclude at all the emphasis that could and should be placed on the otherness of Islamic philosophy and the need to delve into the internal plurality of the Islamic tradition itself, in the very name of the history of effects. Gadamer also shows us that the emergence of the new cannot be done without an awareness of the diversity and richness of the old.

In accordance with Gadamer's hermeneutics, which is less of a methodological proposition than of a phenomenological description, it is not a matter of defending an approach but of saying that when there is use of the concepts of contemporary Western philosophy, whether in a comparatist framework or in the interest of applying Islamic thought to the present, this work cannot be done without taking into account the dialectic of sameness and otherness that exists in the history of the notions at stake.[68] Therefore, given the common history of effects, to think together Gadamer and Avicenna is no longer really to do comparative philosophy, as we are reminded by the example of Heidegger and Mulla Sadra that we mentioned earlier.[69] This seems necessary so that the works *on* the margin of Western philosophy do not remain themselves *at* the margin of Western philosophy, as attempts cut from each other, and not affecting the very heart of academic philosophy. A common conceptual language is needed to build a creative continuity connecting multiple isolated works in which both are affected by the meeting (Husserl/Heidegger and Avicenna or Heidegger and Ibn Arabi/Mulla Sadra, etc.).

We wonder, therefore, to what extent, in the specific case of Islamic philosophy, the very idea of comparative philosophy does not indirectly nourish the idea that there are already two fundamentally different traditions between which it would be necessary to build bridges – bridges that remind us both of the concern for the link and the evidence of the gap between the two banks. It is not about opposing comparative philosophy but about promoting a form of philosophy – or intercultural philosophy – which, going beyond the mere study of historical influences, integrates the cross between the two hermeneutic circles, so that otherness revives works based on sameness.[70]

Notes

1 Nader El-Bizri, 'The Labyrinth of Philosophy in Islam', *Comparative Philosophy* 1, no. 2 (2010): 5.

2 For a similar position, see Muhsin Mahdi, ˌOrientalism and the Study of Islamic Philosophy', *Journal of Islamic Studies* 1 (1990): 93.

3 El-Bizri, 'Labyrinth', 7.

4 We will not enter into debates on the difference between these two expressions because – even if it is less the case for the second – they both presuppose to a certain extent an initial alterity between two traditions, which represents the idea discussed here. See William Sweet, 'Introduction: The Project of Intercultural Philosophy', in *What Is Intercultural Philosophy?* ed. William Sweet (Washington: The Council for Research in Values and Philosophy, 2014), 3–5; and Robert W. Smid, *Methodologies of Comparative Philosophy: The Pragmatist and Process Traditions* (New York: SUNY Press, 2009), 2.

5 El-Bizri is himself the author of many works of comparative philosophy, notably Nader El-Bizri, *The Phenomenological Quest between Avicenna and Heidegger* (Binghamton: Global Publications, 2000).

6 In accordance with Mohammad Azadpur and Christian Jambet, we use the term 'Islamic philosophy' in a sense including both the Peripatetic philosophy and its

influence on philosophers mixing discursive and intuitive approaches, such as Suhrawardi, Mulla Sadra or Qūnawī. And it is precisely the focus on the cultivation of the self, close to the philosophy as a way of life of Pierre Hadot, that permits this continuity. See Christian Jambet, *Qu'est-ce que la philosophie islamique?* (Paris: Galimard, 2011); Mohammad Azadpur, *Reason Unbound: On Spiritual Practice in Islamic Peripatetic Philosophy* (New York: SUNY Press, 2011). For Azadpur, the purification of one's being also allows a rapprochement with contemporary phenomenology (Azadpur, *Reason Unbound*, 21). On this last point, we can also mention the works of Anna-Teresa Tymieniecka, and especially Anna-Teresa Tymieniecka (ed.), *The Passions of the Soul in the Metamorphosis of Becoming* (Dordrecht: Kluwer Academic Publishers, 2003).

7 See Ali Paya (ed.), *The Misty Land of Ideas and The Light of Dialogue. An Anthology of Comparative Philosophy: Western and Islamic* (London: ICAS Press, 2014).

8 Mahmoud Khatami, 'On the Very Idea of Comparative Philosophy: Some Preliminary Remarks for a Meta-Theory', in *The Misty Land of Ideas and The Light of Dialogue. An Anthology of Comparative Philosophy: Western and Islamic*, ed. Ali Paya (London: ICAS Press, 2014), 157.

9 Hans-Georg Gadamer, *Truth and Method*, second revised edition, translation revised by Joel Weinsheimer and Donald G. Marshall (London and New York: Continuum, 2004), 307.

10 Ibid., 366.

11 Ibid., 328.

12 Hans-Georg Gadamer, 'Reply to my Critics', in *The Hermeneutic Tradition: From Ast to Ricoeur*, ed. Gayle L. Ormiston and Alan D. Schrift (New York: SUNY Press, 1990), 283.

13 Gadamer, *Truth and Method*, 368. Emphasis added.

14 Ibid., 328, 575.

15 Gadamer, 'Reply', 282.

16 Gadamer, *Truth and Method*, 328.

17 This is why Gadamer seems important to us, despite the warnings of Seyyed Hossein Nasr. The latter also insists on the need to reformulate with a new language the spiritual message of Islamic philosophy but opposes any rapprochement with contemporary philosophy fundamentally devoid of spiritual intuition. Comparison is only possible with the premodern, Greek and medieval West. Seyyed Hossein Nasr, 'The Meaning and Concept of Philosophy in Islam', in *History of Islamic Philosophy*, part I, ed. Seyyed Hossein Nasr and Oliver Leaman (London and New York: Routledge, 2003), 23–4.

18 Gadamer, *Truth and Method*, 363.

19 Ibid., 457. Gadamer's two corrections to Collingwood's theory correspond precisely to the two poles of the tension of the application because, on the one hand, the

question to which the text responds goes beyond the question that was consciously thought of by the author and 'merges with our own questioning' (Ibid., 367), and, on the other hand, the very answer of the text poses new questions that are as many occasions for questioning the self.

20 Ibid., 301.
21 Ibid., 468: 'Here too, certainly, there is a standard by which understanding is measured and which it can meet: the content of the tradition itself is the sole criterion and it expresses itself in language.'
22 Ibid., 325.
23 Ibid., 387.
24 Ibid., 366.
25 Ibid., xxiii.
26 Bernhard Waldenfels, *Vielstimmigkeit der Rede. Studien zur Phänomenologie des Fremden 4* (Frankfurt am Main: Suhrkamp, 1999), 74.
27 John D. Caputo, *More Radical Hermeneutics: On Not Knowing Who We Are* (Bloomington: Indiana University Press, 2000), 42. Xinli Wang refuses the effectiveness of the Gadamer model to think Chinese philosophy because the common horizon is 'exactly what is missing between two disparate c-p languages such as the Chinese and Western cultural traditions'. Xinli Wang, 'Incommensurability and Comparative Philosophy', *Philosophy East and West* 68, no. 2 (April 2018): 579.
28 Gadamer, *Truth and Method*, xxii. See also Hans-Georg Gadamer, 'Philosophical Apprenticeship', in *The Many Faces of Philosophy: Reflections from Plato to Arendt*, ed. Amélie Oksenberg Rorty (Oxford: Oxford University Press, 2003), 469.
29 Gadamer, *Truth and Method*, 292.
30 Ibid., 305.
31 Ibid., 285.
32 Hans-Georg Gadamer, *Das Erbe Europas* (Frankfurt am Main: Suhrkamp Verlag, 1989), 30.
33 Thomas Pantham, 'Some Dimensions of the Universality of Philosophical Hermeneutics: A Conversation with Hans-Georg Gadamer', *Journal of Indian Council of Philosophical Research* 9 (1992): 132.
34 Hans-Georg Gadamer, 'Europa und die Oikoumene', in *Hermeneutik im Rückblick. Gesammelte Werke* Band 10 (Tübingen: Mohr, 1995), 267.
35 Fred Dallmayr, *Beyond Orientalism: Essays on Cross-Cultural Encounter* (New-York: SUNY Press, 1996), 41.
36 Hans-Georg Gadamer, 'Herméneutique et théologie', *Revue des sciences religieuses* 51 (1977): 386. He makes the same observation about Indian or Chinese traditions of thought, for which 'we cannot even ask whether we are dealing with poetry, religion, or philosophy'. Hans-Georg Gadamer, 'Aesthetic and Religious Experience',

in *The Relevance of the Beautiful*, ed. R. Bernasconi (Cambridge: Cambridge University Press, 1986), 140. So, the term 'revealed religion' can only 'be applied to the Jewish and Christian religions'. Indeed, he 'can ignore Islam, whose religious proclamation represents a special problem', that he cannot go into since he does not know Arabic at all. See Gadamer, 'Aesthetic', 145. He also excludes Islamic thought in Hans-Georg Gadamer, 'Religious and Poetical Speaking', in *Myth, Symbol, and Reality*, ed. A. M. Olson (Notre Dame: University of Notre Dame Press, 1980), 92.

37 Gadamer, *Truth and Method*, 295.
38 Tamara Albertini, 'Ibn Rushd or Averroës? Of Double Names and Double Truths: A Different Approach to Islamic Philosophy', in *After Appropriation: Explorations in Intercultural Philosophy and Religion*, ed. Morny Joy (Calgary: Calgary University Press, 2011), 221.
39 Or, in the other sense, religious otherness can be totally ruled out and the name 'Arabic philosophy' is preferred to that of 'Islamic philosophy'. See Dimitri Gutas, 'The Study of Arabic Philosophy in the Twentieth Century an Essay on the Historiography of Arabic Philosophy', *British Journal of Middle Eastern Studies* 29, no. 1 (2002): 17–18.
40 Tamara Albertini, 'Reintroducing Islamic Philosophy: The Persisting Problem of "Smaller Orientalisms"', in *Oxford Handbook of World Philosophy*, ed. Jay L. Garfield and William Edelglass (Oxford: Oxford University Press, 2010), 392.
41 Ibid., 390.
42 Mathieu Scraire, 'Les sources médiévales du concept gadamérien d'appartenance dans *Vérité et méthode*', *Laval théologique et philosophique* 65, no. 1 (2009): 96–8.
43 Gadamer, *Truth and Method*, 454.
44 Jean Grondin, *Introduction to Metaphysics: From Parmenides to Levinas*, trans. Lukas Soderstrom (New York: Columbia University Press, 2012), 238.
45 Jean Grondin, 'La fusion des horizons. La version gadamérienne de l'*adæquatio rei et intellectus*?' *Archives de Philosophie* 68, no. 3 (2005): 417.
46 Thomas Aquinas, *Truth. Volume I: Questions I-IX*, trans. Robert W. Mulligan (Eugene: Wipf and Stock, 2008), 6. Avicenna, *The Metaphysics of The Healing*, translated, introduced and annotated by Michael E. Marmura (Provo: Brigham Young University Press, 2005), 284. For a study of similarities and differences between Avicenna and Aquinas on the question of the transcendentals, see Jan A. Aertsen, *Medieval Philosophy and the Transcendentals: The Case of Thomas Aquinas* (Leiden, New York and Köln: Brill, 1996), 80–4.
47 Avicenna, *Metaphysics*, 22.
48 Jan A. Aertsen, *Medieval Philosophy as Transcendental Thought: From Philip the Chancellor (ca. 1225) to Francisco Suàrez* (Leiden: Brill, 2012), 100. To see why the Avicennian idea of notions imprinted originally in the soul 'certainly lies behind the Latin medieval theory of transcendantals', see Jules Janssens, 'Elements of Avicennian metaphysics in the *Summa*', in *Henry of Ghent and the Transformation*

of Scholastic Thought: Studies in Memory of Jos Decorte, ed. Guy Guldentops and Carlos Steel (Leuven: Leuven University Press, 2003), 52–8.
49 Alain de Libera, Penser au Moyen Âge (Paris: Seuil, 1991), 104.
50 The Holy Qur'an, text, translation and commentary by Abdullah Yusuf Ali (Beirut: Dar al Arabia, 1968), 55/26–7.
51 Jean Jolivet, 'Aux origines de l'ontologie d'Ibn Sīnā', in Études sur Avicenne, ed. Jean Jolivet and Roshdi Rashed (Paris: Les Belles Lettres, 1984), 24.
52 Therefore, the influence of the theological on this philosophical discourse legitimizes *a posteriori* all the more the recourse to Gadamer, who takes as a model the religious application to oneself for personal salvation.
53 De Libera, Penser, 114. Ricoeur does not seem to do the identification found in Gadamer. Indeed, he integrates Islam to the dialogue between Jerusalem and Athens, 'whose heirs we are' and describes a hermeneutical circle that includes the works of Augustine, Maimonides and Avicenna. Paul Ricoeur, 'Experience and Language in Religious Discourse', in Phenomenology and the 'Theological Turn: The French Debate', Dominique Janicaud et al., trans. Bernard G. Prusak, Jeffrey L. Kosky and Thomas A. Carlson (New-York: Fordham University Press, 2000), 134. Whereas, despite some links, the meeting with 'far eastern civilizations' did not occur 'to the point of radically transforming our tradition', Paul Ricoeur, The Symbolism of Evil, trans. Emerson Buchanan (Boston: Beacon Press, 1969), 22.
54 De Libera, Penser, 112.
55 Gadamer, Truth and Method, 389.
56 Fred Dallmayr, 'Self and Other: Gadamer and the Hermeneutics of Difference', Yale Journal of Law & the Humanities 5, Issue 2, Article 9 (1993): 515.
57 Hans-Georg Gadamer, 'Hermeneutics and Logocentrism', in Dialogue and Deconstruction, ed. Diane P. Michelfelder and Richard E. Palmer (Albany: SUNY Press, 1989), 119.
58 Gadamer, Truth and Method, 468.
59 De Libera, Penser, 25.
60 Alain de Libera, L'art des généralités: théories de l'abstraction (Paris: Aubier, 1999), 636.
61 See, for example, Muhammad Kamal, From Essence to Being: The Philosophy of Mulla Sadra and Martin Heidegger (London: ICAS Press, 2010).
62 For a study of the impact of Avicenna on both the Muslim world and the Latin West, see Jules Janssens, Ibn Sīnā and His Influence on the Arabic and Latin World (Aldershot: Ashgate, 2006). For his influence on Ghazali, see Alexander Treiger, Inspired Knowledge in Islamic Thought Al-Ghazālī's Theory of Mystical Cognition and Its Avicennian Foundation (London: Routledge, 2012).
63 Alessandro Palazzo, 'Eckhart's Islamic and Jewish Sources: Avicenna, Avicebron, and Averroes', in A Companion to Meister Eckhart, ed. Jeremiah M. Hackett (Leiden and Boston: Brill, 2013), 264.

64 See Reiner Schürmann, 'Heidegger and Meister Eckhart on Releasement', *Research in Phenomenology* III (1973): 95–119.
65 Gadamer, *Truth and Method*, 293.
66 Gadamer, 'Reply', 288.
67 Gadamer, *Truth and Method*, 303.
68 El-Bizri proposes to transcend mere comparativism 'by way of a radicalized form of questioning, which refracts and co-entangles variegated intellectual traditions with one another while being based in this on substantiated historical channels of their interconnected transmissions, and in view of inheriting past philosophical legacies within philosophy'. Nader El-Bizri, '*Falsafa*: A Labyrinth of Theory and Method', *Synthesis Philosophica* 62, no. 2 (2016): 297.
69 For an attempt of application of this approach to the notion of *theoria* see Selami Varlik, 'Understanding as Contemplation in Gadamer and Avicenna', in *Philosophy and the Spiritual Life*, ed. Victoria Harrison (London: Routledge, 2019).
70 François Jullien integrates Arab thought in the 'comparatism of ramification' where we observe some historical exchanges, and which he distinguishes from 'comparatism of foreignness' marked by a total heterotopia, as it is the case with China. François Jullien and Joachim Lacrosse, 'La Grèce et la Chine: comparer, dé-comparer. Un entretien avec François Jullien', in *Philosophie comparée: Grèce, Inde, Chine*, ed. Joachim Lacrosse (Paris: Vrin, 2005), 65–6.

Bibliography

Aertsen, Jan A. *Medieval Philosophy and the Transcendentals: The Case of Thomas Aquinas*. Leiden, New York and Köln: Brill, 1996.

Aertsen, Jan A. *Medieval Philosophy as Transcendental Thought: From Philip the Chancellor (ca. 1225) to Francisco Suàrez*. Leiden: Brill, 2012.

Albertini, Tamara. 'Ibn Rushd or Averroës? Of Double Names and Double Truths. A Different Approach to Islamic Philosophy'. In *After Appropriation: Explorations in Intercultural Philosophy and Religion*. Edited by Morny Joy, 221–38. Calgary: Calgary University Press, 2011.

Albertini, Tamara. 'Reintroducing Islamic Philosophy: The Persisting Problem of "Smaller Orientalisms"'. In *Oxford Handbook of World Philosophy*. Edited by Jay L. Garfield and William Edelglass, 389–96. Oxford: Oxford University Press, 2010.

Aquinas, Thomas. *Truth. Volume I: Questions I-IX*. Translated by Robert W. Mulligan. Eugene: Wipf and Stock, 2008.

Avicenna. *The Metaphysics of The Healing*. Translated, introduced, and annotated by Michael E. Marmura. Provo: Brigham Young University Press, 2005.

Azadpur, Mohammad. *Reason Unbound: On Spiritual Practice in Islamic Peripatetic Philosophy*. New York: SUNY Press, 2011.

Caputo, John D. *More Radical Hermeneutics: On Not Knowing Who We Are.* Bloomington: Indiana University Press, 2000.

Dallmayr, Fred. *Beyond Orientalism: Essays on Cross-Cultural Encounter.* New York: SUNY Press, 1996.

Dallmayr, Fred. 'Self and Other: Gadamer and the Hermeneutics of Difference'. *Yale Journal of Law & the Humanities* 5, Issue 2, Article 9 (1993): 101–24.

de Libera, Alain. *L'art des généralités: théories de l'abstraction.* Paris: Aubier, 1999.

de Libera, Alain. *Penser au Moyen Âge.* Paris: Seuil, 1991.

El-Bizri, Nader. '*Falsafa*: A Labyrinth of Theory and Method'. *Synthesis Philosophica* 62, no. 2 (2016): 295–311.

El-Bizri, Nader. 'The Labyrinth of Philosophy in Islam'. *Comparative Philosophy* 1, no. 2 (2010): 5.

El-Bizri, Nader. *The Phenomenological Quest between Avicenna and Heidegger.* Binghamton: Global Publications, 2000.

Gadamer, Hans-Georg. 'Aesthetic and Religious Experience'. In *The Relevance of the Beautiful.* Edited by R. Bernasconi. Cambridge: Cambridge University Press, 1986.

Gadamer, Hans-Georg. *Das Erbe Europas.* Frankfurt am Main: Suhrkamp Verlag, 1989.

Gadamer, Hans-Georg. 'Europa und die Oikoumene'. In *Hermeneutik im Rückblick. Gesammelte Werke* Band 10, 267–86. Tübingen: Mohr, 1995.

Gadamer, Hans-Georg. 'Herméneutique et théologie'. *Revue des sciences religieuses* 51 (1977): 384–97.

Gadamer, Hans-Georg. 'Hermeneutics and Logocentrism'. In *Dialogue and Deconstruction.* Edited by Diane P. Michelfelder and Richard E. Palmer, 114–28. Albany: SUNY Press, 1989.

Gadamer, Hans-Georg. 'Philosophical Apprenticeship'. In *The Many Faces of Philosophy: Reflections from Plato to Arendt.* Edited by Amélie Oksenberg Rorty, 467–71. Oxford: Oxford University Press, 2003.

Gadamer, Hans-Georg. 'Religious and Poetical Speaking'. In *Myth, Symbol, and Reality.* Edited by A. M. Olson, 86–98. Notre Dame: University of Notre Dame Press, 1980.

Gadamer, Hans-Georg. 'Reply to my Critics'. In *The Hermeneutic Tradition: From Ast to Ricoeur.* Edited by Gayle L. Ormiston and Alan D. Schrift, 273–97. New York: SUNY Press, 1990.

Gadamer, Hans-Georg. *Truth and Method.* Second revised edition, translation revised by Joel Weinsheimer and Donald G. Marshall. London and New York: Continuum, 2004.

Grondin, Jean. *Introduction to Metaphysics: From Parmenides to Levinas.* Translated by Lukas Soderstrom. New York: Columbia University Press, 2012.

Grondin, Jean. 'La fusion des horizons. La version gadamérienne de l'*adæquatio rei et intellectus*?' *Archives de Philosophie* 68, no. 3 (2005): 401–18.

Gutas, Dimitri. 'The Study of Arabic Philosophy in the Twentieth Century an Essay on the Historiography of Arabic Philosophy'. *British Journal of Middle Eastern Studies* 29, no. 1 (2002): 5–25.

The Holy Qur'an, text, translation and commentary by Abdullah Yusuf Ali. Beirut: Dar al Arabia, 1968.

Jambet, Christian. *Qu'est-ce que la philosophie islamique?* Paris: Galimard, 2011.

Janssens, Jules. 'Elements of Avicennian Metaphysics in the *Summa*'. In *Henry of Ghent and the Transformation of Scholastic Thought: Studies in Memory of Jos Decorte*. Edited by Guy Guldentops and Carlos Steel, 52–8. Leuven: Leuven University Press, 2003.

Janssens, Jules. *Ibn Sīnā and his Influence on the Arabic and Latin World*. Aldershot: Ashgate, 2006.

Jolivet, Jean. 'Aux origines de l'ontologie d'Ibn Sīnā'. In *Études sur Avicenne*. Edited by Jean Jolivet and Roshdi Rashed, 11–28. Paris: Les Belles Lettres, 1984.

Jullien, François and Lacrosse, Joachim. 'La Grèce et la Chine: comparer, dé-comparer. Un entretien avec François Jullien'. In *Philosophie comparée: Grèce, Inde, Chine*. Edited by Joachim Lacrosse, 65–78. Paris: Vrin, 2005.

Kamal, Muhammad. *From Essence to Being: The Philosophy of Mulla Sadra and Martin Heidegger*. London: ICAS Press, 2010.

Khatami, Mahmoud. 'On the Very Idea of Comparative Philosophy: Some Preliminary Remarks for a Meta-Theory'. In *The Misty Land of Ideas and The Light of Dialogue. An Anthology of Comparative Philosophy: Western and Islamic*. Edited by Ali Paya, 147–78. London: ICAS Press, 2014.

Mahdi, Muhsin. 'Orientalism and the Study of Islamic Philosophy'. *Journal of Islamic Studies* 1 (1990): 93.

Nasr, Seyyed Hossein. 'The Meaning and Concept of Philosophy in Islam'. In *History of Islamic Philosophy*, Part I, Edited by Seyyed Hossein Nasr and Oliver Leaman, 21–6. London and New York: Routledge, 2003.

Palazzo, Alessandro. 'Eckhart's Islamic and Jewish Sources: Avicenna, Avicebron, and Averroes'. In *A Companion to Meister Eckhart*. Edited by Jeremiah M. Hackett, 253–98. Leiden-Boston: Brill, 2013.

Pantham, Thomas. 'Some Dimensions of the Universality of Philosophical Hermeneutics: A Conversation with Hans-Georg Gadamer'. *Journal of Indian Council of Philosophical Research* 9 (1992): 123–35.

Paya, Ali, ed. *The Misty Land of Ideas and The Light of Dialogue. An Anthology of Comparative Philosophy: Western and Islamic*. London: ICAS Press, 2014.

Ricoeur, Paul. 'Experience and Language in Religious Discourse'. In *Phenomenology and the 'Theological Turn: The French Debate'*, Dominique Janicaud et al., translated by Bernard G. Prusak, Jeffrey L. Kosky and Thomas A. Carlson, 127–46. New York: Fordham University Press, 2000.

Ricoeur, Paul. *The Symbolism of Evil*. Translated by Emerson Buchanan. Boston: Beacon Press, 1969.

Schürmann, Reiner. 'Heidegger and Meister Eckhart on Releasement'. *Research in Phenomenology* III (1973): 95–119.

Scraire, Mathieu. 'Les sources médiévales du concept gadamérien d'appartenance dans *Vérité et méthode*'. *Laval théologique et philosophique* 65, no. 1 (2009): 83–104.

Smid, Robert W. *Methodologies of Comparative Philosophy: The Pragmatist and Process Traditions*. New York: SUNY Press, 2009.

Sweet, William. 'Introduction: The Project of Intercultural Philosophy'. In *What Is Intercultural Philosophy?* Edited by William Sweet, 3–5. Washington: The Council for Research in Values and Philosophy, 2014.

Treiger, Alexander. *Inspired Knowledge in Islamic Thought Al-Ghazālī's Theory of Mystical Cognition and Its Avicennian Foundation*. London: Routledge, 2012.

Tymieniecka, Anna-Teresa, ed. *The Passions of the Soul in the Metamorphosis of Becoming*. Dordrecht: Kluwer Academic Publishers, 2003.

Varlik, Selami. 'Understanding as Contemplation in Gadamer and Avicenna'. In *Philosophy and the Spiritual Life*. Edited by Victoria Harrison. London: Routledge, 2019.

Waldenfels, Bernhard. *Vielstimmigkeit der Rede*. Studien zur Phänomenologie des Fremden 4. Frankfurt am Main: Suhrkamp, 1999.

Wang, Xinli. 'Incommensurability and Comparative Philosophy'. *Philosophy East and West* 68, no. 2 (April 2018): 564–82.

5

'The mind is more like matter, the body more like the form': Geulincx against Descartes (and the scholastics) on the sources of difference in minds

Michael Jaworzyn

The influence of the thinker known in the Latin West as Averroes, Ibn Rushd (1126–98), had in many ways faded by the seventeenth century.[1] There were still occasions, though, when aspects of his thought were made the object of criticism – Craig Martin has, for example, drawn our attention to the ways that his name became associated with denial of providence. But one thing that seems to no longer have been a particular concern was the aspect of Averroes's thought which had seemed most pressing to his medieval opponents: the idea that there is one 'material' or 'possible' intellect shared by all human beings.[2] René Descartes, according to Martin, seems to be a particularly good example of this tendency.[3] Martin points out that in the preface to the *Meditations* Descartes cites the Fifth Lateran Council, which among other things condemned the Averroist view of the intellect, but when Descartes does so he refers only to one (not unrelated) aspect of the condemnation: the fear that the human soul might die with the body. He does not mention the suggestion that there is one intellect for all of humanity. Descartes's apparent omission gives the impression of being entirely of a piece with his famous – perhaps deliberate – failure to provide an account of the individuation of minds.[4]

Still, in the case of at least one follower of Descartes, Arnold Geulincx (1624–69), there might be reason to believe that he adopted something similar to the Averroist line of thought regarding the intellect.[5] One scholar, Andrea Strazzoni, takes Geulincx's views – in particular his account of how we attain a certain kind of intellectual knowledge – to reflect a 'traditional, Averroistic strategy to guarantee the universality of knowledge by recognising its objects in the divine intellect', and to have the even more remarkable consequence that Geulincx thinks of human minds as modes of God's mind.[6] Strazzoni, however, does not spell out how exactly Geulincx draws the connection between understanding the human mind as a mode and his account of how we see ideas in God, and does not think Geulincx addressed the question of the individuation of minds.[7] This is understandable – it is true that Geulincx was less than forthcoming here in particular, and not especially systematic in his presentation of the relevant material. I suspect there is more to be said about the issue, though. This is the case even if what Geulincx says does not seem to go all the way to solving every question which might arise in the context; in fact, Geulincx most likely did not intend to provide all the answers, at least not by means of philosophy.[8] But he nevertheless has a lot of interest to say about what makes us the individuals we are, particularly considering his allegiance to Descartes. For Geulincx, as I will show over the course of this chapter, the primary source of everything which is particular to us as individual minds – except for the fact of that individuality itself – is the only possible source of diversity in Geulincx's philosophical system: body in motion.[9]

Two points raised by Geulincx suggest this in particular: (1) the inversion he makes of the way the Cartesian concepts of mind and body were usually incorporated into the scholastic Aristotelian accounts of form and matter, which he connects to a distinction he draws between the individual mind *simpliciter* and the individual mind with all its particular features, and (2) the aforementioned claim that only body in motion is capable of supporting diversity, which in turn is tied to a particular account of the way in which, for Geulincx, God is able to act on us to bring about the various thoughts we have that provide the basis for us conceiving ourselves as individuals.[10] These will be the subjects of the first and second parts of this chapter respectively. The former indicates that although the individuation as such of minds is not owed to body in motion, everything which is particular to us as individuals is owed to body in motion. The latter indicates that while there is more textual evidence than commonly suspected that body plays an active causal role in the way God brings about the modifications of mind – such that body is an 'instrument' elevated by God to play that role – the balance of evidence is that there are better reasons to think that body in motion constitutes a particular variation of what the scholastics would have called a *sine qua non* cause; body is the source of diversity insofar as it is a condition of God's action on our minds, rather than directly being so.

Not much of this can be found in Descartes himself, and it certainly contributes to the impression that the Cartesian tradition was a good deal more wide-ranging than might be supposed when it comes to questions of what makes us who we are. But, as I will show in the concluding section, there are also reasons to regard Geulincx's views as genuinely, if idiosyncratically, Cartesian. Before addressing these points, however, more should be said (albeit briefly) about how for Geulincx our seeing ideas in God is connected to his view of our minds not as substances but as modes of God's mind. Geulincx's view precludes our discerning anything sufficiently particular to us to count as our 'identities' on the basis of our merely being minds. That will form the remainder of this introduction.

Beyond his explicit rejection of more standard Cartesian and scholastic accounts of metaphysical questions about what constitutes an individual subject, substance or thinking thing, Geulincx seems to display a kind of indifference to the metaphysical question of the individuation of minds, and any account of how our minds relate to and depend on God's more generally.[11] I cannot address these issues in any great detail here, but it is necessary to highlight one crucial point: because of Geulincx's rejection of the standard metaphysical and logical accounts of substance, thing (*res*) and mode, the issue should be approached from the perspective of thought (*cogitatio*), from the perspective of our consciousness.[12] Geulincx does offer an alternative to Cartesian and scholastic accounts of substance metaphysics. Although he admits that his own positive account of what a mode is does not exhaust the issue and that further difficulties remain, he tells us that a mode is an abstraction.[13] Both God and human beings are minds, which is to say they are characterized by thought. To say that our minds are modes is then to say that our minds are abstractions from the divine mind; the divine mind is infinite and eternal, but we are limited – 'by that which we do not know', as Geulincx puts it at one stage.[14] According to this line of thought in Geulincx's work, then, 'we differ from it [the divine mind] only insofar as we are limited and imperfect'.[15] A brief passage summarizing the relevant line of thinking – which also highlights how Geulincx takes his own views to follow from Descartes – he puts follows: 'I doubt, I think, I am; and to that extent I am a limited mind; by means of the intellect I remove the limits, I do not invent, do not make a new thing, but uncover an old one, and come upon an unlimited mind; from which first eternity, and from there the remaining attributes of God easily follow.'[16]

We remove our limits, to speak in Geulincx's terms, when we have what he refers to as 'ideas'; to that extent we participate in God.[17] An idea, Geulincx thinks, is equivalent to an eternal truth. These are to be opposed to what Geulincx refers to as 'modes of thinking' in a broad sense, and to sensations or 'sensible species' in particular. The latter are what I will argue form the basis of our individuality as minds.[18] Since we are finite beings (and being unlimited and eternal are equivalent for Geulincx) ideas are not in us, but are in God. When we attain – not, it must be added, by our own power – such ideas, the particular limitations we had in virtue of our lack of knowledge are overcome, and we are 'with God'. This is how we can tell that we are in a certain sense 'from God and in God'.[19] When Geulincx says that we are modes of God, this is best understood as emphasizing the limitations which make us individual, finite minds – but also that we can (perhaps temporally and partially) overcome those limitations: we can be conscious of ideas in God. In fact, in so doing we seem to lose ourselves. There are, for example, good reasons to think that Geulincx is at best ambivalent about the existence of minds as individuals before and after the death of the body. On the one hand, he clearly argues in favour of the immortality of the soul after the body dies.[20] One the other hand, in one of Geulincx's longer discussions of the issue, he puts it this way: 'we may desire that our limits are destroyed, we are released (as the Apostle says) and to be with Christ; for whatever may happen to us, we are in God and will remain in him'.[21]

Rather than asking primarily metaphysical questions about individuation, then, it is necessary to look at conscious thought from within, as it were; Geulincx's apparent proximity to Averroism should accordingly be understood not in terms of metaphysical or ontological claims, but as a question of what might allow us to pick ourselves out as individuals. The question, that is to say, is what enables us to recognize ourselves as modes, as abstractions from the divine mind. And it is difficult, if not impossible, to find anything that enables us to pick out our minds as individual minds on the basis of what we have in us in virtue only of being minds – in virtue being minds, we only have access to what for Descartes would be innate ideas, and which for Geulincx, though not innate, serve a similar function. Descartes for his part says that 'the mere fact that each of us understands himself to be a thinking thing and is capable, in thought, of excluding from himself every other substance, whether thinking or extended, it is certain that each of us, regarded in this way, is really distinct from every other thinking substance and from every corporeal substance'.[22] For Geulincx, though, it must be something other than the mere fact of being a 'thinking thing' which marks us out as particular individuals. This – in a way that will be outlined in the course of this chapter – will turn out to be the kinds of thoughts we have in conjunction with body in motion, and with the particular body we call our own. Body, then, is the only source of whatever it is that makes us the particular beings we are. This we could refer to as our identity, to connect this more explicitly to the terms of this volume – and this is because, for Geulincx, body in motion is the only source of what he terms diversity, or what might be called difference.

In any case, all this indicates that Geulincx departs significantly from the way Descartes is usually understood. As Emilie Grosholz succinctly puts it, Descartes 'can recognize himself as an individual and God as an infinite, perfect individual distinct from his own finite, imperfect self without invoking the corporeal faculties that depend on the "substantial union" of body and soul'.[23] The same cannot be said of Geulincx, and it seems that the Cartesian tradition was no more unified in this respect than in any others.[24]

Mind as the matter and body as the form of the human being

The first key point that on the face of it indicates substantial differences between Descartes and Geulincx when it comes to the roles they each assign to the body is the following: according to Geulincx, in opposition both explicitly to scholastic Aristotelianism and implicitly to most of his fellow Cartesians, 'the mind of man is more like the matter, and the body more like the form'.[25] While the precise extent to which the terminology of form and matter played a role in Descartes's own work is debatable,[26] it is clear enough that Cartesians did not necessarily reject this kind of language, even if they did tend to discard much of the philosophical work it was supposed to do.[27] But when they maintained the terminology, they continued to adhere to its traditional connotations in the parallels they drew: the mind would be compared to the form; body would be aligned with matter. Geulincx seems to have been alone in his reversal of the usual scheme. Here, then, is the first instance of this suggestion in Geulincx's work in full:

> The schools greatly err when they hold that the body is the matter of the human being, and the mind its form; it is the opposite, the mind of the human in fact is just as the matter, and the body just as the form. The form of an armed man is neither man nor horse, but arms: it is in virtue of arms that he is said to be an armed man; but a human is not such by virtue of the mind, but by virtue of having a body related to his mind in a certain way, which we have described above. The human, that is to say, is nothing other than an incorporated being, whose form is without doubt a body, for it is being incorporated by a body that makes it what it is said to be.[28]

A second, briefer reference to the idea can be found in the third part of the *Metaphysica Vera*: 'indeed, mind is as it were our matter, as we demonstrated in Part One; and body and motion are our form, insofar as we are human'.[29]

There were of course various ways of using the form-matter terminology among Geulincx's predecessors and contemporaries – too many, in fact, to make it a sufficiently well-defined question to be able to ask what Geulincx retains of the doctrine when he inverts it as he does. Pasnau makes the point – in discussing whether for Descartes the mind can still be said to count as the form of the body (or more precisely, denying that this is quite the right question to ask) that 'anyone can *say* that the mind is the form of the body, and the notion of form is so capacious that there is bound to be some sense in which that claim comes out true'.[30] It is of course possible that assigning to body the role of form of the mind would be slightly more difficult to do in a way recognizably connected to more traditional accounts of form and matter. In any case, it would take us too far afield to account for every historically viable account of the way the two terms had been employed in order to ascertain exactly what Geulincx might have had in mind in the passages in question.

As it happens, Geulincx is in fact referring to form and matter in a particular sense – a logical sense, rather than a metaphysical or physical one. This much is clear from his example of the armed man being defined not by his humanity but by his having arms, but in any case the relevant notions of form and matter are discussed one of his works of logic. The 'form' in this sense is the *differentia* in the definition; mind and body constitute what Geulincx elsewhere refers to as 'partial essences' of the human being.[31] As was the case with one of the most important scholastic thinkers active in the period before Geulincx, Francisco Suarez (1548–1617), for Geulincx this logical account of form and matter is independent of the physical and metaphysical conceptions.[32] Geulincx does not mean, then, that body should be accounted as a kind of internal efficient cause organizing and bringing about the various accidents of the human being (as it would be if it were to be construed analogously to the physical form) or that it is somehow responsible for the individuation or identity over time of the mind or could be considered its essence (as it would have been in the case of the metaphysical form).[33] Nor does it mean for Geulincx that the combination of the mind and body results in particular kind of unity. It seems reasonable to say that, suggestive as it might seem, this terminology does not of itself indicate that the human body is supposed to perform any of the metaphysical or physical roles form might traditionally have been supposed to have.

Still, despite his use of form-matter terminology in what is apparently a metaphysically non-committal way, similar rhetoric does occur in places where Geulincx clearly has a metaphysical aim in mind. One of the places where Geulincx alludes to form-matter terminology also introduces the possibility that more can be learned about what it is to be a particular mind by spelling out what Geulincx thinks it means for a human being to have a body. Perhaps this is an indication that Geulincx intended the reader to draw on the connotations other usages of form and matter might have had.[34] In any case, Geulincx draws the following distinction in an annotation later in his *True Metaphysics*:

> Body and motion are only understood as an instrument, by means of which we are, not *simpliciter* but as such and such; but such an instrument is not prior to a thing *simpliciter*, but to a thing as such and such, in the same way a hammer and chisel, and similar sculptural tools, are prior to the statue of Mercury, but not to the wood.[35]

The crucial distinction here is between a thing taken *simpliciter* – without qualification – and a thing taken as being a concrete particular with its own particular characteristics. This, I suggest, is a slightly oblique indication that Geulincx's inversion of the form-matter scheme does not only pertain to the definitional point that having a body is what means the predicate human can correctly be ascribed to us as minds. In the previous section we saw that particular minds cannot be distinguished from one another either by reference to their nature as thinking things or by their having ideas in the sense I have suggested Geulincx uses the term 'idea'. Before body and motion are taken into consideration, a mind taken *simpliciter* it seems could only be said to have such ideas, or at least some kind of access to them. Yet body in motion is prior to our minds existing as particular minds; they are insufficiently differentiated from one another until body and motion are used as 'instruments' to do so. Body in motion can be compared to the form of the human being because it is by means of body in motion that we are said to be the particular ways we are – but this is not a merely extrinsic denomination. It has to do with particular and intrinsic features of mind; one cannot be a human being without being a particular human being, that is to say.

This suggestion is not based only on the terminology used by Geulincx in his distinction between something's simply existing and existing as a particular, concrete thing – especially since although his illustration is clear enough (a sculptor's tools are not prior to statues as such, but they are to a particular statue) the language he uses in drawing the distinction could still conceivably be taken to refer to being a thing of a particular kind, and the term 'priority' likewise remains ambiguous. It is also borne out by Geulincx's account of the nature of the human being and the coordinated changes in mind and body which constitute what Geulincx refers to as the 'human condition'. For Geulincx there is no sense in which a mind can be united to a body other than in the actual respective changes in the two: that we say there is a union is derivative of the fact that there are respective changes in the mind and the body that God brings about. In fact, Geulincx even adds in an annotation that to say 'the mind is *united* to the body signifies nothing',[36] and that Descartes himself perhaps was speaking more imprecisely when he used such vocabulary. According to Geulincx, to be a human being is just to be acted on by God on the occasion of the relevant changes in a particular body – a particular body that we call our own only on the basis of God acting on us. Someone who does not have the particular thoughts that are aroused in the mind by God using the body as an instrument is at that time not in fact human, properly speaking.

All this indicates that body and motion are the 'instruments' by which God makes us what we are because they are the instruments by which God affects our minds in order to bring about the various particular thoughts we have. This is what Geulincx has in mind in making use of the sculptural analogy mentioned earlier, and it is best explained by the next point I will look at: Geulincx's argument that neither God nor human minds could be responsible for the diversity of our various thoughts. In so doing, I will show that there remains an ambiguity in how exactly body in motion is used as an instrument on us, and hence how exactly we are made to exist in the particular way we do.

Body in motion and the diversity of our thoughts

I turn now to a claim that Geulincx makes near the beginning of his *Metaphysica Vera*, while still working out the consequences of his version of the Cartesian *cogito*. In addressing the fact that among the many modes of thinking we have, a good deal of those do not depend on us – we cannot bring them about ourselves – he claims that they could only be brought about in us by means of body in motion, because body in motion is the only possible source of what he terms their 'diversity' (*diversitas*). This claim ultimately does not have the wide-ranging consequences one might expect it – Geulincx does not account for the diversity of our minds by reference to body – but it nevertheless gives us vital information about how to account for diversity in our minds.

The argument – which is actually only one of two Geulincx gives (and one intriguingly, but inconclusively, not included in the manuscript[37]) – is brief, and runs as follows. Both human minds and the divine mind are simple, yet we know for a fact that we, as thinking things, have a great variety of thoughts, and that these do not depend on us since we cannot bring them about at will. The simplicity of both kinds of mind precludes either being the source of these thoughts: 'He [God] cannot arouse them through the medium of myself, since thoughts are diverse, and I am a simple thing, in which diverse thoughts cannot originate.'[38] Whatever it is, therefore, by whose intervention we have those thoughts, 'must be capable of various changes, so that by means of it the various objects of thoughts arise'.[39] And the only thing in Geulincx's ontology which seems to be capable of doing so is body. But even body – which, we should recall, is according to Geulincx a single thing – can only play this role because the introduction of motion (by God) into it differentiates it into different 'figures' which we refer to as particular bodies.

In line with the kinds of questions I have been considering here, it is worth addressing – and ruling out – certain possibilities for exactly what kind of 'diversity' he might have in mind; in brief, it seems clear that Geulincx does not mean to account for what, following his sometime student Richard Burthogge (c. 1638–1705), could be referred to as the 'numerication' of minds. Burthogge puts it as follows:

> Again, were Spirits absolutely pure and simple, without any Concretion of Matter, there could be no distinction among them as to *Individuals*, as well as none in relation to Kinds. For since all Individuation (except only that of the Central pure mind) is *Numerication*, and all Numerication arises from Division, and Division has no place but in Matter, or in Things by means of matter. It is evident that there can be no distinction of Spirits to Individuation, if there be no ingredience of matter in their making ... In short, we may observe *in our selves* (that Mind as I have noted before) is *Individuated by Matter*, since even sense is seeing in the *Eye*; Hearing in the *Ear*; Tasting in the *Tongue* &c.[40]

In Geulincx's case, however, as we've already seen, our minds do not enjoy their existence *simpliciter* because of body in motion; it is only that they are as they are – with the particular thoughts they happen to have – because of God's use of body in motion as an instrument to bring about these kinds of thoughts in us. And in fact, the context in which Geulincx had initially mentioned the distinction between a mind's existing *simpliciter* and in a particular way was in response to the possible objection that body and motion would then be prior to our minds. The point that body and motion are prior to our minds as particular minds is intended to preserve the possibility that our minds taken in an unqualified way are, according to Geulincx, at least simultaneous in the order of things with body, if not prior.[41] Ultimately, for Geulincx, the mind is not individuated by being joined to the body; on the contrary, a particular body is primarily said to be ours precisely because we are affected by it.[42]

Nevertheless, we cannot say in this instance that there is any diversity to or in minds without their being joined to bodies – body and motion are the instruments by which the diverse thoughts we have are brought about in us. Still, other arguments provided by Geulincx make it clearer that it is not only the diversity as such that body in motion provides in this context. There is also something – difficult though it is to say what, given that the instrument, the bodily organ, is per se inapt and unsuited to bringing about the resulting particular sensation of which we are conscious – which in the nature of our consciousness experience indicates our being affected by body in motion. The very fact that we sense things in particular ways is something we cannot help but link to particular movements in particular organs of our bodies. So, according to Geulincx, there must be something which body in motion contributes; the question is how it can do so given the natures of the body and mind, given what Geulincx takes up from the Cartesian conceptions of the heterogeneous natures of the two and given Geulincx's own stipulation that a cause must know how to bring about an effect to be able to do so. Geulincx is, if he is known at all, most often known as an occasionalist – which, as Steven Nadler in particular has emphasized, is not just a position regarding the mind–body problem, but certainly includes taking a position on it.[43]

As a matter of fact, Geulincx frequently uses language which suggests that bodies can be said to act on us, and God cannot directly do so.[44] The term 'instrument', which we have already seen Geulincx invoke a few times, would not usually have suggested that there was no causal interaction at all. It would have suggested that there was real interaction, but that body would have been unable to bring it about of itself; Francisco Suarez, for example, says that 'in the most proper sense' an instrumental cause 'concurs in, or is elevated to, the production of something more noble than itself; that is, something beyond the measure of its own proper perfection and action'.[45] Geulincx also often refers to the necessity 'intervention' of body in motion, and refers to our thoughts being arouses 'by means of' [*mediante*] motion.[46] He speaks of the (admittedly ineffable) 'egression' of motion from the eternal mind and its 'ingression' into the human mind.[47] And when Geulincx says that body has no per se power or aptitude to bring about thoughts in us, this does not of itself exclude their doing so when used by God – who, after all, seems to need body in motion to be able to do so. In fact, the use of such bodily instruments seems to be mandated by Geulincx's account of the simplicity of the divine nature and the simplicity of divine action. If it seems odd to say that an omnipotent being such as God could not simply act directly on our minds, without having to use body – especially given what Geulincx will shortly call the inaptness or inadequacy of such an instrument – this nevertheless is what Geulincx says:

> I rightly presume that God cannot do this [bring about thoughts in our minds without the use of a bodily instrument]; he is one and the same, and always in one and the same state; it is necessary that he have an instrument that can be affected in diverse modes in order to arouse diverse modes of thought in us … but no other instrument than body is capable of such diversity.[48]

Although Geulincx does not specify precisely how God would 'elevate' body in motion to the task in hand – it is, he maintains, ineffable – this looks quite different to the occasionalism usually ascribed to him.[49]

To be sure, there are passages where Geulincx seems more explicitly to deny that bodies act on minds at all, and as far as I can see he never suggests the converse of the account given earlier, namely that God can elevate minds to be able to act on bodies as instruments. We can point to the analogy Geulincx draws between two clocks and mind and body, where in both cases the apparent agreement has to do with their being made by the same creator rather than any causal interaction. Or we can point to his equally infamous (in certain circles!) application of the *quod nescis* principle, the claim that in order to do something one must know how to do it, equally to material objects and to human minds: rocks do not know any better than us how to bring about our perceptions of them.[50] Geulincx also at one stage opposes his conception of instruments to causes, which certainly suggests that an instrument as he understood it was not only not a principal cause but not a cause at all.[51]

Likewise, if instruments are actually to be viewed as a kind of genuine efficient cause, then a somewhat peculiar result would be that there would be a certain asymmetry between the kinds of interactions between mind and body. Geulincx is unequivocal that our actions – the actions of the finite mind – remain in us; it is not our action, but God's, if our volitions appear to have effects outside our minds. This Geulincx puts most strikingly and comprehensively in an annotation: 'our will has no influx, causality, determination or efficacy whatsoever in motion'.[52] But he does not seem to think our volitions could be elevated to the status of cause, even if per se unable to bring about the effects they intend. It is true that a follower of Geulincx, Johannes Flenderus (1653–1732 or after), in his *Phosphorus Philosophicus* (a textbook based on Johannes Clauberg's *Logica Contracta*, explicated from a perspective owing as much to Geulincx), did take seriously the possibility that we can call our minds instruments of God.[53] But Geulincx himself never seems to have done so. As a consequence, taking body in motion to be able to act as an instrument on us without our being able to do the same on it introduces a curious impotence to the mind, without resulting in full occasionalism. It would not be entirely unfitting for someone of Geulincx's philosophical temperament, but it would not fit so well with the Augustinian and Platonic influences which he certainly had, for whom the asymmetry would have been inverted.[54]

Still, in my view the combination of passages which seem to deny interaction and the peculiarity of allowing bodies to be elevated to causes while minds remain powerless probably outweighs the terminological considerations in favour of the earlier suggestion. But this alternative is strange in a way too: in the context of this chapter, it seems to mean, for example, that neither God nor bodies act on us in the production of precisely those modifications of our minds with respect to which we are able to pick ourselves out as individuals. Our bodies, and the diversity which only body in motion can display, are only conditions for God's action on us. But God, as mentioned, is not able to act without an instrument capable of a certain kind of diversity because of the simplicity of his action.

The situation is perhaps best explained by viewing it as a transformation – maybe minor, but definite – of what were known in the period and before as *sine quibus non* causes. To use a standard example from the Middle Ages, if a king decrees that a person in possession of a certain coin made of lead will be rewarded with a vastly greater some of more valuable money, this does not mean that the leaden coin has any intrinsic role itself in bringing about the reward.[55] The leaden coin is only a condition; it is the king's having made the decree, and then enacting his decree, which brings about the reward – yet as long as his decree remains in place, it indicates what will happen quite predictably. Restating this in terms closer to what is at stake here, the presence or occurrence of a particular movement in the body is a condition of God's bringing about a particular sensation in the human mind, but not because of any intrinsic, active or necessary causal connection between that bodily movement and the corresponding sensation. But this makes the key difference between the two cases apparent: even though Geulincx maintains that the bodily occurrence which occasions a thought is powerless and unsuited to bringing about its apparent effect, he does not seem to think that the occasion can be dispensed with in the same way a king could give the reward even without the leaden coin. God, he thinks, cannot dispense with our bodies in bringing about the thoughts particular to us – even if, in the final analysis, those bodies contribute nothing causally.[56]

Concluding remarks

Geulincx by all appearances differs from Descartes in at least the respects just outlined, which in turn point to the indispensable role played in accounting for our individuality as particular minds by body in motion – which Geulincx takes to be the only possible source of diversity. When it comes to our having ideas, as Geulincx understands them, we can find no means to distinguish ourselves either from God or from any other mind. Ideas are in God, and, in a certain way, of God; insofar as we are conscious of such ideas, there seems to be nothing particular about our experience. But Geulincx sometimes also says that, with respect to human beings, minds are something like their matter, and the body like their forms; although his usage of form and matter is intended to be logical rather than metaphysical or physical, passages where he elaborates on this metaphor indicate that the references Geulincx makes to form-matter terminology imply something more: it is only on the basis of being joined to a body, and the kinds of thoughts which arise as a result of that, that we are able to find anything particular about our own existence which would allow us to take ourselves as a particular individual. We are only said to be human beings in virtue of the mind actually undergoing various thoughts on the occasion of the relevant changes taking place in our bodies.

The result is that for our experiences, our conscious thought, to be our own and not God's, as it is in the case of ideas, God needs to use body in motion as an instrument to produce the particular kinds of modes of thinking which seem to us to arise as a result of our having a body. And by instrument, Geulincx – despite his vocabulary – means a condition which contributes nothing causally, but without which God would not only not in fact produce such diverse, particular thoughts in us, but not even be able to produce such thoughts at all. Anything particular to us as individuals – except that we are individuals, which does, for all this, remain somewhat mysterious – is brought about in us by God using body in motion as an instrument to do so.

As different as this account of Geulincx's work might seem to how Descartes is often understood, there have been readings of Descartes which look quite similar. To the question 'What moves the mind?', Richard A. Watson once argued that for Descartes the same motion which produces particular bodies must be what produces particular ideas; according to Watson's reading, 'mind – like the material plenum – is intrinsically, essentially empty'.[57] The mind is of itself entirely undifferentiated, and the various innate ideas are contentless – and yet we do have particular ideas. The explanation, he thinks, is that for Descartes, 'the homogeneous mental plenum is differentiated into particular ideas by the motion that differentiates the material plenum into particular bodies. God moves the mind with the motion he introduces into matter.'[58] Other than the reasons he thinks that minds are of themselves undifferentiated, this is close to the view of Geulincx's work I have been putting forward here (and even closer if we accept the understanding of bodily instruments as instrumental rather than a particular kind of *sine que non* condition). Watson does not present this as a reading of what Descartes himself thought, though. Geulincx, on the other hand, seems to embrace what Watson thinks Descartes only reluctantly recognized, if he recognized it at all. Perhaps Geulincx took himself to be advancing a genuinely and straightforwardly – albeit more consistent, by his lights – Cartesian view, or perhaps he self-consciously took himself to be innovating with respect to these questions. Either way, though, Geulincx's work indicates that the Cartesian tradition bore a complex relation to questions of identity and difference.

Notes

1   This brief account is based on Craig Martin, 'Providence and Seventeenth Century Attacks on Averroes', in *Averroes' Natural Philosophy and its Reception in the Latin West*, ed. Paul J. J. M. Bakker (Leuven: Leuven University Press, 2015), 193–212. It is worth emphasizing that although Averroes was considered controversial in certain respects, he was also often taken to be the preeminent commentator on Aristotle – hence his being referred to as 'the Commentator'. See Kara Richardson, 'Averroism', in *The Routledge Companion to Sixteenth Century Philosophy*, ed. Henrik Lagerlund and Benjamin Hill (Abingdon and New York: Routledge, 2017), 137–55, for further details of Averroes's reception, and a useful account of how the Averroistic view of the material intellect developed and contested, in the years prior to the thinkers addressed in this chapter.
2   Richardson, 'Averroism', 145–6.
3   Martin, 'Providence', 196.
4   For examples of the view that Descartes provided no account of the individuation of minds see, for example, Udo Thiel, *The Early Modern Subject: Self-consciousness and Personal Identity from Descartes to Hume* (Oxford: Oxford University Press, 2011), 38. It is worth pointing out a relevant distinction in the literature (which, although I do not always employ in precisely the same way here, since I would rather the terminology arise from the texts being discussed, is nevertheless helpful). Kenneth Barber distinguishes between individuation and discernibility: 'While the ontologist asks what it is *in objects* that *individuates* those objects, the epistemologist searches

for features *in experience* that allow us to *discern* the difference among objects.' Kenneth F. Barber, 'Introduction', in *Individuation and Identity in Early Modern Philosophy: Descartes to Kant*, ed. Kenneth F. Barber and Jorge J. E. Gracia (Albany: State University of New York Press, 1994), 5 (1–11). For Geulincx, as we will see, the former question appears to collapse into the latter.

5   Quotations from Geulincx are from Arnold Geulincx, *Sämtliche Schriften in fünf Bänden*, ed. H. J. De Vleeschauwer (Stuttgart – Bad Cannstatt: Fromann Verlag, 1965–8), 3 vols. (hereafter SS with volume number and page number). Translations are my own, although I have sometimes consulted: Arnold Geulincx, *Metaphysics*, trans. Martin Wilson (Wisbech: Christoffel Press, 1999). I should emphasize here that this chapter is not intended as a contribution to the history of the reception of Ibn Rushd in the Latin West; its main goal is to show that despite Descartes's reputation as the kind of thinker who would not have been very interested in the kinds conceptions of 'identity in difference' this volume is concerned with (and perhaps, despite Descartes's own views, though that is at least debatable), there were more complex discussions and various ways of spelling out ostensibly Cartesian views, and that Geulincx in particular could be said to ascribe a surprising amount of what makes us the particular individuals we are to our being affected by – in a very particular way – body in motion. I am also not saying that Geulincx actually was an Averroist of any description, or even read Averroes (there is no evidence he did, but it is not impossible either), only that the parallels could be instructive, in the context of very different metaphysical systems.

6   Andrea Strazzoni, *Dutch Cartesianism and the Birth of Philosophy of Science; from Regius to 's Gravesande* (Berlin and Boston: De Gruyter, 2018), 99.

7   Ibid.

8   To cite one example, Geulincx does not take 'natural reason' to be able to show us whether the limits which define as particular minds exist before those minds are joined to a body – see SSII 299.

9   I say primary because there are certain aspects of our thinking which on first glance do not quite fit into the distinction we will look at below between ideas and sensible 'species': (1) what Geulincx refers to as 'intelligible species' and (2) what other Cartesians would refer to as the active modes of the mind, the acts of the will – volition and judgement. The first of these – the intellectual modes of thinking by which we subsume objects under metaphysical concepts such as substance, accident and so on – are not directly brought about by the body, but the mind in an obscure way 'follows and imitates' the senses in these instances (see SSII 210). With respect to the latter, although I cannot argue the point here in the detail it deserves, the reason I do not count these as aspects of thought by which we can differentiate ourselves from thought as such is that I would suggest that they are determinations of the primary modes of mind (i.e. sensations) rather than having

any strict conscious existence of their own; the same would apply to judgement regarding ideas, except in that case our affirmation or judgement of the goodness of the object is indistinguishable from God's. Geulincx makes clear in SSII 157 that when we are not joined to a body there is no possibility of change in the mind, which presumably includes these kinds of judgements and volitions.

10 The foundation Geulincx's occasionalism – which in Geulincx's work canonically takes the form of what has become known as the epistemic condition on causation, or in Geulincx's own terms is based on the axiom 'what you do not know how to do is not your action' [*quod nescis quomodo fiat, id non facis* – hereafter referred to as the '*quod nescis* principle'] – is one of the more frequently mentioned aspects of his theory; this constraint even rules out bodies acting as causes, since they too do not know how to produce particular effects. For one prominent recent discussion of this principle, see Steven Nadler, 'Knowledge, Volitional Agency, and Causation in Malebranche and Geulincx', in Steven Nadler, *Occasionalism: Causation among the Cartesians* (Oxford: Oxford University Press 2011), 74–87.

11 See Han van Ruler, '"Something, I Know Not What": The Concept of Substance in Early Modern Thought', in *Between Demonstration and Imagination: Essays in the History of Science and Philosophy Presented to John D. North*, ed. Lodi Nauta and Arjo Vanderjagt (Leiden: Brill, 1999), 365–93, and Mark Aalderink, *Philosophy, Scientific Knowledge, and Concept Formation in Geulincx and Descartes* (Utrecht: Publications of the Zeno Institute of Philosophy, 2009), particularly 384–8, for assessments Geulincx's views of the Aristotelian substance criteria.

12 I argue for this claim in more detail elsewhere. Thought in this context refers to every instance in which we are conscious of something; the most fundamental distinction is between ideas, which we see in God, and what Geulincx refers to as our 'modes of thinking', which are by definition limited. The latter for Geulincx is a very broad category of the modifications of our mind (for Geulincx, as for Descartes, thought [*cogitatio*] is broader than it is often taken to be these days, and includes anything of which we are conscious, including, for example, sensations or sense perceptions).

13 SSII 243–4.

14 SSII 298.

15 SSIII 380: 'tantum quatenus limitati imperfectique ab illa differimus.'

16 SSIII 385: 'dubito, cogito, sum; adeoque sum mens limitata; limites per intellectum tollo, non fingo, no facio rem novam, sed veterem detego, invenioque mentem illimitatam; ex qua facile, primo quidem aeternitas, deinde reliqua Dei attributa sequuntur.'

17 There are differences between how Geulincx uses the word 'idea' at different stages in his career, and his usage should also be distinguished from Descartes's more extended usage. Again, for a more detailed account of ideas in Geulincx, see

Aalderink, *Geulincx and Descartes*, 273–86. Descartes's conception and usage of the term idea is of course one of the most discussed issues among both recent scholars and early Cartesians. (It is a crucial part of the long, and bitter, debate between Arnauld and Malebranche, for example.) For one account of Descartes's use and its history, see Roger Ariew and Marjorie Grene, 'Ideas, In and Before Descartes', *Journal of the History of Ideas* 56, no. 1 (1995): 87–106.

18 The opposition between ideas and sensations is not exhaustive, as mentioned earlier.
19 SSII 286: 'ita nos sumus ex Deo et in Deo'.
20 In particular, in an annotation (SSII 268) Geulincx points out that the simplicity of consciousness means we cannot be annihilated; our being 'dissolved' in God presumably does not, then, constitute annihilation, but something more like an extension of what we already are, since we are 'in' God.
21 SSII 293: 'ita et nos cupiamus limitem nostrum destrui, nos dissolvi (ut inquit Apostolus) et esse cum Christo; quicquid enim de nobis fiat, sumus in Deo et manebimus in eo'.
22 René Descartes, *The Philosophical Writings of Descartes*, trans. Cottingham, Stoothoff and Murdoch (Cambridge: Cambridge University Press, 1984 and 1985), 2 vols., 1:214. Quoted in Thiel, *Early Modern Subject*, 38.
23 Emily Grosholz, 'Descartes and the Individuation of Physical Objects', in *Individuation and Identity*, ed. Barber and Gracia, 54.
24 See Tad Schmaltz, *Early Modern Cartesianisms: Dutch and French Constructions* (Oxford: Oxford University Press, 2017), particularly 5–11, for a recent account of the breadth of Cartesianisms, and the ways one can conceive of the various thinkers associated with Cartesianism without having to face the impossible task of picking out specific 'key doctrines' as criteria for inclusion.
25 SSII 161: 'mens quidem veluti materia in homini velut forma vero corpus ejus est'.
26 The most controversial aspect of this discussion is the question of whether Descartes's occasional references to the mind as a substantial form – which he does undeniably make – actually mean he has any genuine philosophical use for the terminology and if so what relation that might have to the various different ways it was used among the scholastics. See, for example, Pasnau, *Metaphysical Themes*, 596–605.
27 See, for example, Gideon Manning, 'Three Biased Reminders about Hylomorphism in Early Modern Science and Philosophy', in *Matter and Form in Early Modern Science and Philosophy*, ed. Gideon Manning (Leiden and Boston: Brill, 2012), 1–32.
28 SSII 161: 'Ex quo patet, Scholas vehementer errare, dum corpus ponunt materiam hominis, et mentem ejus formam; contra sit, et mens quidem veluti materia in homini velut forma vero corpus ejus est. Sicuti armati forma non est homo vel equus, sed arma; illis enim armatus est hoc quod esse dicitur; ast mente homo

non est quod esse dicitur, sed corpore certo modo se ad mentem illam habere, qui modus a nobis supra descriptus est. Homo enim non est aliud quam incorporatus, cujus sine dubio forma corpus est, nam corpore incorporatus id est, quod esse dicitur.'

29 SSII 195: 'Mens quidem est veluti materia nostra, ut in parte I. demonstrabamus; corpus vero atque motus sunt forma nostra, quatenus homines sumus.'
30 Pasnau, *Metaphysical Themes*, 596.
31 See SSI 187.
32 Helen Hattab, *Descartes on Forms and Mechanisms* (Cambridge: Cambridge University Press, 2009), 57–64, indicates – to oversimplify her account – that the separation of the different ways of taking form and matter exemplified in the work of the scholastic Francisco Suarez could have been responsible for the decline of substantial forms, since the stand-alone physical form, without the metaphysical form underpinning it, was more liable to be simply disproven by more successful physical explanations.
33 See Pasnau, *Metaphysical Themes*, 549–65, or Hattab, *Forms and Mechanisms*, 54–64, for further accounts of the distinction between metaphysical and physical forms. Tad Schmaltz, 'Substantial Forms as Causes: From Suarez to Descartes', in *Matter and Form*, ed. Manning, 149, suggests that Descartes maintains something of the scholastic (particularly Suarezian) view of the physical form, though he indicates that Marleen Rozemond has pointed out to him that the difference between the usage by Descartes and Suarez of differs in that for the latter the kind of efficient causation is supposed to be 'internal'. For Geulincx the requirement that the causation in this characterization of the physical form be 'internal' would rule it out as a viable reading, since he does not allow for any substantial unity between mind and body.
34 For reasons of space – as well as because without any references in Geulincx's work to the accounts of form and matter given by others the choice would be either arbitrary or excessive – this is not the place to account for how exactly one might accommodate Geulincx's positive account of how the mind and body come together in a human being to any particular scholastic accounts of the form-matter distinction.
35 SSII 299: 'Corpus et motus tantum habent rationem instrumenti, quo non simpliciter simus sed tales simus. Jam autem tale instrumentum non est prius re simpliciter, sed re ut tali, sicut coelum et scalprum, et similia statuariorum instrumenta priora sunt Mercurio, sed non ligno.' My attention was initially drawn to this passage by the fact that Wilson's translation renders 'sed non ligno' as 'but not to the material of the statue' (Geulincx, *Metaphysics*, 118) – which would have been a more direct way of once again referring to the question of form and matter. Geulincx himself point to the analogy between wood and the statue of Mercury in the context of matter and form – see SSII 344–5.

36 SSII 270: 'Mentem *unitam* esse corpori, nihil significat. Sic tamen vulgo dicitur, et Cartesius ipse interdum aliquanto liberius indulget isti vocabulo.' Emphasis in the original.
37 See SSII 151.
38 SSII 151: 'Non excitat eas autem mediante me ipso, quia cogitationes sunt diversae, et ego sum res simplex, a quo diversae cogitationes emanare non possunt.'
39 SSII 151: 'variarum mutationum capax esse debet, ut per hoc varia cogitationum objecta exsurgant'.
40 Richard Burthogge, *An Essay upon Reason, and the Nature of Spirits* (London: John Dunton, 1694), 167. For a slightly more detailed account of Burthogge's account of individuation, see Thiel, *The Early Modern Subject*, 73: 'Burthogge's theory oscillates between an objectivist account of individuation of "things themselves" and a subjectivist explication of individuality in terms of our distinguishing between them on the basis of perceived qualities.'
41 See SII 299.
42 SSII 270.
43 For a strong statement of this view, see, 'Occasionalism and the Mind-Body Problem', in Nadler, *Occasionalism*, 6–28. I tend to agree with Nadler about the more general motivations of occasionalism, but because of the subject matter here it is precisely an aspect of the mind–body problem which is of interest.
44 This being so, Geulincx would be ascribing some causal power to a creature, and would not therefore qualify as an occasionalist in the full sense – occasionalism, in its strictest sense, as a doctrine regarding divine action, both rules out creaturely action and assigns to God all action, all causation in the created world.
45 Francisco Suarez, *On Efficient Causality: Metaphysical Disputations 17, 18, and 19*, trans. Alfred J. Freddoso (New Haven: Yale University Press, 1994), 29.
46 SSII 150; SSII 152.
47 SSIII 288. It is not entirely clear whether these terms – *egressio* and *ingressio* – are definitively terms of the exercise of causal power, since Geulincx also uses them to talk about our ineffable entering and leaving the human condition immediately afterwards. But they certainly sound a lot like they are.
48 SSII 177: 'Merito praesumimus Deum id non posse; ipse enim unus idemque, uno eodemque se habet; necessum ergo est, ut instrumento diversimode affecto utatur, si diversos in nobis cogitandi modos suscitare certum habeat (vide quae his affinia diximus parte prima); atqui nullum est aliud instrumentum quod diversimode se habere potest quam corpus.'
49 Geulincx's view, on this reading, looks like a local (rather than general – that is, covering all forms of interaction) case of divine concurrence, and resembles in particular what was known as 'divine premotion' – very roughly, the idea that God must act on the secondary cause as well as the effect, with the caveat that Geulincx's version addresses only the body-to-mind direction of the interaction of mind

and body. For an account of the debates concerning different accounts of divine concurrence in Leiden roughly at the time when Geulincx moved there from Leuven, see Han van Ruler, 'Franco Petri Burgersdijk and the Case of Calvinism within the Neo-Scholastic Tradition', in *Franco Burgersdijk (1590-1635): Neo-Aristotelianism in Leiden*, ed. E. P. Bos and H. A. Krop (Amsterdam: Rodolpi, 1993), 37–65.

50 The image of the two (sometimes more) clocks was the subject of much debate in the German-speaking world in the late 1800s, because Leibniz was accused of having borrowed it – without acknowledgement – from Geulincx. See Mark Kulstad, 'Causation and Preestablished Harmony in the Early Development of Leibniz's Philosophy', in *Causation in Early Modern Philosophy: Cartesianism, Occasionalism, and Preestablished Harmony*, ed. Steven Nadler (University Park: Pennsylvania State University Press, 1993), 93–117, for a recent account summarizing the debate.

51 SSII 153: 'agant inquam velut instrumenta, non velut causa'.

52 SSII 297: 'Voluntas nosta nullum habet influxum, causalitatem, determinationem, aut efficaciam in motum'.

53 Johannes Flenderus, *Phosphorus philosophica novissimus, seu Logica contracta Claubergiana illustrata commentario logico-metaphysico* (Amsterdam: Janssonius-Waesbergius, 1731), 123–4.

54 On the point regarding the relation between Augustinian views, Platonism and occasionalism, see Richard Sorabji, *Time, Creation, and the Continuum* (London: Duckworth, 1983), 297–306.

55 This example is drawn from William J. Courtenay, 'The King and the Leaden Coin: The Economic Background of "*Sine Qua Non*" Causality', *Traditio* 28 (1972): 185–209.

56 It should be noted that a *sine qua non* cause (or condition) was often taken as a necessary condition, unlike the case described here – see, for example, Andrea Sangiacomo, 'Sine Qua Non Causation: The Legacy of Malebranche's Occasionalism in Kant's *New Elucidation*', *Oxford Studies in Early Modern Philosophy* 9 (forthcoming). Still, Geulincx's denial that God can directly intervene in the world without the use of bodily instruments could quite easily be taken to be a noteworthy limitation of God's power.

57 Richard A. Watson, 'What Moves the Mind: An Excursion in Cartesian Dualism', *American Philosophical Quarterly* 19, no. 1 (January 1982): 77 (73–81).

58 Ibid., 79.

Bibliography

Aalderink, Mark. *Philosophy, Scientific Knowledge, and Concept Formation in Geulincx and Descartes*. Utrecht: Publications of the Zeno Institute of Philosophy, 2009.

Ariew Roger and Grene, Marjorie. 'Ideas, In and Before Descartes'. *Journal of the History of Ideas* 56, no. 1 (1995): 87–106.

Barber, Kenneth F. 'Introduction'. In *Individuation and Identity in Early Modern Philosophy: Descartes to Kant*. Edited by Kenneth F. Barber and Jorge J. E. Gracia, 1–11. Albany: State University of New York Press, 1994.

Burthogge, Richard. *An Essay upon Reason, and the Nature of Spirits*. London: John Dunton, 1694.

Courtenay, William J. 'The King and the Leaden Coin: The Economic Background of "*Sine Qua Non*" Causality'. *Traditio* 28 (1972): 185–209.

Flenderus, Johannes. *Phosphorus philosophica novissimus, seu Logica contracta Claubergiana illustrata commentario logico-metaphysico*. Amsterdam: Janssonius-Waesbergius, 1731.

Geulincx, Arnold. *Sämtliche Schriften in fünf Bänden*. 3 vols. Edited by H. J. De Vleeschauwer. Stuttgart – Bad Cannstatt: Fromann Verlag, 1965–8.

Grosholz, Emil. 'Descartes and the Individuation of Physical Objects', In *Individuation and Identity in Early Modern Philosophy: Descartes to Kant*. Edited by Kenneth F. Barber and Jorge J. E. Gracia, 41–58. Albany: State University of New York Press, 1994.

Hattab, Helen. *Descartes on Forms and Mechanisms*. Cambridge: Cambridge University Press, 2009.

Kulstad, Mark. 'Causation and Preestablished Harmony in the Early Development of Leibniz's Philosophy'. In *Causation in Early Modern Philosophy: Cartesianism, Occasionalism, and Preestablished Harmony*. Edited by Steven Nadler, 93–117. University Park: Pennsylvania State University Press, 1993.

Manning, Gideon. 'Three Biased Reminders about Hylomorphism in Early Modern Science and Philosophy'. In *Matter and Form in Early Modern Science and Philosophy*. Edited by Gideon Manning, 1–32. Leiden and Boston: Brill, 2012.

Martin, Craig. 'Providence and Seventeenth Century Attacks on Averroes'. In *Averroes' Natural Philosophy and Its Reception in the Latin West*. Edited by Paul J. J. M. Bakker, 193–212. Leuven: Leuven University Press, 2015.

Nadler, Steven. 'Knowledge, Volitional Agency, and Causation in Malebranche and Geulincx'. In Steven Nadler, *Occasionalism: Causation Among the Cartesians*, 74–87. Oxford: Oxford University Press, 2011.

Pasnau, Robert. *Metaphysical Themes. 1274–1671*. Oxford: Oxford University Press, 2013.

Richardson, Kara. 'Averroism'. In *The Routledge Companion to Sixteenth Century Philosophy*. Edited by Henrik Lagerlund and Benjamin Hill, 137–55. Abingdon and New York: Routledge, 2017.

Schmaltz, Tad. *Early Modern Cartesianisms: Dutch and French Constructions*. Oxford: Oxford University Press, 2017.

Schmaltz, Tad. 'Substantial Forms as Causes: From Suarez to Descartes'. In *Matter and Form in Early Modern Science and Philosophy*. Edited by Gideon Manning, 99–121. Leiden and Boston: Brill, 2012.

Sorabji, Richard. *Time, Creation, and the Continuum*. London: Duckworth, 1983.
Strazzoni, Andrea. *Dutch Cartesianism and the Birth of Philosophy of Science; from Regius to 's Gravesande*. Berlin and Boston: De Gruyter, 2018.
Suarez, Francisco. *On Efficient Causality: Metaphysical Disputations 17, 18, and 19*. Translated by Alfred J. Freddoso. New Haven: Yale University Press, 1994.
Thiel, Udo. *The Early Modern Subject: Self-consciousness and Personal Identity from Descartes to Hume*. Oxford: Oxford University Press, 2011.
van Ruler, Han. 'Franco Petri Burgersdijk and the Case of Calvinism within the Neo-Scholastic Tradition'. In *Franco Burgersdijk (1590–1635): Neo-Aristotelianism in Leiden*. Edited by E. P. Bos and H. A. Krop, 37–65. Amsterdam: Rodolpi, 1993.
Watson, Richard A. 'What Moves the Mind: An Excursion in Cartesian Dualism'. *American Philosophical Quarterly* 19, no. 1 (January 1982): 73–81.

6

My identity differs: On why I am not myself in light of Hume, Beauvoir and Zen Buddhist writings

Andrew K. Whitehead

Introduction

Comparative philosophical research concerning the no-self doctrine of later Mahāyāna Buddhism remains, to a large extent, secondary to that concerning the no-self doctrine of early Buddhism. With regards to the latter, scholarship has mainly focused on a comparison between Buddhism and the works of David Hume, no doubt as a result of the apparent similarities between the two. This tendency notwithstanding, it is worth noting that there are also gross discrepancies between Hume's conception of identity and the no-self doctrine of Buddhism, discrepancies that become all the more glaring through a comparison with the later Buddhist schools of Chan and Zen. With this in mind, the greater portion of this chapter consists in outlining Hume's position and providing a Zen critique. Suggesting an alternative approach, I compare the Zen Buddhist no-self doctrine to Simone de Beauvoir's existentialist account of self as project. Though unconventional, this approach highlights the need to broaden the parameters for comparative research concerning philosophical interpretations of the Buddhist no-self doctrine. It is my contention that the Zen notion of this central concept lends itself more easily to comparisons with existentialist philosophies than it does to epistemological or psychological ones.

The celebrated and long-standing comparative philosophical journal *Philosophy East and West* has published over 180 articles dealing with both David Hume and Buddhism, and these as early as 1951's Volume 1 Number 1. In fact, there is an overwhelming tendency to take Hume's inclusion in the east-west comparative philosophy toolkit for granted, an inclusion considered self-evidently warranted and uncritically accepted. This tendency notwithstanding, it is worth noting (and has been noted, albeit sparingly) that there are also gross discrepancies between Hume's conception of identity and the no-self doctrine of Buddhism – discrepancies that become all the more glaring through a comparison with the later Buddhist schools of Chan and Zen. It is my contention that a number of fundamental presuppositions operating in Hume's philosophy preclude any reconciliation of his conclusions with those of Buddhism. This chapter is therefore only the first step in a much larger project of critically re-examining comparisons between Hume and Buddhism on the basis of fundamental incommensurability. With this in mind, I suggest an alternative approach, comparing the Zen Buddhist no-self doctrine to Simone de Beauvoir's existentialist account of self as project. In what follows, I first discuss Hume's conception of self, and then I question the viability of its comparison with the no-self doctrine of Zen Buddhism, suggesting further investigation into the merit of alternatively comparing this latter with Beauvoir's conception of self as project.

The Humean conception of self

First, it is worth providing a general introduction to some key concepts employed in Hume's writings, namely his notions of perception, impression and idea. According to David and Mary Norton, these terms can be understood as follows:

Perception: 'Every thing that enters the mind', the general name for impressions and ideas.[1]

Impression: one of the two kinds of perception, ideas being the other; impressions are 'all our sensations, passions and emotions, as they make their first appearance' in the mind. There are two kinds of impression: (1) impressions of sensation that 'without any antecedent perception' arise in the mind; and (2) impressions of reflection, or secondary impressions, those that 'proceed from some of these original ones, either immediately or by the interposition' of ideas. 'Of the first kind are all the impressions of the senses, and all bodily pains and pleasures: Of the second are the passions, and other emotions resembling them.'[2]

Idea: one of the two kinds of perception, the other being impressions, from which ideas are derived. Perceptions (i.e. ideas and impressions) are 'whatever can be present to the mind, whether we employ our senses, or are actuated with passion, or exercise our thought and reflection. ... When we reflect on a passion or an object which is not present, this perception is an idea.'[3]

My treatment of Hume concerns perceptions of self and whether and how such perceptions are the products of impressions or ideas. For Hume, perceptions of self are never congruent with individual impressions. There is no impression, or sense-perception, of an invariable self. As James Giles writes: 'We are never, says Hume, aware of any constant invariable impression that could answer to the name of self. What we experience, rather, is a continuous flow of perceptions that replace one another in rapid succession.'[4] Perceptions are never lasting and are always different, albeit to differing degrees. Hume's investigation into attributions of identity to a self begins with the concession that any perceived identity of a self does not differ in its construct from the perceived identity of any other thing. Specifically, for the purposes of this comparison, Hume's project can be reformulated as an investigation into how and why the fundamental distinction between self and other, maintained through varying experiences, seems to denote an invariable self against and through which all others are discriminated and perceived.

According to Hume, our immediate experience fails to account for the perception of an underlying essential self. Even the idea of a self, given the fashion in which ideas are generated and established, proves non-sensical. As David Appelbaum and Ingrid Turner Lorch write: 'Hume claims that sense perceptions or impressions are the sole origin of all ideas and that an examination of sense perception lends no credence to any belief that a soul substance underlies and endures through perception.'[5] Hume reflects on experience and finds himself unable to support the belief in an unchanging essential self. Experience evidences only the variability and inconstancy of those perceptions that give rise to the idea of a 'theatre of the mind' upon which impressions of a world are cast. One does not consistently encounter the same impression of self through varying acts upon this stage. Instead, one is repeatedly presented with similar differing impressions and ideas which are then taken to be identical and hence to refer to an identical self. The resulting idea of self, however, is not 'real'. Hume writes: 'It must be some one impression, that gives rise to every real idea. But self or person is not any one impression, but that to which our several impressions and ideas are suppos'd to have a reference.'[6]

Hume concedes the inherent reinforcement of identities through their perpetual re-iteration. He writes:

> When we attribute identity, in an improper sense, to variable or interrupted objects, our mistake is not confin'd to the expression, but is commonly attended with a fiction, either of something invariable and uninterrupted, or of something mysterious and inexplicable, or at least with a propensity to such fictions.[7]

In this sense, the conventional use of language by which one identifies a self and attributes identity to it coincides with the reification of an underlying and constant self. Such a self remains unaccounted for to the extent that there is no experience supporting this attribution of identity.

What is experienced, according to Hume, is a series of varying, autonomous and independent perceptions imagined to pertain to a self, and never the self as such. He writes:

> For my part, when I enter most intimately into what I call myself, I always stumble on some particular perception or other, of heat or cold, light or shade, love or hatred, pain or pleasure. I never can catch myself at any time without a perception, and never can observe any thing but the perception.[8]

With respect to the expression 'self', Hume insists that, in every instance, a close examination of what is generally agreed upon as the referent for this expression fails to successfully discover anything that could possibly correspond to it. His insistence rests on his understanding of what is, and is not, perceived. What is perceived, as a sense-impression, is nothing more than a particular sensation that comes to be attributed to a subject who experiences it. What is not perceived is any impression of a self that stands in distinction from such experiences. However, the absurd positing of a self ensues. This positing, according to Hume, results from the initial attributions of identity to the various perceptions that the self is believed to encounter.

Attributing identity to things in the world facilitates an attribution of identity to an experiencer. On this point, Hume writes:

> In order to justify to ourselves this absurdity, we often feign some new and unintelligible principle, that connects the objects together, and prevents their interruption or variation. Thus we feign the continu'd existence of the perceptions of our senses, to remove the interruption; and run into the notion of a soul, and self, and substance, to disguise the variation.[9]

In order for the operations of identification to unite disparate impressions and ideas, it is necessary to concede that perceptions of such impressions and ideas continue through time. In other words, in order for the contents of such perceptions to be determined as continuous, despite their variance, it must either be assumed that the perceptions themselves are continuous or that the stage upon which all perceptions are cast is continuous. Hume finds that neither of these assumptions can account for attributions of identity through experience. Instead, what is experienced is a continuous flow of varying and inconstant impressions and ideas. Discussing perceptions of identity, he writes: 'They are nothing but a bundle or collection of different perceptions, which succeed each other with an inconceivable rapidity, and are in a perpetual flux and movement.'[10] However, this definition of identity, for Hume, is absurd: ideas of identity are false. This notion of falsity bears directly on the problem of personal identity. Hume writes: 'The identity, which we ascribe to the mind of man, is only a fictitious one, and of a like kind with that which we ascribe to vegetables and animal bodies. It cannot, therefore, have a different origin, and must proceed from a like operation of the imagination upon like objects.'[11]

Through perpetual re-instantiations of the self–other distinction, perceptions (ideas) of the self and perceptions (ideas) of others are conventionalized in a similar fashion. In other words, the mind or self, conceived as the storehouse of all conscious activity, is falsely reified as the essential and continuous underlying basis of all experience. However, this false reification depends on the mind's being distinctly perceived in varying situations in which it fails to resemble itself beyond the formal resemblance of its operations, which are all given as though through a discrimination of self from other. In this sense, one has not one but many ideas of self. The perception of the identity of an invariable self is the perception of an idea that is generated through a multiplicity of varying perceptions of ideas of self. According to Hume: 'Identity is nothing really belonging to these different perceptions, and uniting them together; but is merely a quality, which we attribute to them, because of the union of their ideas in the imagination, when we reflect upon them.'[12] Perceptions are never continuous, but are, instead, disjointed and distinct. Upon reflection, the mind notes similarities between the attendant ideas and comes to imagine that such similarities imply a genuine identity between them. These operations are then reflected upon, and the false idea of a self is posited in perception, ultimately serving to occasion an identification of similar occurrences of such perceptions as self.

Though the mechanism by which such identification takes place is the same as that which allows for the uniting of any perceptions of objects, the nature or 'reality' of perceptions of self, for Hume, is 'unreal'. Giles writes: 'As Hume has told us, there is no impression … of the self; there is only the smooth and uninterrupted progress of thought within our imagination.'[13] It is only when one feigns the reality of the false idea of the self that the mind is able, upon reflection, to imagine an uninterrupted flow of perceptions as belonging to and/or constituting one and the same perceiver. According to this reading, Hume's account of the confounding of instances of similar perceptions with instances of an identical self requires that the mind must first identify that pivot point from which perceptions are observed as similar. The mind must first identify itself.[14] Only upon such an identification does it become possible for the discrimination of other identities to occur. According to L. Stafford Betty:

> Hume points to the memory as the basis of the self. Just as the memory makes it possible for the mind to confound resemblance of impressions with identity of impressions – to make that presumptuous leap from resemblance to identity – so it is also the basis of the next step, which is to account for the identification of impressions by an 'identity' on which this identification is based.[15]

The sequence in which identifications take place – that is, whether identifications of similar perceptions result in a need for the identification of the identity that gives way to such identifications or whether the identification of the identity that gives way to all identifications necessarily precedes such identifications – need not concern us here. It is sufficient to note that the identification both of self and of others is rooted in resemblances perceived through memory. Elaborating his position, Hume writes: 'The memory not only discovers the identity, but also contributes to its production, by producing the relation of resemblance among the perceptions. The case is the same whether we consider ourselves or others.'[16] The relation of resemblance among perceptions of the self is established by memory. The perception of this relation is then misconstrued to be the discovery of their identity. Varying perceptions that merely resemble each other are related in such a way as to produce the idea of their identity (by remembering the varying perceptions and comparing them), which is found in memory (specifically the memory that 'discovers' they are the same). Sense-impressions generate ideas that are related through memory of resemblances. In their own turn, these resemblances are perceived, informing further experience through their feigned relations, ultimately coming to be misconstrued as belonging to similar processes of identification, which resemble each other to the extent that they confound varying related resemblances with the identity of identifications. They come to posit a self.

Hume's treatment of the self, according to this reading, fails to offer any active means for expelling the mind's fictions. According to Appelbaum: 'Hume … concludes that perception is passive, consciousness involuntary, incapable of self-direction, and discontinuous.'[17] It is out of this notion of the discontinuity and independence of perceptions that the main thrust of the Zen criticism of Hume will develop.

A Zen critique of Hume: Suggesting an alternative

According to Vasubandhu, 'he who meditates on emptiness does not exist'.[18] Interestingly enough, this seems to address the dissolution of self in Hume. If the self is perceived in the imagination as the idea of the relation that identifies and discovers the identity of varying and inconstant resemblances by means of memory, then reflection on the illusory nature not only of the relation but also of the varying and inconstant resemblances themselves, undermines the operations by which any self is perceived. By undermining the distinctions of conventional worlds, the distinction that enables such distinctions becomes superfluous.

According to Thomas Kasulis:

> In their raw givenness within the state of nonthinking, phenomena are open or empty (this is sometimes referred to as 'suchness'). Yet, in their 'presencing' (genjō), they coalesce into meaningful matrices appropriate to their context or 'occasion'. Thus the same meaningless phenomena can configure themselves in multiple possible matrices of meaning ('there are many worlds everywhere'). This attention to meaning-in-the-making is the major theme developed in 'Genjōkōan" Dōgen's most famous philosophical essay and one he himself highlighted when he started collecting his own writings.[19]

The conditions that constitute the 'cause' of the meaning of the occasioned phenomenal matrices are understood as conventionally interconnected and co-dependent. Instances of identity, for Zen Buddhism, are meaningfully articulated at the contextual intersection of these conditions, which, in their interrelatedness, serve as the cause, or as the occasion, for their presencing as such.

Conversely, according to D. C. Mathur: 'Hume's concept of experience ... was "atomistic" and as such a postreflective one. Reflective introspection revealed to Hume that the mind was nothing but a series of disjointed impressions and ideas with no "real" relations between them.'[20] For Hume, things, despite being experienced as though in a continuous and uninterrupted flow of perception, are in fact identifications as relations between many unique and disjointed perceptions. However, for Hume, such relations are false. They are only concoctions of the imagination. Hume's atomism goes so far as to note that 'every distinct perception, which enters into the composition of the mind, is a distinct existence, and is different, and distinguishable, and separable from every other perception, either co-temporary or successive'.[21] For Hume, perceptions are real; in fact, only perceptions are real. Moreover, they are also distinct and unrelated.

Describing Hume's atomism, Betty finds that '[he] holds that each split second of perception is a unique and essentially complete unit datum in itself'.[22] The relations between such units are generated out of their resemblances reflected upon in memory. Therefore, such relations are not real. As Appelbaum writes:

> Perception being discrete, atomic and linearly successive, consciousness is characterized by sequences of perceptions, each arising in some fashion after the other. We can examine the relations between the single perceptions. But in doing this, we may neglect to recognize the basic implication of the independence of perceptions.[23]

For Zen, on the other hand, out of specific contexts in specific conventional worlds, distinctions are based on a presupposition of relation. Each distinction can never stand in isolation, but only in relation to some other distinction that is either implicitly or explicitly placed against it. There are relations, and these are of such a nature as to allow for the discrimination of distinct existences. Along these lines, Kasulis argues for a functional reading of the self in Zen. He writes: 'Insofar as one is functional – that is, related to something – the Zen Buddhist has a specific meaning objectifiable by the thought of an external observer or by one's own subsequent retrospective analysis. Within the functionality itself, however, there is merely relatedness.'[24] The objectification of the discriminated occurs in virtue of the attribution of contextual identities, an attribution that validates the contextual objectification it projects. For example, contextually, a Zen master is discriminated and objectified out of a specific relation (e.g. a private meeting with a Zen monk) as a Zen master in virtue of the conventional truth (the relational discrimination) of his being a 'Zen master', a truth that validates and confirms that the Zen master (the one in the private meeting with a monk) corresponds to the reference 'Zen master' and is therefore, situationally, a Zen master. This is how the self appears in conventional reality.

Hume insists on the reality of sense-impressions and of the ideas that represent them. The self fails to be perceived as a sense-impression and is, therefore, a false idea of the imagination. Interestingly enough, by not subjecting the self to the same criteria as all other perceived identities, Hume's no-self doctrine seems to imply an essential underlying self. Mathur writes:

> [Hume] did not perceive that in accounting for personal identity in terms of our 'feigning' or 'imagining' such a unity into our discrete data he was already assuming an 'I' which, if not a metaphysically distinct substantial entity, must have a greater continuity than was allowed by his theory of the self as a series of 'loose and separate' perishing particulars.[25]

Hume's insistence that memory is responsible for the feigning of a self seems to imply that there is something, which comes to be identified as the self, that continues through various perceptions and is able to posit relations between them based on resemblances that it has perceived. Some thing oscillates between perceptions and 'bundles' them together based on the resemblances that have been perceived. Insofar as Hume understands perceptions to be unrelated and atomistic, he requires that this something be real. The flow of perceptions, as flow, is also required if Hume is to be able to account for the identity of things. This flow is constituted by the successive perceptions arising from singular perception units. According to Appelbaum: 'The temporal flow brings with it a continual succession of perceptions – sensations, emotions, and thoughts. Moreover, since each perception perishes, it must be replaced by a totally new one. Significantly, each perception therefore arises independently.'[26] The disjointed series of independent and 'totally new' perceptions, once related by resemblance in memory, generates the illusory reality of their identity. Such is the case both with the identity of others and with the identity of self.

The identification of the varying perceptions, in turn, allows for this series to appear smooth and uninterrupted. This illusory continuance then serves to reinforce the identification of the series as continuous by facilitating their relation and perpetuating the illusory continuance. Appelbaum writes: 'Because the sequence of perceptions tends to be gradual, consciousness, failing to note the change from each single perception to the next, attributes the succession of actually discrete and independently existing perceptions to a single object which it then projects into an external world.'[27] Hume develops his no-self theory starting from the supposition that all perceptions exist independently. Perceptions, for Hume, are the only indication of reality. However, claiming that all perceptions are atomistic unit data, Hume is forced to account for the attribution of identity without recourse to a premise of continuity. This proves problematic for Hume's argument, insofar as he is then compelled to rely on the mental faculty of memory to account for the attribution of identity. Hume's no-self doctrine thereby posits a continuity that it cannot theoretically account for. In an attempt to circumvent this problem, Hume finds that perceptions are given as though in a 'flow', once memory has discovered the identity of the objects of the varying perceptions. Hume escapes the essentialization of the self by conceding that his atomistic perceptions flow together. In this sense, he forfeits the fundamental principle of his empiricism in order to avoid forfeiting it. He forfeits the atomistic nature of perceptions in order to account for how these data units are related. Unwilling to concede the continuity of self, which would be required for his theory to hold water, Hume provides a circular argument without realizing its implication. The implication (and the necessary outcome of this reading) is that self and other are co- and interdependently generated. Perceptions cannot stand in isolation from each other or anything else.

In a movement away from the intellectualization of reality, Zen discussions on the no-self doctrine are existential as opposed to epistemological or psychological. The self only exists relationally, in specific situations, and often in preestablished roles. The human self is therefore a relational being of engagements, and is understood as existing as a specific person occupying a specific position in the context of the relation in which it finds itself. Existentially, no thing exists independently. All things exist only relationally, including perceptions. This remains the case not only with regards to the self but also with regards to all things conventionally existent. In other words, engagements in conventional worlds are the relations that occasion discriminations of self and other. The Zen use of the no-self doctrine, as a skilful means use, undermines these relations, thereby disrupting the operations by which discriminations are produced. In this sense, conventional worlds consist of relational being, and all distinct discriminations are determined by the relational context. The interrelational occasion of the world and its constituent phenomena applies equally to both the relational identity of things and that of selves. For these and similar reasons, it is interesting to note that

> Hume ... did not really believe in the philosophy he expounds in the *Treatise*. Not only did he not believe it, he loathed it. At one point he damns his conclusions as a 'monstrous offspring' and a 'malady'. As the *Treatise* unfolded in front of its author, it became more and more obvious to him that his philosophy was one not to be delivered by but delivered from.[28]

In accordance with Zen, the no-self doctrine must be read in light of the insistence on practice for the sake of liberation from attachments. It is a soteriological tool with which to disrupt the conventional worlds and their contexts in order to show no-thing. It allows practitioners to understand the relational existence of themselves and others, a relational existence that occasions their discrimination. All selves stand in relation, as relation, to all others in the context of their conventional world. Relations, denoting a particular contextual engagement in which discriminations arise, are able to perpetually shift and reaffirm the relational existence of engagements. Conventionally, persons are these engagements. Without a self, the person becomes an expressive discrimination of the relational. According to Kasulis: 'From the Zen perspective, the person does not perform action; rather, action performs the person.'[29] Out of relational engagements, as contexts in conventional worlds, discriminations of identities constitute distinct individuals who stand in relation to one another. In this way, action performs the person.

This Zen conception of the person coincides with Simone de Beauvoir's existentialist development of self as project in a number of ways, especially with her equation of action with self. This equation rests on her equation of possession with action. She writes: 'The only reality that belongs entirely to me is ... my act; even a work fashioned out of materials that are not mine escapes me in certain ways. What is mine is first the accomplishment of my project.'[30] What a person is truly able to possess as his or hers is nothing above and beyond his/her actions. Their sense of self, therefore, also rests on actions. Since such actions are always situated in a context, the self found in those actions is also situated in a context. Finding oneself situated in a given context, one also finds a disposition to act in accordance with one's distinct situation. Beauvoir identifies the drive to act as the basis of humanity, determining that 'spontaneity, the drive to engage the world and make it ours, is the truth of our humanity'.[31] This understanding can be compared to that of Zen, where attachment and craving are understood to perpetuate the conventional worlds of illusory identities. These, in turn, lead to greater attachment and craving. The drive to engage the world, whether understood positively or negatively, generates contextual relations that occasion distinctions of a self that engages and acts upon such a world. To this extent, the 'truth of our humanity' is indeed marked by our engagements with the world.

As an existentialist, Beauvoir contends that existence precedes essence. Through relational engagements, distinctions of self arise, seemingly determining the reality of the subject and its engagements in the world. Beauvoir writes: 'I take up projects in the world to make the world mine, to make myself essential.'[32] The world becomes conventionally reified in such a way that it seems to be the world of the subject, a subject who is discriminated out of this world. Through engagements with the world, the self's existence is affirmed. This confirmation, in turn, leads to attachment and craving, ultimately perpetuating discriminations for engagement. To the extent that this remains the case, Zen would disagree with Beauvoir's conclusion that 'what is mine is therefore first what I do. But as soon as I have done it, the object goes and separates itself from me; it escapes me.'[33] Zen would argue that such an understanding fails to take account of the law of dependent origination. If the self is nothing outside of the relations in which it finds itself engaged, and if such engagements perpetuate the illusion that is the conventional world (which provides the context for this relation), then all engagements contribute to the construction of the identities that provide the manifestations of relational contexts within which the self can, and does, later engage. 'It' does not escape me. 'It' occasions my very identity to the extent that it occasions further relational contexts within which I may appear: 'The effects of actions that have been performed continuously from an infinite past intermingle with each and every thing that exists, with everything that breathes and lives. These effects are manifest here and now in the substrate of my whole existence.'[34]

To this extent, Beauvoir does not follow through on her position. If it is through concrete relational engagements that one makes oneself essential, then the essence of a person must lie in his/her relational engagements alone. From the perspective of Zen Buddhism, Beauvoir takes too much liberty in identifying humanity with freedom. It is important to note that

> When Beauvoir identifies us with freedom, she is not using the term to designate the transcending nature of our being. As human I am perpetually transcending myself toward a yet to be defined future in which I seek to establish myself in my concrete particularity. I am a way of being that makes myself be by reaching beyond myself toward something other than myself.[35]

The use of the active verbs 'seek', 'makes' and 'reaching' seems to denote an essential self that undertakes the drive for engaging in projects and acts for the sake of essentializing itself.

However, such an essential self is found only in the relational contexts. Zen avoids this difficulty by connecting those conventional discriminations that constitute the relational occasioning of appearances of the distinction between self and other, as opposed to using an underlying actor behind the actions that allow for the actor's existence. Beauvoir seems to forget her unique use of possession and how it relates to action and essence. What is mine is my act, and it is mine to the extent that I find myself in it. In this sense, relational contexts, as engagements, are where the self is found. One does not have relationships, but becomes essentialized through one's engagements with the worlds of convention. As Kasulis writes: 'In both secular Japan and Zen Buddhism, the person is not something that has meaning or has relationships; rather, one achieves meaning through relationships.'[36]

This seems strikingly similar to Beauvoir's notion of making oneself essential through projects. In both cases, one attains meaning through engagements. A self becomes meaningful, in the sense of becoming conventionally existent as a discriminated distinct identity, only to the extent that a relative engagement provides meaningful relational positions. One's relational position is always found in a conventional context, in a world of convention. The conventional world presents itself as though against a subject – a subject driven to engage in its particular relational contexts. Beauvoir writes: '[Man] cannot suddenly spring forth into the world in the pure ipseity [selfness] of his being without the world suddenly springing forth in front of him.'[37] There are no instances of a person standing apart from the world in which he/she is meaningfully distinguished. Instead, one is only a self through one's engagements in the conventional worlds that 'spring forth' in and through these engagements.

Hume's inability to adapt his epistemological project to the existential implications he encounters compel him to make unnecessary concessions, ultimately rendering his bundle theory of the self incomplete and problematic. Any comparison of Hume and Buddhism must take account of the vast divergence of their projects (epistemological vs. existential), and the consequential ordering of fundamental implications thereof. Hume aims to account for the existential by means of the epistemological, whereas Buddhism aims to account for the epistemological by means of the existential. To this extent, a comparison of Beauvoir and Buddhism should and does yield greater similarities and, in turn, greater terrain for critical engagement and exchange. While the two are obviously irreconcilable (for instance, due to their disparate volitional valuations of craving and attachment), the overlap of their conceptions cannot be ignored in terms of its comparative worth.

Notes

1 David Hume, *A Treatise of Human Nature*, ed. David Norton and Mary Norton (Oxford: Oxford University Press, 2000), 579.
2 Ibid., 577.
3 Ibid., 576.
4 James Giles, 'The No-Self Theory: Hume, Buddhism, and Personal Identity', *Philosophy East and West* 43, no. 2 (1993): 177.
5 David Appelbaum and Ingrid Turner Lorch, 'Tracking the Discontinuity of Perception', *Philosophy East and West* 28, no. 4 (1978): 469.
6 Hume, *A Treatise of Human Nature*, 164.
7 Ibid., 166.
8 Ibid., 165.
9 Ibid., 166.
10 Ibid., 165.

11 Ibid., 169.
12 Ibid.
13 Giles, 'The No-Self Theory', 190.
14 The critical reading of Hume I have adopted is not new. It is entertained in the vast majority of the comparative literature dealing with Hume and Buddhism. It is also one of the 'standard' readings of Hume in Humean scholarship. For example, David Fate Norton and Mary J. Norton draw very similar conclusions. In fact, they note that Hume himself eventually abandons his project, finding that it is too difficult to resolve. In their commentary, they write: '[Hume] is convinced, on the one hand, that if "perceptions are distinct existences, [then] they form a whole only by being connected together". He is also convinced, on the other hand, that "no connexions among distinct existences are ever discoverable by human understanding". And he cannot now see how to reconcile these two insights or "principles", nor is he prepared to renounce either as false. The notion of personal identity arises from reflection on the way in which the past perceptions of the mind naturally introduce one another, but Hume is unable to explain the principles, that "unite our successive perceptions in our thought or consciousness" or to discover any satisfactory theory of personal identity. Candidly admitting that this issue is too difficult for him to solve, he holds out the hope that someone else may find a solution to it.' Hume, *A Treatise of Human Nature*, 145.
15 L. Stafford Betty, 'The Buddhist-Humean Parallels: Postmortem', *Philosophy East and West* 21, no. 3 (1971): 242.
16 Hume, *A Treatise of Human Nature*, 170.
17 Appelbaum and Loch, 'Tracking the Discontinuity of Perception', 469.
18 Quoted in Goodman, 'Vaibhasika Metaphoricalism', *Philosophy East and West* 55, no. 3 (2005): 379.
19 James W. Heisig, Thomas P. Kasulis and John C. Maraldo (eds), *Japanese Philosophy: A Sourcebook* (Honolulu: University of Hawaii Press, 2011), 144.
20 D. C. Mathur, 'The Historical Buddha (Gotama), Hume, and James on the Self: Comparisons and Evaluations', *Philosophy East and West* 28, no. 3 (1978): 259.
21 Hume, *A Treatise of Human Nature*, 169.
22 Betty, 'The Buddhist-Humean Parallels', 238.
23 Appelbaum and Loch, 'Tracking the Discontinuity of Perception', 470.
24 T. P. Kasulis, *Zen Action Zen Person* (Honolulu: University of Hawai'i Press, 1981), 132.
25 Mathur, 'The Historical Buddha (Gotama), Hume, and James on the Self', 261.
26 Appelbaum and Loch, 'Tracking the Discontinuity of Perception', 470.
27 Ibid.
28 Betty, 'The Buddhist-Humean Parallels', 251.
29 Kasulis, *Zen Action Zen Person*, 139.

30 Simone de Beauvoir, *Philosophical Writings*, ed. Margaret A. Simons (Chicago: University of Illinois Press, 2004), 93.
31 Ibid., 82.
32 Ibid.
33 Ibid., 93.
34 Heisig, Kasulis and Maraldo, *Japanese Philosophy*, 127.
35 Beauvoir, *Philosophical Writings*, 83.
36 Kasulis, *Zen Action Zen Person*, 132.
37 Beauvoir, *Philosophical Writings*, 98.

Bibliography

Appelbaum, David and Ingrid Turner Lorch. 'Tracking the Discontinuity of Perception'. *Philosophy East and West* 28, no. 4 (1978): 469–84.

Beauvoir, Simone de. *Philosophical Writings*. Edited by Margaret A. Simons. Chicago: University of Illinois Press, 2004.

Betty, L. Stafford. 'The Buddhist-Humean Parallels: Postmortem'. *Philosophy East and West* 21, no. 3 (1971): 237–53.

Giles, James. 'The No-Self Theory: Hume, Buddhism, and Personal Identity'. *Philosophy East and West* 43, no. 2 (1993): 175–200.

Goodman, Charles. 'Vaibhasika Metaphoricalism'. *Philosophy East and West* 55, no. 3 (2005): 377–93.

Heisig, James W., Thomas P. Kasulis and John C. Maraldo, eds. *Japanese Philosophy: A Sourcebook*. Honolulu: University of Hawaii Press, 2011.

Hume, David. *A Treatise of Human Nature*. Edited by David Norton and Mary Norton. Oxford: Oxford University Press, 2000.

Kasulis, Thomas P. *Zen Action Zen Person*. Honolulu: University of Hawai'i Press, 1981.

Mathur, D. C. 'The Historical Buddha (Gotama), Hume, and James on the Self: Comparisons and Evaluations'. *Philosophy East and West* 28, no. 3 (1978): 253–69.

Individual identity and cultural practice: Relationalism in modern protestant theology

Harald Matern

Introduction

In July 2014, a conference took place at the University of Manchester. Its topic was the impact of 'postliberalism' on modern societal theory. Is modern political liberalism with its inherent 'individualism' in itself a bad thing, opposing an image of humanity rooted in Christianity because of its notion of undeniable individual rights? Or, as John Milbank put it in the *Oxford Journal of Law and Religion* in 2012, isn't there a hidden, but inherent link, between the concept of human rights and political absolutism?[1]

Questions like these may not be of particular interest to all cultures globally. In fact, many might argue that discussions of this kind only demonstrate the academic administration of self-made problems, deeply rooted in Western dualism and political culture and intrinsically linked to the Christian tradition. I would not oppose such lines of thought, but what I want to explore in the following is the question if this very tradition does not host different modes of thinking about personal identity that may offer not a solution to this dilemma but a framework that does not even produce a tension of this kind. In order to do this, and, subsequently, ask for a different contribution to a global discussion on difference and identity, and religion, we should first get a more detailed picture of this 'Western' problem. What is the opposition between liberal and post-liberal all about?[2]

What Milbank opposes in his views is neither the idea of respecting the individuality of a person nor the concept of the modern democratic state. Moreover, his intervention points at the question of how the political and legal concept of individual rights could possibly be *founded*. If individual rights were granted by human nature or by the modern state, so the argument evolves, they would be nothing but a moral or political extrapolation of facticity.[3] Thus, in their *Politics of Virtue*, Milbank and Adrian Pabst argue for a different account of political thinking – one that champions embeddedness and tradition over individuality.[4] It is in the social relations of persons and the narrative of a certain tradition where human dignity – rather than individual rights – can and should be derived. In opposition to this, the very idea of prolonging the political ramifications based on the classic 'Western' narrative of a 'Cartesian' subject socially embedded in an ongoing struggle marked by negativity of each individual against the other rather than a positive account of personality leads, according to Milbank and Pabst, to destructiveness.[5] It is 'atomising and authoritarian' at the same time, as reflected in modern-liberal democracies that lack a certain type of inner commitment, 'loyalty and collective belonging'.[6] This commitment should then be granted not by a state conceived as 'one' nor by a sort of grassroots democracy of the 'many', but by a 'few' who 'defend democracy non-democratically', by means of cultivating traditional religion, educating the masses led by an ideal of virtuous personality, inserting the ideas of reciprocity and responsibility into economics and encouraging global leadership of such morally led communities like the European Union – or Great Britain.[7]

While Milbank represents one trend in current British thought, on the other side of the ocean we can observe similar currents of thought, linked to names like George Lindbeck and Stanley Hauerwas. These representatives of the so-called 'post-liberal theology' argue in a comparable way: modern society and modern political ethics lack a proper foundation for what they try to guarantee by the mere force of law. Here it is the narrative structure of the biblical tradition that contributes to the formation of the individual self in a way that guarantees its inner freedom from social and political determinations.[8] While the focus on the narrative structure of individual self-interpretation seems to me an important contribution to current thinking about personal identity, especially in an attempt to enter the stage of global-philosophical discussions, the apparent immunization of Christian theology against public discourse in both thinkers could, in my opinion, provide yet another source for a different kind of 'absolutism' – this time a particularistic one.

I will come back to this point later on. First I want to try to systematize the question I shall raise on the background of the outlined discourse.

Individual identity – a European 'grand narrative' and its post-liberal transformation

The thinkers I have cited are competing against a narrative that plays an important role in modern Western public discourse. A masterly adaptation of this is found in Oxford historian Larry Siedentop's recent account of *Inventing the Individual. The Origins of Western Liberalism*.[9] In this book, Siedentop narrates European history as deeply influenced by Christianity – not only politically but also ideologically. The formation of Western political modernity is, as he claims, deeply linked to the development of the symbolic sources of the Christian religion. These sources politically furthered and symbolically reflected the formation of a type of society within which the individual's rights are respected and held high due to the fact that each member of mankind is individually connected to God – be this in a conscious or unconscious manner. On the other hand, the Christian idea of God not only strengthens this concept but originated it by representing the Divine in one individual person, Jesus Christ. Thus, the history of political thought in Europe should be read as an account of the struggle to secularize this concept of the relation between God and man, or to 'translate' it into political reality.

The idea of the theological roots of modern Western liberalism is not a private invention of Siedentop's. We can find it in modern classics like Karl Löwith but also in contemporary thinkers as diverse as the French philosopher Jean-Luc Nancy and the Canadian philosopher Charles Taylor. In very different ways but united in this common notion, Nancy and Taylor contribute to the view that modern Western liberalism is strongly connected to the Christian tradition.[10] And even more: they claim that Christianity has thoroughly contributed to the formation of the modern Western notion of individual *identity*. Though they differ in various important points, these thinkers converge in some aspects concerning this notion: Individual identity is not an isolated substance but a structure that consists of various relations. The basic ones of these are corporality and the plurality of phenomena in the objective and social worlds. These relations converge in one point, where they become conscious. Individual self-conscience is a relational structure. But more: as a relational structure in itself points out to difference rather than to oneness, the plurality of the world is at the same time the place where the individual discovers the very notion of transcendence. 'Transcendence' here means a sense of being related to things or persons other than me, a general openness. In Nancy, this openness, not as in somebody being open to something but as an openness per se, is the core of what we call individual identity. At the same time, it is the centre of the Christian tradition. The point of this argument is that individuality and sociality are of the same origin – perhaps not in an epistemological but in an ontological or transcendental sense. Individual identity is in itself already a social concept.

If that is so – than where is the problem the post-liberalists are pointing at and struggling against? Where then is to be found the isolated individual and the social atomism against which they argue? The problem lies deeper. Perhaps no modern Western thinker would argue against what I have briefly outlined – in a conceptual manner. But the problem that is at stake in the debate above-mentioned is not in the first place a conceptual but an ethical one. The claim of post-liberal ethics is to describe social reality and (assumed) individual identities within a political framework blamed as defective, one, which, effectively, impedes identity-building in a desirable manner. As a remedy, they offer strong, community-based concepts of identity where belonging and embeddedness take the place of constitutional relations of the self. In order to realize such normative ideal they oppose what they call 'liberal theology' – much in the same way as Karl Barth did in Germany and Switzerland in the early–mid twentieth century. Liberal theologians, so the narrative evolves, have far too easily accepted the premises of Enlightenment philosophy, the destruction of classical metaphysics and the turn to what has come to be called 'subjectivity', usually associated today with whiteness, maleness, violence and, in the end, solitude. An example of this stereotype may be found in Fichte's early writings from 1794/5: 'The I posits itself.'[11] It will be worth considering this point later. For now, I simply raise the question as to whether the opposition between the supposed 'individualism' of 'liberal theology', that goes hand in hand with political liberalism (left or right) and, on the other side, the community-oriented narrative formation of personal identity together with an internally bonded society is real or is an academic straw fire which redirects energies philosophers of religion and theologians could use for better goals instead. It is possible, I will argue, that here two sides of an ethical opposition are constructed that could belong together, at least from a continental perspective. Let us have an even closer look.

Anyone could agree, I assume, that individuality and sociality are, conceptually, explicable on the level of epistemology and, perhaps, ontology. But ethics has to become a practical reality and that means that it must at some point of its development become law (at least this is the case in the Western Liberal tradition). Law, in turn, must recur to fixed concepts in order to establish social order. The individual in law is not the same as it is in philosophy and, perhaps, in the Christian tradition. Law, when trying to establish and reinforce human rights, uses a *negative* concept of the individual. The individual here is defined by what it is *not*, by its *borders*, which under all circumstances must be defended. In this negative concept of individuality and individual freedom, which has its roots in the ethical thinking of Immanuel Kant and Johann Gottlieb Fichte, lays a danger, as the post-liberals point out. This danger consists in substantializing individuality while at the same time refraining from defining it *positively*. By describing individual identity as a project of borders, the individual facticity in the perspective of Western liberalism is equivalent to what it is by its determining factors on the social level. This is what Milbank challenges when he distinguishes between 'human dignity' and 'human rights'. A *positive* account of human individuality must rely on what it *is* or *can be*, not on what it *is not*. Here, religion comes into play. What it positively is, for the individual is not determined by the facticity of her corporeal, social or historical situation. It is rather the narrative tradition within which it is formed and by whose terms it will interpret itself. Individual freedom and individual dignity then appear to be derived from the concrete communities within which this individual self-interpretation takes place. And even more: not only does a positive account of individual identity arise only within these narratives, but this narrative identity is the only valuable founding source of human dignity.

So far, so good. But isn't this just another form of social determinism? If the narratives I live by and which are transported by the community I live in really *do* predetermine the way I interpret myself, where is the possibility to opt out? Isn't the Christian community, as described by Milbank, just another 'dispositive', which by its discursive power undermines my very being me? What would the positive contribution of such a conception be to our description of social reality? In Milbank, it is the very *content* of the narrative of *this* community that not only distinguishes it from others but in which it excels. Christianity's contribution to public discourse is that it is – itself. And even more: by claiming that theology methodically starts *beyond* the social sciences and public reason, there is an underlying tendency towards implicitly 'theologising' the public perception of reality. Should the Western contribution to thinking about personal identity already be exhausted at this point? And where would there be a place for difference?

In my opinion, what here is intended to be a step forward towards something like a second naiveté turns out to result in two steps backwards when it comes to ethics. In fact, this seems to be not a post-liberal but a premodern world view, with a Christian elitism trying to qualify for the leading ideology. While the critique of political liberalism(s) seems to be striking, the alternative offered – at least in

Milbank and Pabst – is anything but tempting in terms of ethics, especially, I think, when it comes to the role of religion within the politics of identity and difference.

While it is important to ask for the positive role and contribution of (traditional) religious thought to our understanding of human identity, the claim of absoluteness of one particular group, even if restricted to the members of this group, cannot be an accurate answer to the plurality of our present world. This is, in my opinion, not only true for a philosophical perspective but for a theological one as well. To think about the contribution of Western Christianity to the narrative construction of identity cannot and should not mean to erase the distinctive role of difference(s). In the following, I will sketch some thoughts on this debate by drawing upon the German-speaking tradition. I will focus especially on the role of relations within the construction of personal identity – an aspect that sometimes seems to be neglected in far too schematic criticisms of 'liberal' theology.

This is, naturally, not meant to offer *the* solution to the question of how to give individual identity within its framework of social relations a proper formulation and foundation. It is moreover an attempt to make an offer for resuming and enriching the discussion, and I am well aware of its particularity. What I will try to point out is that the critique of theological liberalism offered by Milbank and others simply misses the point, both at the conceptual and at the ethical level. Instead of 'only' looking back and negating modernity we could very well have a closer look at contributions formulated within modernity if we are to preserve what has been achieved in terms of liberal ethics.

Individual identity and religious practice: A relationalist account of the constitution of personal identity

We have seen that contemporary post-liberal thinkers challenge the European master narrative about the genealogy of the modern-liberal concept of human individuality in the Christian tradition. What Christianity has to say about human individuality is, if we follow Milbank, something quite different to the modern discourse on human rights (as an example of a liberalist approach to that question) has to offer. The price for this conceptual turn is, as I have pointed out, the restriction of Christian theology and philosophy of religion to the internal semantics and identity-forming processes of the communities they refer to. While this is explicit in Lindbeck and Hauerwas, it is implicit but not less real in Milbank, too. The risk I see in this endeavour is either to ghettoize Christianity or to theologize public discourse through the backdoor.

I want to offer two examples of a different mode of dealing with the social and political problems of modernity.[12] These could inspire us to resume the debate and perhaps, to reconcile the (apparently) opposing points of view. Both examples, Friedrich Schleiermacher and Paul Tillich, stem from the German-speaking, so-called 'liberal' tradition of philosophical theology.[13] Both thinkers I shall refer to are theologians and philosophers. Both are emphatically modern. The positions of both are, as we shall see, not accurately addressed by the global critiques against liberalism (both theological and political) of their post-liberal challengers, at least not when it comes to their ethical side.[14] By doing this I want to approach the political problem outlined earlier in terms of philosophical theology, taking up the challenge set up especially by Milbank: theologies of the self should be accounted for as political theologies contributing to the politics of identity and difference.

The heuristic question I use to address both thinkers has three aspects: First, I want to outline briefly in what way individual identity is conceived of. Second, I will point out what role religion plays in the respective concept. Third, I want to turn the perspective towards the projected role of religion in the public domain, hence, to its political side. As Joshua Daniel has recently put it, the task for political ethics as well as political philosophy is 'to recover a conception of individuality that recognizes the significance of the self's social constitution without claiming that being socially constituted is the point of an individual self's existence'.[15] If religion or religion-inspired thinking can contribute to achieving this goal, it is well and good. But this should not be at the price of post-liberally encapsulating itself or trying to insinuate an implicit Christian content of public discourse that only the religious specialist can uncover.

Friedrich Schleiermacher: Individual identity as performance

The first example I want to present is a modern 'classic'. Friedrich Schleiermacher, theologian and philosopher, is not only important to this question because of his importance in shaping the methodical proceedings of German-speaking philosophical theology. He is also important because he is one of the protagonists of the Early Romantic emphasis on 'individuality'.

In order to understand the meaning of individuality in Schleiermacher's thought we must consider the background of his work. Having been educated at a Moravian Seminary, Schleiermacher began his university teaching at a time when Kantian and early Fichtean subject-philosophy had not only destroyed classical metaphysics but had also in a certain way undercut the plausibility of religious thought. Schleiermacher turned against both subjects – against the restriction of the normative dimension of human personality to critical reason and against the reduction of religion to morality. In his famous and broadly acclaimed *Speeches on Religion* (1799) he challenged both by claiming that religion, in the first place, is a matter of '*Gefühl*' (feeling) and '*Anschauung*' (intuition), and, secondly, that it is a universal phenomenon that cannot be reduced either to metaphysics or to morality.[16] While the universality of the subject and object of religion – a human's feeling and intuiting the universe – in this early stage of Schleiermacher's work leads to the idea that the goal of religion is ultimately to dilute all individual borders (and differences), he rapidly changes his mind. As early as in 1804/5, in his first lectures on philosophical ethics, he claims that '*Eigenthümlichkeit*' (individuality) and identity are, side to side with spontaneity and receptivity, the main aspects that not only determine the way in which the human mind perceives and organizes the world but by which the order of human sociality and culture should be understood.[17] 'Religion', as one of the main aspects of human culture, is then about the topic of individually conceiving the world and giving this conception an individual expression. The privileged form in which religion expresses itself is art. Religion, as he concludes in these lectures, is the part of human society and cultural life, where the individuality of man is thematic. Religion is an individual performance and in religious communities it finds the only place within culture where this individuality is the sole focus. Individual expressions are meant here to be part of a reciprocal process of enrichment, within which individual persons enter in a mutual process of recognition. Individuality is not real if it is not performed. While this process recognition can take place in politics or economics as well, the reason for it in religion is the other's otherness that contributes to my personal formation and *vice versa*.[18]

As Schleiermacher remarks in his late work in dogmatic theology, the church shall be a place where, in addition to the performance of human individuality, the awareness for the fragmentary character of individual identity is held awake, firstly because everyone knows that he or she is not Christ, the prototype of human religious consciousness, and secondly, because everyone remembers that she or he has not been the same forever. This pietist idea, that religion is a result of a '*Bekehrungserlebnis*' (conversion experience), lays the ground here for the conception of a community in which dissent and learning is possible: everyone knows that humans can improve while the memory of having been wrong will remain even in the best.[19]

Even if the Schleiermacherian approach in its attempt to construct the church as an exemplary or even paradigmatic community where a special notion of human individuality is cultivated through religious communication seems not too far from what I criticized in Milbank earlier on, their concepts differ at least in two important points: Schleiermacher never doubted that the common ground on which religious and non-religious people would meet is the common reason which structures public life decision-making processes. And he was, secondly, always aware that in order to clarify the importance of religion to non-religious people, one would have to describe it in a functional manner rather than restrict the *thinking about religion* to *religious thinking*. His concept is far from that reductionalist or even neo-foundationalist view.

Individual identity becomes real when it is performed within a community that is grounded on plurality and difference. A person's identity is also shaped by the performances of others from which it differs. The grounds for this lay in the idea of Christ overcoming sin (the symbol for humans being shut off against each other) as a common structure within his individual personality. This does indeed sound very much like the liberal European metanarrative of how society should work sketched earlier in this chapter. However, Schleiermacher's account of individual identity is far from tending towards social atomization. Rather, he underlines the importance and even necessity of relations, especially to other humans, for individual identity to become real. In this relationalist account of personal identity, plurality and difference, on a social level but also in a biographical perspective form the very ground for what is only real when performed in interaction. Does taking sin seriously imply an ontology of violence with the ethical consequence of a struggle of every man against his neighbour? I do seriously doubt that. In the perspective of (German) liberal relationalism it rather provides one example of why interaction and communication within a plural society are a resource of meaningful order.

Paul Tillich: Individual personality as process and cultural enactment

Historically, it is a large step from Schleiermacher to the next philosophical theologian I would like to focus on now. The German-American philosopher and theologian Paul Tillich participated in the First World War as a field chaplain and held various teaching positions in Germany before he had to flee from Nazi-Germany because of his socialist convictions. He then taught at Union Theological Seminary in New York until 1965 and later on held a University Professor position at Harvard University.

Like Schleiermacher, Tillich approached the Christian religion from a philosophical background and wanted to be both: a Christian thinker and a thinker about Christianity. And as with Schleiermacher, in Tillich we find a universalist notion of religion. But, in opposition to Schleiermacher, Tillich did not restrain 'religion' to a particular cultural activity. Moreover, for him religion is the intentional content of all human cultural activity.[20]

What is, then, individual identity in Tillich's thought – and what role does religion play in this concept? How is this expressed in terms of ethics? Human identity is formed within the group, as Tillich puts it in his recently edited lectures on 'Advanced problems of Systematic Theology', which he held at Union during 1936 and 1938.[21] The knowledge of a human about himself or herself receives its main imprint within the social formations, in which we learn about the function and order of human culture. And even religion only comes into play in the context of a group. The consciousness of being part of something that is formed not only by mere coincidence but has a collective history and a collective goal that in itself is 'more' than the sum of the individual ideas concerning this goal – this consciousness is where we come to develop our notion of 'transcendence', of something before and beyond mere social facticity.[22]

As with Schleiermacher, positive religions – Tillich's 'broad' concept of religion notwithstanding – have a certain function within human culture. Concrete religions are the social place where the notion of transcendence itself is thematized. In these groups, communication about the transcendent ground and goal of all things takes place in a symbolic manner. Religious symbols thematize their meaning not only for the social collective but for the individual person herself.

Although this seems to lead to a far more collectivist approach to personal identity, Tillich defines identity as a balancing process that mediates between individuality and participation, self-integration and self-transcendence. Human existence is shaped by 'contingency, individualisation, altogether finiteness' – but this is exactly what should be overcome. Anthropology should be interpreted in terms of creation and Christology.[23] For Tillich, '[the doctrine of] Creation expresses that this our finiteness, contingency and separation and corresponding anxiety, strangeness and solitude is overcome in something infinite, necessary and united'.[24] Christology is an essential anthropology because it shows the eschatological nature of humanity, the normative idea of its being 'beyond essence and existence, including both'.[25]

From such a perspective it makes absolutely no sense to speak of isolated individuals:

> Man as having a world or as being free, is individual personality and social community at the same time. [...] Personality is that process of life which actualizes the universal structure of being in a free reasonable individual. Therefore personality always has the two poles, the individual self which is radically separated from the universal life and the universal life, its structures and forms, which shapes the individual. Mediating is the rational structure of the individual or its freedom from and, consequently, for his Self and his world.[26]

Again, one could describe the idea of personal identity as a process within social relations – and relations to a world – to be furthering an ontology of violence rather than peace. But the very idea of a 'religious' substance of human existence and culture (the products of the process described) is misunderstood when interpreted as championing effects like social 'atomization'. Rather, what is offered here in terms of an eschatological-Christological anthropology is the attempt to develop a perspective on human identity as mediating difference. Fully to affirm human individuality on the grounds of its connectedness with other beings within a world is what religion is all about, if we follow Tillich.

And we are maybe stunned when studying the final pages of Tillich's late *Systematic Theology* from 1963. Not only is the goal of humankind as a whole a topic here (symbolized in the 'Kingdom of God'), but we find broad explanations of the eternal destiny of the individual. The Christian symbol of the 'eternal life', according to Tillich, means that individual decision-making and development of character have an 'eternal' meaning. 'Eternal' here does not signify any time or place 'after' the historical life, but it refers to the normative dimension of human existence. It is an 'Eternal Now'.[27] The whole life of the individual, here, is conceived as a process, in which something takes place that Tillich calls 'essentialization'. This term is derived from the German Idealist philosopher Friedrich Wilhelm Joseph von Schelling. It means that individual identity not only has structural elements, such as corporeity, sociality and self-consciousness, but that these elements are as a whole comprised in a process of becoming during which sense-ful and sense-adverse developments take place. Essentialization is the process of normative evaluation that mediates between facticity and final destiny.[28] It is in human culture where the enactment of this process takes place in everyday life – eschatology is by no means about a temporal future.

Looking at Tillich we note a certain ambiguity. Not only the seemingly collectivist approach to human individuality but also the somewhat difficult idea of 'essentialization' seem to indicate that Tilich is not far from current post-liberalism. But as Schleiermacher differs from it, so too does Tillich – and in similar ways. Tillich does not only try to validate the plausibility of the contents of his insights from the Christian tradition in philosophical terms that are meant to be understood by public reasoning, but he even claims that his universalist concept of religion points at something everyone could understand while looking closely enough at the formational stages of her individual consciousness. In Tillich, we have a deeply felt emphasis on the value of human individuality that is intended to be understood as a contribution to public discourse. But he is far from anything one could interpret as 'individualist' – which has its counterpart in the ghettoization of specific religious groups. It is not by accident that throughout his whole life Tillich had his problems with what he felt of as the narrowness of church groups. A relationalist account of human identity – as offered in the tradition of (German) theological liberalism – can be criticized for many things, but not for being 'liberal' in the abhorred sense some of its critics would like to give it.

Before I make some concluding remarks, I would like to highlight a question that could help us understand better the emphasis on human individuality in both thinkers referred to. This is especially important given the emphasis on communication, cultural production and social bonds we have seen in the examples given.

Ethical touchstones

What I would like to schematize is an internal examination of the accuracy of Schleiermacher's and Tillich's respective concepts of personal identity. As we have seen, both are quite similar in certain aspects. However, do their emphases on individuality lead to a world view that champions factual individuality?

We can examine that by taking a quick look at both thinkers' ideas about gender. Whatever way we conceive of gender and sex – as biologically given facts or as cultural superimpositions that have to be transcended by queer performances – it is clear that gender is an important part of individual identity. Now, both thinkers I referred to have been criticized for their views on gender identity. In the case of Schleiermacher, it is his emphasis on women being the more receptive and men the more active gender, a rather traditionalist way of thinking.²⁹ On the other hand, we know very well that Schleiermacher personally held women in high regard – be it as the leaders of intellectual salons or as persons who showed an interest for his emotional life.³⁰ I think the most adequate place to examine his intentions – disregarding the fact that he was a child of his own time – are his remarks on 'friendship'. Friendship in Schleiermacher's thought is the social relation within which the individual tends to another due to a love that lacks any interest in possessing or assimilating the other.³¹ It is the individuality of character that concerns the friend.

In my opinion, this romantic concept of friendship is Schleiermacher's paradigm of social relations. Here, we find a balance of particularity and identity in both individuals, and it is here where the essentially social character of self-consciousness is formed. This 'platonic' love between two persons could then, if we think further, find any kind of expression, if it is true that individuality means the corporeal and communicative performance of personality as a whole.

With Tillich, the case is a bit different. Like Schleiermacher, he tries to 'transcend' the category of gender and thematizes the interpersonal relation as one of 'love' in quite similar terms.³² While Tillich surely does not have any obvious gender-issues (in terms of direct theological treatment), he has been strongly criticized for the universalist claim of his description of human existence. Does what he describes as 'human' represent only a male experience? Or is he, to some extent, excluding women from his system?³³ I think this critique is partly right. For example, Tillich describes the religious conscience as 'courage to be' in the teeth of the general existential 'fear' that is part of the universal human condition.³⁴ This could indeed be interpreted as a kind of 'heroic' conception of the self that not only has a certain connotation of violence but seems to be rather anti-individualistic as well. But I would argue that we misinterpret Tillich if we take his descriptions of fear as an objective and normative claim about the psychological condition of human beings. 'Fear' here means something similar as what we find in Kierkegaard's critique of Hegel. Fear is a structural concept that has the meaning that although there is a *reason* for our being-in-the-world we cannot be sure about its *ground*: Why, in an ultimate sense, are we here, and why is there a world at all? In a relation of love towards the next – whatever gender she or he has or is – we grow conscious of the same contingency we find in ourselves.

This, in my opinion, is the descriptive strength of both, Schleiermacher's and Tillich's concepts of individual identity, that in the end there is something in the individual that remains opaque to my attempts to understand. Moreover, it is this opacity that in religious (and cultural) practice finds symbolic expressions of manifold characters. Finally, it is through this opacity of personal identity that differences can be treated affirmatively, as structures that, when enacted, tend to create meaning.

Conclusion

If we look back to what I outlined in the beginning of my chapter, the intended meta-critique of 'Western liberalism' becomes clearer. With my references to Schleiermacher and Tillich I wanted to indicate that if we simply accept the overall label of 'individualism' as produced by Milbank, Lindback and Hauerwas, we are about to lose a certain point of view on individual identity, cultural practice and the importance of differences (in identity) which has been very vivid in the German-speaking tradition. Championing individual identity and religiously affirming it must in no sense mean to detach it from its social context. Thinking of human individuality as a performative process that integrates and re-integrates multiple relations (including the social ones) is what one could call the contribution of these thinkers to liberal thought. Staying aware of the fluidity and fragmentariness of personal identity and its enactment through social processes is one of the contributions of religion to public life.

Without having to accept all of this and even without accepting the master narrative of the religious roots of modern liberalism, I think, we should think twice before accepting neither the 'theologization' of public discourse nor the encapsulation of religion in its own semantics and communities. Any critique of 'individualism' – despite its validity – should have in mind that individual identity can be thought of differently than in terms of 'isolation' and 'egotism'. To underline this, in my opinion, is an important contribution of the symbolic sources of the Christian tradition that could be of importance also when debating the role of religion for the constitution of identities on a global level.

Notes

1 John Milbank, 'Against Human Rights: Liberty in the Western Tradition', *Oxford Journal of Law and Religion* 1, no. 1 (2012): 203–34.
2 In the following, I will assume a stance that in the Anglophone world was made popular, too, by Nancey Murphey. She claims (among other things) that it is ethics which not only secures theology's position as a science but also should be the very

field where theology and social theory should be debated, compare only Nancey C. Murphey, 'Theology and Ethics in the Hierarchy of the Sciences', in *Anglo-American Postmodernity. Philosophical Perspectives on Science, Religion, and Ethics*, ed. Nancey Murphy (Boulder: Westview, 1997), 155–72.

3 John Milbank, 'Human Dignity, Not Rights: Breaking Up Modernity's Uneasy Marriage' (2014). Retrieved from: http://www.abc.net.au/religion/articles/2014/03/04/3956588.htm (accessed 30 May 2018).

4 John Milbank and Adrian Pabst, *The Politics of Virtue: Post-Liberalism and the Human Future* (London: Rowman and Littlefield, 2016).

5 Ibid., 18.

6 Ibid., 1 and 185.

7 Ibid., 239.

8 See for instance G. A. Lindbeck, *The Nature of Doctrine: Religions and Theology in a Postliberal Age* (Louisville and London: Westminster John Knox Press, 1984) and G. A. Lindbeck, 'The Gospel's Uniqueness: Election and Untranslatability', *Modern Theology* 13 (1997): 423–50. On Lindbeck see K. Surin, '"Many Religions and the One True Faith": An Examination of Lindbeck's Chapter Three', *Modern Theology* 4 (1988): 187–208 and T. W. Tilley, 'Incommensurability, Intratextuality, and Fideism', *Modern Theology* 5 (1989): 87–111. See also S. Hauerwas and W. Willimon, *Resident Aliens: Life in the Christian Colony* (Nashville: Abingdon, 1989), S. Hauerwas, *A Better Hope: Resources for a Church Confronting Capitalism, Democracy and Postmodernity* (Grand Rapids: Brazos, 2000) and S. Hauerwas, *The Hauerwas Reader*, ed. J. Berkman and M. G. Cartwright (Durham: Duke University Press, 2001); S. Hauerwas and R. Coles, *Christianity, Democracy, and the Radical Ordinary: Conversations between a Radical Democrat and a Christian* (Eugene: Wipf and Stock, 2008). Hauerwas's position draws on the same basic idea like Lindbeck's (the narrative structure of Christian personal and social identity) but differs in the ethical outcome from Milbank's. Although joined in their critic of liberalism, the strongest difference is, in my view, the notion of the church as people and democracy as the preferable form of Christian politics (Hauerwas) as opposed to a view of the church as institution/exemplary state mirrored by or mirroring a monarchy (Milbank). To summarize Lindbeck's and Hauerwas's positions as I have, neither pays full respect to the differences between them nor to the internal differentiation of their respective positions. I approach both 'from outside' in order to make a point from a different tradition.

9 Larry Siedentop, *Inventing the Individual: The Origins of Western Liberalism* (London: Allen Lane, 2014).

10 Charles Taylor, *Sources of the Self: The Making of Modern Identity* (Harvard: Harvard University Press, 1989), Charles Taylor, *A Secular Age* (Harvard: Harvard University Press, 2007), Jean-Luc Nancy, *Être singulier pluriel* (Paris: Editions

Galilée, 1996), and Jean-Luc Nancy, *L'Adoration (Deconstruction du Christianisme 2)* (Paris: Editions Galilée, 2010).

11 J. G. Fichte, *Grundlage der gesamten Wissenschaftslehre* (Hamburg: Meiner, 1997), 16. My translation.

12 I would like to hold fast to the conviction that we ('Western' people, of whatever gendered and racial identity) are modern – and that we truly have been so for a couple of centuries.

13 On the difference between the uses of 'liberal' in the German-speaking and the Anglophone traditions see Douglas Hedley, 'Should Divinity Overcome Metaphysics? Reflections on John Milbank's Theology beyond Secular Reason and Confessions of a Cambridge Platonist', *The Journal of Religion* 80 (2000): 271–98; for a very different account of 'liberal' theology in current British thought, see I. Bradley, *Grace, Order, Openness, and Diversity: Reclaiming Liberal Theology* (London and New York: Bloomsbury, 2010).

14 One can even show that some aspects of Radical Orthodoxy are indeed 'modern' and 'liberal' themselves, see Paul Hedges, 'Is John Milbank's Radical Orthodoxy a Form of Liberal Theology? A Rhetorical Counter', *Heythrop Journal* XLVIII (2009): 1–24.

15 J. Daniel, *Transforming Faith: Individual and Community in H. Richard Niebuhr* (Eugene: Pickwick 2015), 12.

16 See Friedrich D. E. Schleiermacher, *Über die Religion. Reden an die Gebildeten unter ihren Verächtern (1799). Mit einer Einleitung herausgegeben von Andreas Arndt* (Hamburg: Meiner, 2004), passim. The distinction between religion, metaphysics and moral is the subject of the second speech.

17 F. D. E. Schleiermacher, *Der christliche Glaube. Nach den Grundsätzen der evangelischen Kirche im Zusammenhange dargestellt (1830/31)*, ed. M. Redeker (Berlin and New York: de Gruyter, 1999).

18 See for recent and excellent Anglophone accounts of this see F. C. Beiser, 'Schleiermacher's Ethics', in *The Cambridge Companion to Friedrich Schleiermacher*, ed. J. Mariña (Cambridge: Cambridge University Press, 2005), 53–72 and J. Mariña, *Transformation of the Self in the Thought of Friedrich Schleiermacher* (Oxford: Oxford University Press, 2008).

19 Schleiermacher, *Der christliche Glaube*, §123.3.

20 See Paul Tillich, 'Über die Idee einer Theologie der Kultur [1919]', in Paul Tillich, *Die religiöse Substanz der Kultur. Schriften zur Theologie der Kultur* (Gesammelte Werke, Vol. 9) (Stuttgart: Evangelisches Verlagswerk, 1967), 13–31, translated with an interpretative essay in Victor Nuovo, *Visionary Science: A Translation of Paul Tillich's 'On the Idea of a Theology of Culture' with an Interpretive Essay* (Detroit: Wayne State University Press, 1987), 17–40. See also Russell Re Manning, 'The Religious Meaning of Culture: Paul Tillich and Beyond', *International Journal of Systematic Theology* 15 (2013): 437–52.

21 Paul Tillich, *Advanced Problems in Systematic Theology: Courses at Union Theological Seminary, New York, 1936-1938. Herausgegeben und mit einer historischen Einleitung versehen von Erdmann Sturm* (Berlin and New York: de Gruyter, 2016).
22 Ibid., 164ff and197ff.
23 Ibid., 104.
24 Ibid., 105.
25 Ibid., 122.
26 Ibid., 144.
27 This is also, of course, the title of one of Tillich's most popular works, a volume of sermons, many of which were delivered in the period during which Tillich was writing his *Systematic Theology*. Paul Tillich, *The Eternal Now* (New York: Scribners, 1963).
28 Paul Tillich, *Systematic Theology, 3. Life and the Spirit: History and the Kingdom of God* (Chicago: The University of Chicago Press, 1963), 420.
29 There is one excellent study analysing the way in which gender is treated and how it informs Schleiermacher's understanding of religion, see E. Hartlieb, *Geschlechterdifferenz im Denken Friedrich Schleiermachers* (Berlin and Boston: de Gruyter, 2006). See also R. Richardson, *The Role of Women in the Life and Thought of the Early Schleiermacher (1768-1806): An Historical Overview* (Lewiston: Edwin Mellen Press, 1991) and P. E. Guenther-Gleason, *On Schleiermacher and Gender Politics* (Harrisburg: Trinity, 1997).
30 K. Nowak, *Schleiermacher: Leben, Werk und Wirkung* (Göttingen: Vandenhoeck & Ruprecht, 2002) and R. Crouter, *Friedrich Schleiermacher: Between Enlightenment and Romanticism* (Cambridge: Cambridge University Press, 2008).
31 F. D. E. Schleiermacher, *Brouillon zur Ethik (1805/06). Auf der Grundlage der Ausgabe von Otto Braun herausgegeben und mit einer Einleitung versehen von Hans-Joachim Birkner* (Hamburg: Meiner, 1981), 50–2; 60.
32 Paul Tillich, *Love, Power, and Justice: Ontological Analyses and Ethical Applications* (Oxford: Oxford University Press, 1954).
33 The first to issue such a critique was Donald MacKinnon, 'Tillich, Frege, Kittel: Some Reflections on a Dark Theme', *Explorations in Theology 5* (London: SCM Press, 1979), 129–37. See also Judith Plaskow, *Sex, Sin, and Grace: Women's Experience and the Theologies of Reinhold Niebuhr and Paul Tillich* (Lanham: University Press of America, 1980). Perhaps the best critique of this kind is T. Fessenden, '"Woman" and the "Primitive" in Paul Tillich's Life and Thought: Some Implications for the Study of Religion', *Journal of Feminist Studies in Religion* 14, no. 2 (1998): 45–76. See also R. S. Baard, 'Tillich and Feminism', in *The Cambridge Companion to Paul Tillich*, ed. R. Re Manning (Cambridge: Cambridge University Press, 2008), 273–87; for a metacritical approach see R. Re Manning, 'Life, Sex, and

Ambiguity', in *Les ambiguïtés de la vie selon Paul Tillich*, ed. M. Dumas, J. Richard and B. Wagoner (Berlin: de Gruyter, 2017), 39–50.

34 Paul Tillich, *The Courage to Be* (Yale: Yale University Press, 1952).

Bibliography

Baard, Rachel S. 'Tillich and Feminism'. In *The Cambridge Companion to Paul Tillich*. Edited by Re Manning, 273–87. Cambridge: Cambridge University Press, 2008.

Beiser, Frederick C. 'Schleiermacher's Ethics'. In *The Cambridge Companion to Friedrich Schleiermacher*. Edited by J. Mariña, 53–72. Cambridge: Cambridge University Press, 2005.

Bradley, Ian. *Grace, Order, Openness, and Diversity: Reclaiming Liberal Theology*. London and New York: Bloomsbury, 2010.

Crouter, Richard. *Friedrich Schleiermacher: Between Enlightenment and Romanticism*. Cambridge: Cambridge University Press, 2008.

Daniel, Joshua. *Transforming Faith: Individual and Community in H. Richard Niebuhr*. Eugene: Pickwick, 2015.

Fessenden, Tracy. '"Woman" and the "Primitive" in Paul Tillich's Life and Thought: Some Implications for the Study of Religion'. *Journal of Feminist Studies in Religion* 14, no. 2 (1998): 45–76.

Fichte, Johann G. *Grundlage der gesamten Wissenschaftslehre*. Hamburg: Meiner, 1997.

Guenther-Gleason, Patricia E. *On Schleiermacher and Gender Politics*. Harrisburg: Trinity, 1997.

Hartlieb, E. *Geschlechterdifferenz im Denken Friedrich Schleiermachers*. Berlin and Boston: de Gruyter, 2006.

Hauerwas, Stanley. *A Better Hope: Resources for a Church Confronting Capitalism, Democracy and Postmodernity*. Grand Rapids: Brazos, 2000.

Hauerwas, Stanley. *The Hauerwas Reader*. Edited by J. Berkman, M. G. Cartwright. Durham: Duke University Press, 2001.

Hauerwas, Stanley and Coles, Romand. *Christianity, Democracy, and the Radical Ordinary: Conversations Between a Radical Democrat and a Christian*. Eugene: Wipf and Stock, 2008.

Hauerwas, Stanley and Willimon, William H. *Resident Aliens: Life in the Christian Colony*. Nashville: Abingdon, 1989.

Hedges, Paul. 'Is John Milbank's Radical Orthodoxy a Form of Liberal Theology? A Rhetorical Counter'. *Heythrop Journal* XLVIII (2009): 1–24.

Hedley, Douglas. 'Should Divinity Overcome Metaphysics? Reflections on John Milbank's Theology beyond Secular Reason and Confessions of a Cambridge Platonist'. *The Journal of Religion* 80 (2000): 271–98.

Lindbeck, George A. 'The Gospel's Uniqueness: Election and Untranslatability'. *Modern Theology* 13 (1997): 423–50.

Lindbeck, George A. *The Nature of Doctrine: Religions and Theology in a Postliberal Age*. Louisville and London: Westminster John Knox Press, 1984.

MacKinnon, Donald. 'Tillich, Frege, Kittel: Some Reflections on a Dark Theme'. *Explorations in Theology 5*, 129–37. London: SCM Press, 1979.

Mariña, Jacqueline. *Transformation of the Self in the Thought of Friedrich Schleiermacher*. Oxford: Oxford University Press, 2008.

Milbank, John. 'Against Human Rights: Liberty in the Western Tradition'. *Oxford Journal of Law and Religion* 1, no. 1 (2012): 203–34.

Milbank, John. 'Human Dignity, not Rights: Breaking up Modernity's Uneasy Marriage' (2014). Retrieved from: http://www.abc.net.au/religion/articles/2014/03/04/3956588.htm (accessed 30 May 2018).

Milbank, John. *Theology and Social Theory*. Oxford: Oxford University Press, 1990.

Milbank, John and Pabst, Adrian. *The Politics of Virtue: Post-Liberalism and the Human Future*. London: Rowman and Littlefield, 2016.

Murphy, Nancey C. 'Theology and Ethics in the Hierarchy of the Sciences'. In *Anglo-American Postmodernity. Philosophical Perspectives on Science, Religion, and Ethics*. Edited by Nancey Murphy, 155–72. Boulder: Westview, 1997.

Nancy, Jean-Luc. *Être singulier pluriel*. Paris: Editions Galilée, 1996.

Nancy, Jean-Luc. *L'Adoration (Deconstruction du Christianisme 2)*. Paris: Editions Galilée, 2010.

Nowak, Kurt. *Schleiermacher: Leben, Werk und Wirkung*. Göttingen: Vandenhoeck & Ruprecht, 2002.

Nuovo, Victor. *Visionary Science: A Translation of Paul Tillich's 'On the Idea of a Theology of Culture' with an Interpretive Essay*. Detroit: Wayne State University Press, 1987.

Plaskow, Judith. *Sex, Sin, and Grace: Women's Experience and the Theologies of Reinhold Niebuhr and Paul Tillich*. Lanham: University Press of America, 1980.

Re Manning, Russell. 'Life, Sex, and Ambiguity'. In *Les ambiguïtés de la vie selon Paul Tillich*. Edited by M. Dumas, J. Richard and B. Wagoner, 39–50. Berlin: de Gruyter, 2017.

Re Manning, Russell. 'The Religious Meaning of Culture: Paul Tillich and Beyond'. *International Journal of Systematic Theology* 15 (2013): 437–52.

Richardson, Ruth. *The Role of Women in the Life and Thought of the Early Schleiermacher (1768–1806): An Historical Overview*. Lewiston: Edwin Mellen Press, 1991.

Schleiermacher, Friedrich D. E. *Brouillon zur Ethik (1805/06). Auf der Grundlage der Ausgabe von Otto Braun herausgegeben und mit einer Einleitung versehen von Hans-Joachim Birkner*. Hamburg: Meiner, 1981.

Schleiermacher, Friedrich D. E. *Der christliche Glaube: Nach den Grundsätzen der evangelischen Kirche im Zusammenhange dargestellt (1830/31)*. Edited by M. Redeker. Berlin and New York: de Gruyter, 1999.

Schleiermacher, Friedrich D. E. *Über die Religion. Reden an die Gebildeten unter ihren Verächtern (1799). Mit einer Einleitung herausgegeben von Andreas Arndt*. Hamburg: Meiner, 2004.

Siedentop, Larry. *Inventing the Individual: The Origins of Western Liberalism*. London: Allen Lane, 2014.

Surin, Kenneth. '"Many Religions and the One True Faith": An Examination of Lindbeck's Chapter Three'. *Modern Theology* 4 (1988): 187–208.

Taylor, Charles. *A Secular Age*. Harvard: Harvard University Press, 2007.

Taylor, Charles. *Sources of the Self: The Making of Modern Identity*. Harvard: Harvard University Press, 1989.

Tilley, Terrence W. 'Incommensurability, Intratextuality, and Fideism'. *Modern Theology* 5 (1989): 87–111.

Tillich, Paul. *Advanced Problems in Systematic Theology: Courses at Union Theological Seminary, New York, 1936–1938. Herausgegeben und mit einer historischen Einleitung versehen von Erdmann Sturm*. Berlin and New York: de Gruyter, 2016.

Tillich, Paul. *The Courage to Be*. Yale: Yale University Press, 1952.

Tillich, Paul. *The Eternal Now*. New York: Scribners, 1963.

Tillich, Paul. *Love, Power, and Justice: Ontological Analyses and Ethical Applications*. Oxford: Oxford University Press, 1954.

Tillich, Paul. *Systematic Theology, 3. Life and the Spirit: History and the Kingdom of God*. Chicago: The University of Chicago Press, 1963.

Tillich, Paul. 'Über die Idee einer Theologie der Kultur (1919)'. In *Die religiöse Substanz der Kultur. Schriften zur Theologie der Kultur* (Gesammelte Werke, Vol. 9), 13–31. Stuttgart: Evangelisches Verlagswerk, 1967.

8

One's other self: Contradictory self-identity in Ueda's phenomenology of the self

Raquel Bouso

Introduction

The sixth volume of the Japanese philosopher Ueda Shizuteru's (b. 1926) collected works, which is entitled *In the Course of the 'Ten Ox-Herding Pictures' Path* [道程「十牛図」を歩む (*Dōtei 'jūgyūzu' o ayumu*)], is devoted to the classic Zen parable presented in the *Ten Ox-Herding Pictures* (十牛図 *jūgyūzu*).[1] The ten images and accompanying short poems were in all likelihood originally conceived in order to be used in Zen training.[2] In the Buddhist tradition, the herding of an ox is usually read as an analogy for training the mind on the path to enlightenment. As a philosopher, Ueda reflects on this path by way of a 'phenomenology of the self' (自己の現象学 *jiko no genshōgaku*).[3] On the one hand, this approach can be regarded as a hermeneutics of both the figurative and written language of the Zen ox narrative. On the other, Ueda's phenomenological aim suggests that his reading surpasses the Zen context, giving this type of experience a broad reach as a meaningful and philosophically fruitful event relevant to all humans.[4]

After analysing the ten pictures in detail in the first part of the book, in the sixth section, which forms the second part, Ueda offers his interpretation of how the transformative process of existential self-awareness and self-knowledge occurs. In his explanation of this process, he focuses on the last three ox-herding images, which respectively depict an empty circle, a landscape and two people.[5] In so doing he identifies three spheres as places of self-awareness: 'absolute nothingness' (絶対無 *zettai mu*), 'nature' (自然 *shizen*) and 'human beings' (人間 *ningen*). In his interpretation, Ueda establishes a dialogue with well-known German thinkers such as Martin Buber (1878–1965), Johannes Scheffler (better known as Angelus Silesius, 1624–77), Meister Eckhart (1260–1328) and Friedrich Nietzsche (1844–1900).[6] Ueda concludes the essay by claiming that the end of the path is nothing but a new beginning, thus emphasizing the dynamic aspect of the suggested itinerary of comprehension for the Zen parable. Therefore it would not be so much a matter of reaching a definitive result but an ever-opening and an ever-deepening process of self-understanding.

My main goal here is to examine how Ueda understands the human being as a place of self-awareness in this particular work. Specifically, my concern is the openness to the other involved in the process of reaching one's own true identity through self-negation. According to Ueda, only when one's self is negated can a true encounter with the other take place, since the other is for the first time allowed to be as he or she is. Following a Zen perspective – but in dialogue with the philosophy of Nishida Kitarō and European Existential Phenomenology and Hermeneutics – Ueda maintains that the fundamental difference between the identity of the self and the other disappears into a state where the individual becomes emptiness. In Zen, this is said to happen in the silence and stillness of sitting meditation or *zazen*. Then, the person that arises from *zazen* is again one individual facing another individual but now the encounter takes place at the very boundary between the self and the other. Thus, for Ueda the answer to the problem of the confrontation with the other that occurs in worldly existence can be found in the infinite openness that permeates this existence. This openness becomes manifest in the aforementioned space between self and other where a true encounter may transpire.

The complementarity of the contrasting elements of negation and affirmation, emptiness (as sameness) and opposition (as difference) is of decisive importance here. This interpretation of the encounter that takes place in the common ground of the open space is highly illuminating. For this reason, Ueda's standpoint could certainly be of interest if applied to social and intercultural relations since instead of searching a synthesis or a sublation in a dialectical relation based in dissimilarity, Ueda offers a way of grasping the paradox of identity and difference as two different modes of a single process. Much philosophical discussion about the self–other encounter has focused on the problem of identity. A strong emphasis on the subjective and individualistic aspects of identity runs the risk of solipsism. Conversely, lacking a clearly defined and affirmed sense of identity can lead us to consider it impossible to demand individual responsibility. Thus, it seems necessary to understand the role of nullification in the interpersonal encounter as we will examine in the next section, for it might help us to undermine the boundaries we draw between ourselves and others and to discern whether Ueda's view is able to mitigate those pitfalls.

True self as selfless self in Buddhism

The ox-herding parable consists of ten images, and each of them is accompanied by a short poem and a brief text, which serves as a commentary or preface. The first seven images form a narrative sequence, while the last three images can be interpreted as overlapping and not necessarily, or at least conspicuously, connected to the previous narrative. Ueda regards them as a sort of self-portrait (自画像 *jigazou*).⁷ By means of this self-description, the self expresses itself through three linguistic dimensions – figurative, verbal and conceptual – which Ueda regards as a correspondence within a primordial event, between poetic self-awareness and conceptual self-understanding. Thus, the self-knowledge gained along the depicted path can be considered as a linguistic event. Indeed, experience, language and comprehension are three interrelated dimensions elaborated by Ueda in his philosophy.⁸ Nevertheless, our focus now lies in Ueda's interpretation of the Zen understanding of the process of self-knowledge as an awakening (自覚 *jikaku*) to the true self (真の自己 *shin no jiko*), in turn regarded as a selfless self (自己ならざる自己 *jiko narazaru jiko*). We will later return to the expression of the self, captured in these three images, and especially the last one, where an I–thou/self–other encounter occurs, which reveals the interpersonal dimension of the self. Let's consider first the meaning of these notions in their original Buddhist context.

Buddhism correlates our suffering with delusion, which stems from our ignorance and egoistic attachments. It has been said that 'the Buddhist project is to eliminate suffering by overcoming the idea that there is an "I" for whom life can have meaning'.⁹ Instead of projecting our desires onto reality, we should accept it as it is presented. In line with this stance, Zen's main concern is to awaken from the self-centred ego – enslaved by itself, by its desires – to our true selfhood and thereby to achieve a more authentic and unrestricted way of being. According to tradition, through meditation, Buddha concluded that what we directly experience is what actually is, but the root of our discontent lies in the fact that 'we project onto the immediately accessible phenomena a desire for things to be otherwise: to be "mine" rather than simply "to be"; to be enduring instead of transient; to be substantial – to be independently existing entities – instead of interdependent processes'.¹⁰ Since we fail to see and accept reality as it is due to the distortion of our egocentric projections, through meditative praxis we should be able to cease making those projections and therefore to cease suffering.

Following Buddha's analysis and contrary to the Hindu analysis of the self as *ātman*, the unchanging inner true self, Indian Buddhist thinkers held that in this life we do not have a fixed identity from moment to moment. With the notion of *anātman*, or 'non-self', Buddhists rejected the Hindu belief in *ātman*, conceived both as an independently existing agent behind our sensory functions and as a personal identity inaccessible to ordinary sensorial experience. Hindu extended belief was that the core of the person was only attainable as a state of pure indiscriminate awareness through long and arduous and Yogic psychophysical disciplines. The counterargument in this discussion was that the self cannot be identified with any of the specific physical or mental features of the individual person, nor their experiences, and therefore there is no agent that causes or undergoes the processes of psychophysical changes. Even if a meditative state of temporary sensory cessation might be admitted, Buddhists argued that there is no reason to assume that there is a deeper, substantial, permanent, transcendent reality in the form of either the individual (*ātman*) or the absolute (*brahman*) beyond appearances. For the Buddhists, the phenomenal world as such is real, as is our transient and changing self. This disagreement, of course, entailed not only philosophical but also soteriological implications, for it affected deep-seated beliefs such as *karma* (action) and *samsara* (the cycle of suffering).

If what we ordinarily call 'I' is only a delusion, a form of fixation and attachment because in truth it is not substantial, permanent and self-dependent, or, as Walpola Rahula puts it, 'the idea of self is an imaginary, false belief which has no corresponding reality', how could then Buddhists explain our sense of personal identity?[11] The various Buddhist schools have proposed different answers to this question. Early Buddhist texts describe the basis of personal identity as a causal continuity between aggregates (physical bodily forms, sensations or feelings, sense perceptions, volition and consciousness).[12] That is, according to these, there is a causal series of continuously changing dispositions and conscious events, which constitutes personal identity. This Buddhist theory of self is often interpreted as a denial that the self exists and thus basically nihilistic. But looking at ancient texts, it seems that Buddha's middle way rejected both extremes of eternalism and annihilationism. Indeed, there is a self, but this self is called a non-self or no-self insofar as it is a set of interrelated and changing psychophysical processes but not a substantive unchanging entity.

Thus, the realization of the true self as a non-self emerges from the Buddhist idea that the very concept of self is a fiction, an artificial construction: our sense of identity can be seen as a mere product of our interests and limitations, a sort of self-delusion devoid of reality. For this reason, to realize our own true self entails recognizing that there is 'no-self' as such but rather a non-abiding self, which will result in the dissipation of craving and attachment. To gain this perspective it is important to understand the causes that give rise to the experience that we mistakenly interpret as belonging to a permanent self. Then, once one overcomes the illusion of a self, one acknowledges that preventing his or her own suffering equally extends to the suffering of others.

This latter point is central to Zen Buddhism. Zen follows Mahāyāna Buddhist developments when it teaches that to realize the truth of the self is at the same time its truth, in accordance with the truth of all beings. As a Mahāyāna school, in Zen, it is primarily the *bodhisattva* ideal that distinguishes its position from the early Buddhist schools on the aim of self-cultivation. To put it simply, since the *bodhisattva* takes a vow not to enter into *nirvana* until all beings have become enlightened, it embodies compassion and altruism and an other-centredness. The purpose of the Mahāyāna ideal is to become compassionate towards all beings and care about relieving their suffering. The *bodhisattva* came to reflect an ideal of true selflessness in this manner.

In addition, Mahāyāna schools develop the early Buddhist doctrine of dependent origination that explains the causal connection between a number of mental states that ultimately lead to the creation of suffering. The meaning of dependent origination was that everything depends on something else, and so everything is connected to everything else. For example, the Madhyamaka School linked this with the claim that not only the self but also all things lack substance or 'self-nature' (S. *svabhāva*), in Nāgārjuna's terms. The argument that everything arises in dependence on causes and conditions was used to show that all things are empty, maintaining that anything compounded lacks intrinsic nature.[13] This is not the place to explore all the issues involved in this claim. Yet, it is worth noting that Zen develops this standpoint in accordance with the teaching that all beings are capable of attaining Buddhahood, namely, the potential for enlightenment that is described in Mahāyāna Buddhism as 'Buddha-nature'. Therefore, contrary to the self-enclosed self, wherein one is not able to go out of oneself, the true self is characterized as selflessness, a self without self. Thus, Zen teaches that by letting go of one's own ego-self, one can realize the true self of all beings – that is, that like one's self, all beings lack of intrinsic nature (substance or self-nature).

We can find this position, for instance, in Zen master Dōgen (1200–53), whose most famous statement in this regard is often quoted by the philosophers of the Kyoto School: 'To model yourself after the way of the buddhas is to model yourself after yourself. To model yourself after yourself is to forget yourself. To forget yourself is to be authenticated by the totality of phenomena.'[14] As Peter Harvey notes, for Dōgen, 'selfless compassion is what is naturally expressed when one acts in a spontaneous way – from one's underlying Buddha-nature – free from reflection and desire, which comes from self-centredness.'[15] This means that developing wisdom through a disciplined life would enable this inner goodness to be expressed in actions and ensure that good actions become the only natural thing to do. Zen's aim would then be to bring out the true self that normally lies hidden within.

Therefore, as we have seen, the Buddhist conception of personal identity does not rely on an unchanging essence or an ontological entity but on acknowledging the continuities and interactions among the ongoing processes that constitute our temporary selves. In this way, every attempt to fix the boundaries of our personal identity is called into question from both temporal and spatial perspectives (in our constantly coming to be and ceasing to be). Identity is found in the interconnected processes that form the self and these processes are always conditioned by the surrounding factors that also form the self. In view of this constitutive interdependence, it can be said that personal identity expands its limits to be more comprehensive and this is fundamental reason why becoming aware of ourselves also implies becoming aware of others. Mahāyāna Buddhism therefore emphasizes that wisdom is inextricable from compassion and even places the extinction of suffering that involves freedom from these conditionings (*nirvana*) in the very midst of this conditioned phenomenal world (*samsara*). In this manner, the Buddhist understanding of true self can be ontologically understood not only as a 'non self' (a contingent and interdependent self without essence or substance) but also in a moral sense as 'un-selfishness' or 'without ego-centeredness'. In which case, the search for the true self could provide an opportunity for breaking up our self-enclosing ego and opening to others.

The search for self-identity

If Ueda's starting point for his phenomenology of the self is Zen self-awareness of our true self conceived as a selfless self, how can a person validate such an understanding? According to Ueda, the place to start seeking the true self is the question, 'Who am I?' (自己とは何か *jiko to wa nani ka*). The search starts when the lack of meaning of one's own existence, felt in a state of anxiety and uneasiness, becomes for the first time a real doubt. It is possible to establish a clear parallel here with the starting point of Ueda's mentor, Nishitani Keiji (1900–1990), as expressed in his main work *Religion and Nothingness*, where he states that the essence of religion is the result of a religious quest, and that the encounter with nihility triggers this search.[16] This happens when our existence becomes problematic and we ask ourselves why we live or should keep living. Ueda writes that it is a problem that concerns us personally, since everyone has to face one's own life and death (一人生まれ一人死す *hitori umare hitori shisu*) alone. Only then does the possibility of a 'fundamental conversion from non-self-awareness to self-awareness' (無自覚から自覚への根本的転換 *mujikaku kara jikaku e no konponteki tenkan*) open up. Ueda adds that from a philosophical perspective, this first step differs from the standpoint of rational ethics, because it does not entail a voluntary decision, but it is beyond the domain of the will. It demands a sort of 'releasement' close to the Eckhartian (and later Heideggerian) expression *Gelassenheit*.[17]

However, according to Ueda, after the existential impasse, the following self-questioning is not necessarily being pursued further. What truly makes one decide to follow the path of self-realization are words of wisdom, namely one's first evidence of truth. The decisive drive to further pursue self-transformation results from following in another's footsteps. Typically, it comes out of hearing inspiring teachings that seem capable of guiding and helping to improve one's way of life. For instance, in the context we are dealing with, it happens when one can for the first time pay full attention to the Zen literature about the possibility of attaining a true self.[18] Even if one still harbours doubts as to the attainment of truth, the words that captivate someone's attention may sound as though they are specially uttered for them. In Ueda's interpretation this differs from the philosophical standpoint. All philosophical speculation needs to be validated empirically.[19] If we consider that philosophy typically questions reflectively, for Ueda, this merely theoretical or speculative dimension needs to be complemented with a lived experience. Therefore, cultivation is the privileged methodological route to self-understanding.

The next step is ongoing practice. The underlying assumption is that changing habits through discipline and instruction changes a person. Ueda draws a parallel between this way of living and that of the contemplative attitude of the herdsman in the ox-herding parable: once the ox has been tamed, the herdsman is depicted as being back at home, as if he were praying showing gratitude and praise. In Ueda's interpretation, this picture would then represent a mode of religious existence.[20] It could be said that the above-mentioned moral and philosophical standpoints must be complemented within a religious one, which is characterized in the manner of an everyday practice of self-cultivation. One example of this sort of practice is found in Zen discipline training as a way to realize the true self. It consist of various practices including sitting meditation in silence (座禅 *zazen*), the active service of working on daily duties, gardening and other forms of work

(作務 *samu*), and wandering – namely, the practice of Zen in nature (行脚 *angya*), and the practice of encountering and dialoguing with a master (参禅 *sanzen*).[21] It is worth noting the correspondence between silent quietness, daily work in natural surroundings and dialogue in Zen training, and the last three ox-herding pictures (i.e. the empty circle, nature and the interpersonal encounter; see the Figures 8.1, 8.2 and 8.3 respectively).

As a result, just like pure gold mined from the earth or a full moon coming out of the clouds, in Ueda's words, the self appears as what it is.[22] In the detailed analysis of the self in its true aspect, the last three images of the parable are said to illustrate three ways of expressing the self-awareness of the selfless self: in Figure 8.1, the empty circle as the infinite opening that Mahāyāna Prajñāparamita sutras call 'emptiness', which becomes a very important notion in the philosophy of the Kyoto School, often referred to as 'absolute nothingness';[23] in Figure 8.2, the landscape of a flowering tree by the river, that is, nature being as it is by itself; and Figure 8.3, two people indicating the meeting between an old and a young man, as an illustration of the I–thou encounter. Accordingly, Ueda suggests that it is by encountering nothingness, nature and other people that the self comes to realize its own selflessness.

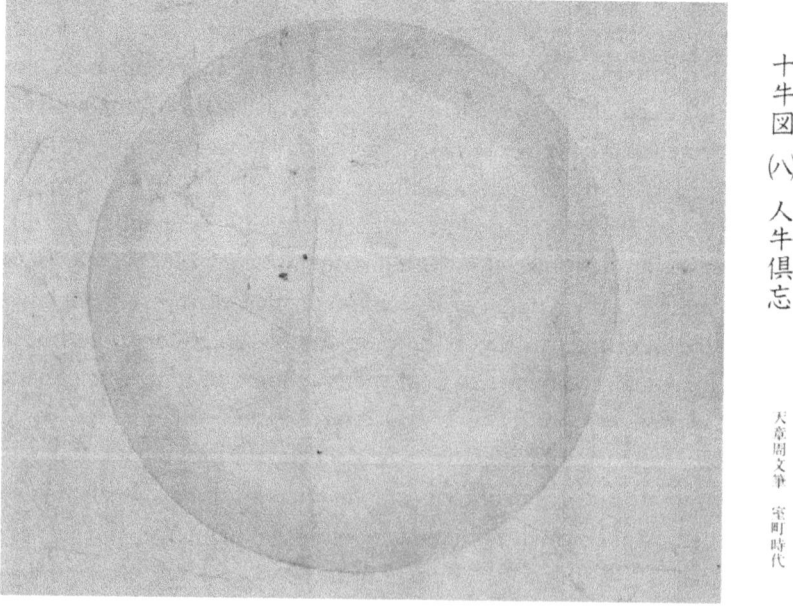

Figure 8.1 *Both Man and Ox Forgotten*, traditionally attributed to Tenshō Shūbun (active ca. 1423–60), fifteenth century. Ink and light colours on paper handscroll (32 × 181.5 cm). Museum of Shokoku-ji Temple, Kyoto, Japan.

Figure 8.2 *Returning to the Fundamental, Back to the Source*, traditionally attributed to Tenshō Shūbun (active ca. 1423–60), fifteenth century. Ink and light colours on paper handscroll (32 × 181.5 cm). Museum of Shokoku-ji Temple, Kyoto, Japan.

Figure 8.3 *Entering the City with Hands Hanging Down*, traditionally attributed to Tenshō Shūbun (active ca. 1423–60), fifteenth century. Ink and light colours on paper handscroll (32 × 181.5 cm). Museum of Shokoku-ji Temple, Kyoto, Japan.

A transition is needed to accord with one's true self, that is, with unconditioned selflessness: one must leap into pure nothingness; embody the selflessness of the true self in all its immediacy beyond the dualism of subject and object; and finally selflessly recognize one's other self in the encounter with the other. Firstly, absolute nothingness works by conforming to a desubstantializing dynamic in such a way that unconditioned selflessness discloses itself as the formless, namely a self free of all form, or formlessness itself. Secondly, self-negation is followed by an affirmation. In religious terms, this is symbolized by the resurrection after death. The formless takes on concrete form like the depictions of the flowing river or the blooming flower. Those natural elements embody the selflessness of the human being in a non-objective manner. Nature here does not refer to the tangible world of natural things but rather to the truth of the being of all that exists, as it exists in being from oneself.[24] Nature is seen as the locus of the selfless freedom of the self. Finally, in the encounter with an other, one may see one's self in the other. The self is selflessly cut open and becomes a double self: an I and a Thou. The closed ego is now opened to the other, since it is aware that its self-identity includes also its self-negation, so that, for the selfless self the other's concerns are one's own concerns. The in-between serves one as a selfless inner field, while the other becomes the locus for the existential question (Who am I?) about the self.

Considering Ueda's interpretation, nothingness, nature and the other as the threefold manifestation of selflessness become instances that allow the self to open itself in an ecstatic movement (脱自の運動 datsuji no undō). Therefore, the self becomes a sort of centrifugal place, namely a place for the aforementioned transition (運動の場になる undō no ba ni naru), where one can practice self-negation. In order to clarify this point, Ueda borrows Nishida Kitarō's term 'topological self' (場所的自己 bashoteki jiko) suggesting that the self comes to be understood as a place.[25] In Ueda's interpretation, the figures depicted in the three images (empty circle, landscape, two people) point towards an understanding of reality as groundless and relational, where nature and human beings are intrinsically interconnected. Yet, how does he derive the idea of the self as a 'place' from this interpretation? And what is the place for a true interpersonal encounter?

Contradictory self-identity: The self as a place and one's other self

According to Ueda, the manner in which we encounter people and even objects in the world, all of them encompassed within a 'limitless' or 'infinite openness' (限りない開け *kagirinai ake*), is determined by the nature of the place in which the encounter occurs. We have also mentioned the locative understanding of the self that Ueda borrows from Nishida's philosophy. On the one hand, Ueda relates the notion of place (場所 *basho*) to the Heideggerian 'world' from the expression 'being-in-the-world' (*In-der-Welt-sein*). For Martin Heidegger, *Dasein* is the self as the subject of existence, and the basic structure of the self is to be in the world. On the other hand, by adapting this conception to Nishida's *basho*,[26] Ueda denotes the place, space or world where the self lives and in which it is characterized.[27] Therefore, to be is to be located, or in other words, the self is 'context-dependent'.[28] In Ueda's phenomenology, the self becomes aware of its locative character, an idea clearly indebted to Nishida's philosophy.

Nishida's philosophical starting point orbited around the idea that in the sheer occurrence of things, there is no subject, no predicate.[29] By virtue of this standpoint he prioritized the original unity of reality and the flux of experience rather than the individual. While maintaining this insight, the later development of his understanding of the self led him to elaborate the idea of 'place' (*basho*) and his predicate logic.[30] His notion of place offers 'a base out of which subject and object separation and opposition arises in epistemology. *Basho* connects the subject and object, the self and the world as its synthetic base'.[31] Nishida calls the condition of the human being in the world the 'self-identity of absolute contradiction' (絶対矛盾の自己同一 *zettaimujun no jikodōitsu*), to account for the dialectic of individuality and universality, self and other, affirmation and negation.[32]

In his logic of *basho*, Nishida distinguishes between the place of being (the realm of physical facts), the place of relative nothingness (the realm of consciousness) and the place of absolute nothingness. The latter is where 'active intuition' (行為的 直観 *kōiteki chokkan*) takes place, hence it has been defined as a sort of 'interresponsive field' which 'is engaged when you recognize that you are located in and part of the world while simultaneously acting and performing in that world'.[33] In his attempt to pay more philosophical attention to the concrete historical and cultural world, in his latter works, Nishida identifies the three *basho*: the 'natural world' of things, the 'life world' of conscious self-awareness and the 'historical world' of the self of contingency and indeterminacy. It is possible to see here a parallel with Ueda's interpretation of the last three ox-herding images and Nishida's ontological and epistemological structure of the three *basho*-worlds,[34] especially if we consider that all of them overlap and work as one single and dynamic reality.

According to Arisaka Yoko, after abandoning his theory of pure experience, in his new embodied theory, if he could give an account of the action-mediated reality, an inherently shared world, he could found intersubjectivity.[35] However, she asserts that in Nishida's mature theory there is no 'intersubjectivity', because the notion of 'subjectivity' is thoroughly replaced by the notion of embodied active selves that emerge from the field of concrete experience-qua-reality.[36] In the same vein, Ueda notices similarly that in Nishida's locus classicus for the I–Thou relationship, his essay 'I and Thou' (私と汝 'Watakushi to nanji', 1932), when he speaks of the world of reality where I and Thou are reciprocally opposed, his perspective is not that of an intersubjective relation but that of a dialectical self-determination of the world in which the I and Thou meet.[37] Arisaka argues that in late Nishida, the fundamental relation between selves, the 'inter' part of 'intersubjectivity', is concretely retained as well as his notion of co-determination in negation. Indeed, following the classic principle *omnis determinatio est negatio* (all determination is negation), in this field of social and historical actions and things constantly co-emerging, the co-emerged 'selves' interact with each other. The field as a whole is also determined as objective social reality, which in turn determines the actions of the selves. Then, 'reality' is thoroughly shared from the outset, through a perspectively concrete organization that could simultaneously indicate numerous acting selves:

> Experientially, to the extent that these 'objects of action' that generate different 'selves' are *concrete*, the ways in which the objects 'indicate' have social and historical content; they are not simply 'objects' but objects of a such and such kind that emerged out of a long series of transactions and emplacements.[38]

Let us now turn to the way in which Ueda integrates Nishida's 'topology' in his hermeneutic-existential phenomenology. Although we have seen that Ueda follows the idea of being-in-the-world as the basic condition of human existence, he modifies Heidegger's notion. He argues that the tendency to be closed in upon ourselves present in our mode of existence contrasts with being open to the place wherein the self is located, that is, self-understanding as existing in the world. Ueda explains that every place comprises a specific 'meaning-space', each with its own temporal and historical connections. In the Heideggerian sense, 'world' would be a connection of meanings. The world is the final place that comprehends all the various places since all the places are interconnected with each other in a multilayered fashion. Instead, according to Ueda, we live in the world and at the same time in an 'infinite openness' that encompasses it. In his view, if only the world is considered as a space of meaning, our understanding is limited. If the world is the final horizon of meaning, only that which appears on the horizon is what is (this or that individual thing) for us. Thus, for Ueda we live in a 'double openness' or a 'two-foldness' of the world (二重世界 *nijū sekai*; yet, he often uses the German term *Doppelerschlossenheit*), one limited and the other unlimited. Openness without limits beyond the limited world is necessary for opening up new meanings, that is to say, other horizons of understanding. The web of interrelated meanings that penetrate the world, insofar as it is surrounded by an infinite openness, might be regarded as possessing an infinite depth. This infinite openness possesses the character of indeterminacy that Nishida's *basho* of absolute nothingness assumes.

Here Ueda makes his contribution to a line of argument posited in modern phenomenology and hermeneutics. For him, philosophy has elucidated the fact that the horizon phenomenon is intrinsic to the structure of experience, but it has neglected the beyond-the-horizon that also belongs to the structure of that horizon. For Ueda, as in Heidegger's and Hans-Georg Gadamer's philosophies, the term 'horizon' points to an existential-hermeneutical perspective, namely the view of the world according to our pre-comprehension (*Vorverständnis*). It means that our comprehension is determined by our historically-determined situatedness, and thus hermeneutics must take into account what is at work behind statements,[39] and can be an invitation to a critical examination of one's own prejudices – an effort of constant revision of any interpretation.[40] This understanding was somehow already present in the Husserlian notion of the 'lifeworld' (*Lebenswelt*), that is, the lifeworld which is 'pregiven' and 'already there' (*vorgegeben*): a key notion that called for further clarification of the relation between the immediate world of perception and the cultural and historical sphere, for it has a social and intersubjective character.[41] In Ueda, the concept of the horizon of my world, and horizon in the historical sense where I am placed, presupposes a cultural world as a shared background of meaning. This is congruent with the phenomenological view of truth as a process of constitution of meaning settled by means of intersubjectivity within a historical horizon. Here we are concerned with encounter and communication with others who share our horizon of meaning.

Ueda speaks of being in relation as an integral part of what it is to be in the world. In this regard, in his reading of the tenth ox-herding picture (Figure 8.3, two people), he suggests that the relational aspect of selfhood is underlined against the concept of the self as the autonomous, isolated individual. The closedness of the world and the self-enclosed subject belong together. Likewise, the openness of the world and the openness of the selfless self are mutually interdependent.[42] On the one hand, the horizon structure of experience conditions things in such a way that they appear to be meaningful to us. On the other, according to the two-foldness of the world, the same thing that we experience as an individual entity on this side of the horizon, beyond the horizon, can be something of infinite depth because its unknowability. Due to this openness, the innerworldly horizon is now open to create new and in-depth meanings. The infinite openness that both envelops and transcends the world imparts a decisive quality to our existence in the world. In this manner, the encounter and communication with others becomes different because the relationship to the other no longer takes place in a context of subject–object structure.

At this point, as Ueda himself notes, his interpretation of the I and Thou relationship departs from Buber's. As it is well known, this encounter (*Begegnung*) stands at the centre of Buber's thought. Buber also speaks of a twofold world in his celebrated work *Ich und Du* but in different terms: 'The world is twofold for man in accordance with his twofold attitude. The attitude of man is twofold in accordance with the two basic words he can speak.'[43] For him, the human is totally isolated in a world of objective experience. His concern is to overcome the one-sided egocentrism of the 'I' that objectifies everything it comes in contact with. His aim seems to be to transform an indifferent world into a personal world. Buber calls the world of experience the 'It-world' (*Es-Welt*) because it is impersonal until one enters into a relationship with it. In the world of experience, every particular 'Thou' is transformed into an 'it'. At the same time, the meeting of I and Thou may lead to one's realization of self, since by addressing the person or object 'over and against' oneself, one enters the intimacy of personal contact. It happens when the 'I' encounters the 'Eternal Thou'. With a relationship to the 'Eternal Thou', the particular 'Thou' is incapable of becoming a thing.[44] For Buber, the basic urge to encounter a Thou occurs in three spheres: in the phenomenal world of nature where creatures represent the Thou; in the world of man where man himself is the Thou; and in the spiritual world where the ultimate encounter is with the 'Eternal Thou'. The 'Eternal Thou' can be identified with God, seen as already immanent in the world.

Buber and Ueda place great importance on the dialogical aspect of language.[45] Interpersonal relations also play a significant role in the realization of the self for both thinkers. Buber's three spheres (natural, human and spiritual) remind us of the three places postulated by Ueda in his reading of the last three ox-herding images. However, Ueda understands the 'Thou' without reference to an 'Eternal Thou'.[46] He considers the pair 'I-Thou' to be in reciprocal dependency as well as in reciprocal self-sufficiency, and he locates this relation in absolute nothingness or 'infinite openness'.⁴⁷ Ueda conceives the interpersonal encounter in the following terms:

> Instead of being directed immediately to the one encountered, [one] first sinks selflessly into the nothingness of the ungrounded groundlessness of the 'in between', in order then, arisen from the depths of nothingness, resurrected, to enter in the vis-à-vis of the I-Thou.⁴⁸

An interpersonal encounter is a complex situation, given that it involves the reception of the other that is not the self and the simultaneous presentation of the I that is independent of the other. Yet, because the world is imbued with infinite openness, Ueda affirms, using Buddhist terms, that all things confronting the subject and all things confronted by the subject are 'Buddhas, bodhisattvas, and sentient beings'.⁴⁹ Moreover, Ueda uses the religious term 'worship' to describe the reception of the object by the self that faces the other, when it returns to the state of nothingness and from the condition of boundless depth: 'Worship is the acceptance of the fundamental fact that "the other" exists.'⁵⁰ But the reception of the other that is not the self also requires the expression of the self as the self: 'a clear and immediate actualization, on each and every occasion, of the fact that the self is the self even as if receives the other as the other'.⁵¹ Therefore, the question of who is the other ('Who are you?') becomes the concrete question, to which there is not a specific answer, but rather the question requires a response that depends on specific circumstances. In Ueda's view, worldly existence (世界内存在 *sekai nai sonzai*) is the locus of this question, and the answer is found in the infinite openness that embraces this worldly existence. Thus each and every encounter creates the space between the self and the other where they interrelate.

John C. Maraldo remarks that contrary to other interpretations of the last ox-herding picture in terms of the oneness of the two people depicted, Ueda places the emphasis in the 'realm between' the two, 'who are really just the selfless unfolding the one' and this 'undercuts separateness and strict duality yet recognizes difference'.⁵² Although Ueda does not mention the philosopher Watsuji Tetsurō here, this 'betweenness' could be regarded as indebted to Watsuji's significant contribution to theories of intersubjectivity in Japanese philosophy. In brief, looking at the Japanese word for 'human being' (人間 *ningen*), Watsuji realized that it includes the meaning of the self both as individual and as relational. According to Watsuji, while the first character in the word 人 '*nin*' points to the self as individual, the second character of the word 間 '*gen*' suggests 'the public' domain:

> We Japanese have produced a distinctive conception of human being. According to it, *ningen* is the public domain and, at the same time, the individual human being living within it.⁵³

Then, for Watsuji, one cannot be fully human unless one is an individual and is also in relation to other human beings. In consequence, Watsuji's conception of ethics was related to the study of human beings as individual and social in the betweenness (*aidagara* 間柄) among selves in the world.⁵⁴ Therefore, *ningen* here names both the individual, the human being involved in social networks and the 'space' between human beings where their relationships take place. It can be said that Watsuji's view of the self as intrinsically social illuminates a trait that characterizes much of Japanese ethics where the communal aspect has often been stressed at the expense of the individual.⁵⁵

While probably agreeing with Watsuji that the relation with others is intrinsic to selfhood, Ueda also follows Nishida's dialectics, which includes the difference and negation aspects that constitute the self in the relational field where active and embodied selves encounter one another. Ueda tries to preserve both the sameness and the alterity of the other, and both the selflessness and the autonomy of the self. The nullified self still preserves its identity, the other is accepted as different and at the same time both share a common selfless ground in the space where they interrelate. Hence, similarly, Nishitani Keiji speaks of a 'non-duality of self and other' (自他不二 *jitafuni*) where self and other are one and simultaneously each one remains what it is in itself.⁵⁶ In his essay devoted to the I and Thou relation in Zen Buddhism, Nishitani develops this idea in the following terms:

> *Self and other are not one, and not two*. To be not one and not two means that each self retains its absoluteness while still being relative, and that in this relativity the two are never for a moment separated. While the I to be the I acknowledges the Thou in relation to the Thou's own absolute non-differentiation, and this permits itself to become absolutely the Thou, at the same time it takes the Thou to itself. Situated within this absolute nondifferentiation which opens up in the I, the I is the I itself – I am I.⁵⁷

In this relation, that both unites and separates, Nishitani maintains that for harmony to be possible, or love in the religious sense, the self must empty or negate itself to be 'other-centered', and so, I can be Thou and Thou can be I. Likewise, Maraldo concludes that Ueda's message is that 'to allow another to be fully other, to be himself or herself, one must be selfless. The other is the selflessness of the self.'⁵⁸

It is worth noting that according to Ueda none of the figures in the tenth ox-herding picture represent the true self. Rather the self is to be found in the encounter between them. The encounter indicates a living action, and so, a dynamic conception of the self that is expressed by the movement from the true self back to itself: the open, giving self, as opposed to a closed, substantialized self. As an example of mutual self-negation in the encounter, Ueda mentions the Japanese greeting. For Ueda, 'a form of greeting is originally an elemental expression and a way of exercising human self-understanding in interhuman encounters where the essence of the human being is being expressed.'[59] The act of bowing is regarded as a self-emptying of attachments and selfish motivations.[60] Once one rises up from the bow, the formality of talking about the weather can be seen as a way of sharing a common ground and enabling a true encounter. In this common ground one experiences absolute non-differentiation as neither-I-nor-Thou. As a result, both are at once absolutely free and completely the equal of one another.

At the end of this quest for meaning or truth, the self that undergoes a transformation and becomes a new self does not find a new fixed and definitive identity. The threefold manifestation of the self that the images portray indicates a process, not an objectified thing. For Ueda, nothingness, nature and communication are different aspects of a dynamic process of transformation. The self is the place where this transformation occurs, constantly changing and hence open, but at every moment fully concrete and individual. By means of its self-negation, the self opens up to openness. The dynamic movement in infinite openness takes place in every encounter, both with the other and with nature. Behind this understanding of the non-self lies the core of the Buddhist view of reality, including that of the self as impermanent, non-substantial and interdependent. As we have seen, the basic idea of true self as non-self and selfless self is clearly borrowed from Zen Buddhism, yet Ueda further develops its philosophical potential with insights taken from both Japanese and Western philosophies.

Notes

1 Shizuteru Ueda, *Dōtei 'jūgyūzu' o ayumu* [In the Course of the 'Ten Ox-Herding Pictures' Path], in *Ueda Shizuteru shū* [The Ueda Shizuteru Collection], 6 (Tokyo: Iwanami Shoten, 2003).

2 This Zen Buddhist classic narrates with images, verses and comments how a herdsman finds his lost ox, illustrating through ten stages the progress of a man's

self-becoming according to the way of Zen. There is a famous version by thirteenth-century Chinese master Kuo-an (Jap. Kakuan). In his German writings, Ueda usually quotes the German translation of Tsujimura Kōiji and Hartmut Buchner, *Der Ochs und sein Hirte: eine altchinesische Zen-Geschichte* (Pfullingen: Neske, 1975).

3 An earlier writing on the Ox-herding pictures by Ueda together with Seizan Yanagida was published with this subtitle *Jūgyū- jiko no genshōgaku* (*The Ten Ox-Herding Pictures: A Phenomenology of Self* (Tokyo: Chikuma Shobō, 1982)). In his collected works, the tenth volume (Tokyo: Iwanami Shoten, 2002) also bears the title of *Jiko no genshōgaku* (*A phenomenology of Self*). Our suggestion here is that Ueda with his hermeneutics of these pictures attempts to go beyond the cultural framework of Zen tradition.

4 This article is part of a research project on Japanese Philosophy, supported by the Spanish Ministry of Economy and Competitiveness, Grant FFI2015-65662-P.

5 The last three pictures, which respectively depict an empty circle, a landscape and an encounter between two people, hereinafter are referred to as Figure 8.1: Picture Eight, *Forget Both Self and Ox*; Figure 8.2: Picture Nine, *Return to the Origin, Back to the Source*; and Figure 8.3: Picture Ten, *Entering the Marketplace with Extended Hands*.

6 Ueda finds a correspondence between the three images and some exponents of European *Geistesgeschichte* (from the German 'spirit' and 'history', often translated into English as 'intellectual history'): between the empty circle and the Nothingness of the Godhead in Meister Eckhart (and to a certain point Nietzsche's radical nihilism); between nature and Angelus Silesius's famous verses 'The rose is without why; it blooms simply because it blooms'; and between the interpersonal encounter and Martin Buber's work *Ich und Du* (1923).

7 Ueda, *Dōtei 'jūgyūzu' o ayumu* [*In the Course of the 'Ten Ox-Herding Pictures' Path*], 208.

8 Cf. Shizuteru Ueda, 'Silence and Words in Zen Buddhism', *Diogenes* 170, 43, no. 2 (1995): 1–21; Raquel Bouso, 'Lenguaje y silencio. Experiencia y comprensión en Ueda Shizuteru', in *Atti del Convegno 'Comparatismi e Filosofie'*, ed. Maria Donzelli (Naples: Liguori, 2006).

9 Mark Siderits, *Buddhism as Philosophy: An Introduction* (Aldershot: Ashgate; Indianapolis: Hackett, 2007), 205.

10 Thomas P. Kasulis, 'The Buddhist Concept of Self', in *A Companion to World Philosophies*, ed. Elliot Deutsch and Ronald Bontekoe (Malden and Oxford: Blackwell, 1997), 402.

11 Walpola Sri Rahula, *What the Buddha Taught* (Oxford: Oneworld Publications, 2011), 51.

12 For instance, Richard Gombrich argues that the mistranslation of *anātman* as 'not having a self or essence' was how later Buddhist came to interpret it, but the

Pali grammar and a comparison with the *Vedānta* show that the original meaning was '*is* not *ātman*' rather than 'does not *have ātman*': 'as time went by the term was taken as a possessive compound and also taken to refer to everything, so that it became the one-word expression of the Buddha's anti-essentialism.' Richard Gombrich, *What the Buddha Thought* (London: Equinox, 2009), 70.

13 Nāgārjuna, *Mūlamadhyakakārikā: The Philosophy of the Middle Way*, ed. and trans. D. J. Kalupahana (Albany: State University of New York Press, 1986), XV/1-2; 228-9.

14 Dōgen, *Shōbōgenzō Genjōkōan*, trans. Thomas P. Kasulis in *Japanese Philosophy: A Sourcebook*, ed. James W. Heisig, Thomas P. Kasulis and John C. Maraldo (Honolulu: University of Hawai'i Press, 2011), 145.

15 Peter Harvey, *An Introduction to Buddhist Ethics: Foundations, Values and Issues* (Cambridge: Cambridge University Press, 2011), 144.

16 Keiji Nishitani, *Shūkyō to wa nanika* [What Is Religion?], in *Nishitani Keiji chosakushū* [Works by Nishitani Keiji], 10 (Tokyo: Sōbunsha, 1961), 6-7; translated by Jan Van Bragt as *Religion and Nothingness* (Berkeley, Los Angeles and London: University of California Press, 1982), 4-5.

17 Awakening is a problem to the self. In one's search for the true self one's very way of being becomes stuck as one becomes through and through a problem to oneself. Ueda, *Dōtei 'jūgyūzu' o ayumu* (*In the Course of the 'Ten Ox-Herding Pictures' Path*), 223. (On this point he is believed to differ from the standpoint of rational ethics.) (The translation of the quotations is mine unless otherwise indicated.)

18 About Suzuki Daisetsu T., Ueda writes elsewhere: 'The written word is important, of course, but what causes one to actually *believe* in something is this kind of vibrant, free, and unpremeditated functioning of a living human being' (Shizuteru Ueda, 'The Practice of Zen', *The Eastern Buddhist* 27, no. 1 (1994): 16). Ueda affirms that the influence of other people is the most crucial factor in starting Zen meditation and Zen instruction. When he felt that Zen was a way out of the impasse he suffered, Suzuki was the person who inspired him in this way.

19 For the first time it becomes possible to listen to teachings. What has been heard and deeply understood must be appropriated in living form and become part of oneself. (On this point he is believed to differ from the standpoint of philosophy.) And this is precisely the way the self works. Ueda, *Dōtei 'jūgyūzu' o ayumu* (*In the Course of the 'Ten Ox-Herding Pictures' Path*), 223.

20 The way (of practice) is a concrete *embodiment* in which the *teaching* regarding the way of being of the self becomes the *concern* of the self. Practice only becomes practice when it is inherited. It is not a matter of repeating a habit. The self is not something that has to do with exercise. Practice is not drill or exercise. It is leaving the Dharma-gate of asceticism for that of tranquillity. If I may be permitted to set up a parallel, catching the ox represents logical existence in practice; riding the ox returning home, aesthetic existence in practice; and forgetting the ox and the

herder, religious existence in practice. Ueda, *Dōtei 'jūgyūzu' o ayumu* (*In the Course of the 'Ten Ox-Herding Pictures' Path*), 223.

21 Ueda, *Dōtei 'jūgyūzu' o ayumu* (*In the Course of the 'Ten Ox-Herding Pictures' Path*), 248. See it explained in detail, for instance, in Shizuteru Ueda, *Zen no fūkei* [*A Landscape of Zen*], in *Ueda Shizuteru shū* [*Ueda Shizuteru* Collection], 5 (Tokyo: Iwanami Shoten, 2002).

22 Ueda, *Dōtei 'jūgyūzu' o ayumu* (*In the Course of the 'Ten Ox-Herding Pictures' Path*), 223.

23 In a non-substantial sense, absolute nothingness is transformed into a 'nothingness of nothingness'. In the classical diction of Mahāyāna in general, emptiness is 'sky is also empty'. It is therefore said, 'form is emptiness, emptiness is form'. Ueda, *Dōtei 'jūgyūzu' o ayumu* (*In the Course of the 'Ten Ox-Herding Pictures' Path*), 235.

24 Note that the Japanese term for 'nature', 自然 *shizen* (in Chinese *ziran*) is usually translated as 'self-soing', 'self-going', 'being free' or 'spontaneous'. In Chinese texts, like *Daodejing*, designates what unfolds of its own accord as opposed to the will and designs of the self. In ancient Japanese, the first character in *ziran* (*zi* 自) appears in the term '*onozukara*' 自ずから to indicate that which originates from itself, as well as in the term '*mizukara*' 自ら to refer to that which originates from oneself, or from the body.

25 Ueda, *Dōtei 'jūgyūzu' o ayumu* [*In the Course of the 'Ten Ox-Herding Pictures' Path*], 249.

26 Compare Kitarō Nishida, *Hataraku mono kara miru mono e* (From That Which Acts to That Which Sees), in *Nishida Kitarō Zenshū* (*Collected Works of Nishida Kitarō*), 4 (Tokyo: Iwanami Shoten, 1987), 208–89.

27 In this regard, Nishida wrote: 'What is considered the "individual self" is nothing more than a thing that is thinkable as the individual determination of the world that determines itself' (Kitarō Nishida, *Tetsugaku no konpon mondai* (*Fundamental Problems of Philosophy*), in *Nishida Kitarō zenshū* (*Collected Works of Nishida Kitarō*), 7 (Tokyo: Iwanami Shoten, 1988): 203).

28 In his philosophical anthropology, Lluís Duch speaks about ambiguity as human 'natural place', 'human adventure' is a pending task and an open horizon, always a provisional 'context-dependent' construction. See Lluís Duch, *La religión en el siglo XXI* (Madrid: Siruela, 2012), 62–4.

29 For an English translation of Nishida's seminal work *Zen no kenkyū* (1911), see Kitarō Nishida, *An Inquiry into the Good*, trans. Masao Abe and Christopher Ives (New Haven: Yale University Press, 1990).

30 As Thomas Kasulis observes, *basho* is a common word in Japanese meaning 'place' but Nishida uses it with multiple nuances, like 'the sense of where or how an experience or a judgment in experience *takes place*. Basho also *topicalizes* an experience by establishing a standpoint or engulfing context for the way something is judged and it *localizes* every judgment in terms of its larger experiential context.'

Thomas P. Kasulis, *Engaging Japanese Philosophy: A Short History* (Honolulu: University of Hawai'i Press, 2018), 463. For an interpretation and translation into English of Nishida's writing on 'Basho', see Kitarō Nishida, *Place and Dialectic: Two Essays*, trans. John W. M. Krummel and Shigenori Nagatomo (Oxford and New York: Oxford University Press, 2012).

31 Yasuo Yuasa, 'Foreword', in *Encounter with Enlightenment: A Study of Japanese Ethics*, by Robert E. Carter (New York: SUNY, 2001), xxix.

32 In English, see for instance 'Logic and Life', in Nishida, *Place and Dialectic*, 113 passim.

33 On this concept, see Kitarō Nishida's essay written in 1938, 'Kōiteki Chokkan', in *Tetsugaku ronbunshū I* (*Philosophical Essays* I), *Nishida Kitarō Zenshū* (*Collected Works of Nishida Kitarō*) 8, (Tokyo: Iwanami Shoten, 1988), 541–71. See Kasulis, *Engaging Japanese Philosophy*, 467.

34 Sometimes Nishida links the meaning of world to that of *basho*, as 'to be in' and 'the place where a thing is'.

35 Yoko Arisaka, 'The Ontological Co-Emergence of "Self and Other" in Japanese Philosophy', in *Between Ourselves: Second-Person Issues in the Study of Consciousness*, ed. Evan Thompson (Charlottesville: Imprint Academic, 2001), 205.

36 Ibid., 207.

37 Kitarō Nishida, *Mu no jikakuteki gentei* (*The Self-Conscious Determination of Nothingness*), in *Nishida Kitarō Zenshū* (*Collected Works of Nishida*), 6 (Tokyo: Iwanami Shoten, 1987), 406 and Shizuteru Ueda, *Nishida Kitarō*, in *Ueda Shizuteru shū* (The Ueda Shizuteru Collection), 1 (Tokyo: Iwanami Shoten, 2001), 345.

38 Arisaka, 'The Ontological Co-Emergence of "Self and Other" in Japanese Philosophy', 206.

39 See Jean Grondin, *Introduction to Philosophical Hermeneutics*, trans. Joel Weinsheimer (New Haven and London: Yale University Press, 1994), in particular, 92–3.

40 Jean Grondin, *L'hermeneutique* (Paris: Presses Universitaires de France, 2006), 28–9.

41 For example, Husserl defines world-life as 'the world of sense-experience constantly pregiven as taken for granted unquestioningly and all the life of thought which is nourished by it', Edmund Husserl, *The Crisis of European Sciences and Transcendental Phenomenology*, trans. D. Carr (Evanston: Northwestern University Press, 1970), §17, 47. And then he develops further this position as follows: 'In this world we are objects among objects in the sense of the life-world, namely, as being here and there, in the plain certainty of experience, before anything that is established scientifically, whether in physiology, psychology, or sociology' (Husserl, *The Crisis of European Sciences*, § 28; 105), and 'If we have made this clear to ourselves, then obviously an explicit elucidation of the objective validity and of the whole task of science requires that we first inquire back into the pregiven world. It is pregiven to us all quite naturally, as persons within the horizon of our fellow

men, i.e., in every actual connection with others, as "the" world common to us all' (Husserl, *The Crisis of European Sciences*, §33, 121–2).

42 Compare 'The "actor" [i.e. the one who acts] exists as a self within the world and at the same time penetrates to the infinite openness in which there is no self; this actor might thus be called "a self that is not a self"', Ueda, 'The Practice of Zen', 23.

43 Martin Buber, *I and Thou*, trans. W. Kaufmann (New York: Charles Scribner's Sons, 1970), 1.

44 In *I and Thou*, Buber wrote that 'The basic word I-You establishes the world of relation'. It is worth noting that the 1923 edition adds 'Basic words do not signify things but relations' while in the 1957 edition this sentence is substituted by the following: 'Basic words do not state something that might exist outside them; by being spoken they establish a mode of existence' (Cf. Buber, *I and Thou*, 1970).

45 Despite the fact that this goes far beyond what can be suggested here, their interest in dialogue seems to derive from their traditional dialogical literary heritage: in the case of Ueda with Zen 問答 *mondō* and in the case of Buber with Hassidic tales.

46 Likewise, Nishitani objects that a universal such as God acts as a kind of obstruction to absolute individuality: 'I and Thou are absolutes, each in its own respective subjectivity. And second, both I and Thou are, because of their relationship to one another, at the same time absolutely relative.' Nishitani, 'The I-Thou Relation in Zen Buddhism', in *The Buddha Eye: An Anthology of the Kyoto School*, ed. Frederick Franck (New York: Crossroad, 1991), 49. Ueda pursues this argumentation further in relation to Meister Eckhart's understanding of God. Compare Shizuteru Ueda, *Jiko no genshōgaku* (*The Phenomenology of Self*), in *Ueda Shizuteru shū* (*The Ueda Shizuteru Collection*), 10 (Tokyo: Iwanami Shoten, 2002), 296–308.

47 Shizuteru Ueda, *Jiko no genshōgaku* (*The Phenomenology of Self*), 102–7.

48 Shizuteru Ueda, 'Ascent and Descent I: Zen in Comparison with Meister Eckhart', *The Eastern Buddhist* 16, no. 1 (1983): 68.

49 Ueda, 'The Practice of Zen', 24.

50 Ibid.

51 Ibid., 25.

52 John C. Maraldo, 'Zen, Language and the Other: The Philosophy of Ueda Shizuteru', *The Kuroda Institute*, Fall/Winter (1989): 22.

53 Tetsurō Watsuji, *Rinrigaku: Ethics in Japan*, trans. Yamamoto Seisaku and Robert E. Carter (Albany: State University of New York Press, 1996), 15.

54 For the contribution of this position towards an 'ethics of care', see Erin McCarthy, 'Towards a Transnational Ethics of Care', in *Neglected Themes and Hidden Variations: Frontiers of Japanese Philosophy*, 2, ed. Victor S. Hori and Melissa Anne-Marie Curley (Nagoya: Nanzan Institute for Religion and Culture, 2008).

55 'Watsuji's intellectual journey took him from a rejection of Japanese social conformity together with an admiration for Western individualism, to a rejection of that particular brand of individualism and rediscovery of the worth of community

in Japanese culture and practice. Watsuji's objection to the ethics of individualism is that it loses touch with the vast network of interconnections that serves to make us what we are, namely individuals inescapably immersed in the space/time of a world, together with others [...] Community is to be found in the "betweenness" between people, the space in which people can interact with other people thereby eliminating the isolation rampant in Western thought and culture.' Robert E. Carter, *Encounter with Enlightenment: A Study of Japanese Ethics* (New York: State University of New York Press, 2001), 125.

56 Nishitani, *Shūkyō to wa nanika* (What Is Religion?), 309; *Religion and Nothingness*, 280.
57 Nishitani, 'The I-Thou Relation in Zen Buddhism', 56.
58 Maraldo, 'Zen, Language and the Other: The Philosophy of Ueda Shizuteru', 25. Elsewhere Maraldo comments that in Nishitani it is not clear how the 'great death' in Zen leads to great compassion and to the Christian 'love of neighbour' and that in his later years, he took the question of awakening as prior to political and social problems. Maraldo sees also this lack of clarification in merely claiming that awakening or zazen practice is all that is needed to be ethical, or in invoking an ethics of compassion as merely situational and without clear principles. This is an important issue related with our topic here since, as Maraldo notices and it follows from our discussion, the Kyoto School philosophers recognized the potential of the alternative normativity in Zen. For his perceptive analysis of this issue and his proposal of a *declarative* normativity in Zen – according to which the two forms of expressing the ideals, norms or precepts, the imperative and the descriptive, are inherently aligned – see John C. Maraldo, 'The Alternative Normativity of Zen', in *Confluences and Cross-Currents: Frontiers of Japanese Philosophy*, 6, ed. Raquel Bouso and James W. Heisig (Nagoya: Nanzan Institute for Religion and Culture, 2009).
59 Shizuteru Ueda, 'Emptiness and Fullness: Śūnyatā in Mahāyāna Buddhism', *The Eastern Buddhist* 15, no. 1 (1982): 35.
60 Ueda, *Dōtei 'jūgyūzu' o ayumu* (*In the Course of the 'Ten Ox-Herding Pictures' Path*), 274ss.

Bibliography

Arisaka, Yoko. 'The Ontological Co-emergence of "Self and Other" in Japanese Philosophy'. In *Between Ourselves: Second-Person Issues in the Study of Consciousness*. Edited by Evan Thompson, 197–208. Charlottesville: Imprint Academic, 2001.

Bouso, Raquel. 'Lenguaje y silencio. Experiencia y comprensión en Ueda Shizuteru'. In *Atti del Convegno 'Comparatismi e Filosofie'*. Edited by Maria Donzelli, 239–61. Naples: Liguori, 2006.

Buber, Martin. *I and Thou*. Translated by W. Kaufmann. New York: Charles Scribner's Sons, 1970.

Carter, Robert E. *Encounter with Enlightenment: A Study of Japanese Ethics*. Foreword by Yuasa Yasuo. New York: State University of New York Press, 2001.

Duch, Lluís. *La religión en el siglo XXI*. Madrid: Siruela, 2012.

Gombrich, Richard, *What the Buddha Thought*. London: Equinox, 2009.

Grondin, Jean. *Introduction to Philosophical Hermeneutics*. Translated by Joel Weinsheimer. New Haven and London: Yale University Press, 1994.

Grondin, Jean. *L'hermeneutique*. Paris: Presses Universitaires de France, 2006.

Harvey, Peter. *An Introduction to Buddhist Ethics: Foundations, Values and Issues*. Cambridge: Cambridge University Press, 2011.

Heisig, James W. 'Non-I and Thou: Nishida, Buber, and the Moral Consequences of Self-Actualization'. *Philosophy East and West* 50, no. 2 (2000): 179–207.

Heisig, James W., Thomas P. Kasulis and John C. Maraldo, eds. *Japanese Philosophy: A Sourcebook*. Honolulu: University of Hawai'i Press, 2011.

Husserl, Edmund. *The Crisis of European Sciences and Transcendental Phenomenology*. Translated by D. Carr. Evanston: Northwestern University Press, 1970.

Kasulis, Thomas P. 'The Buddhist Concept of Self'. In *A Companion to World Philosophies*. Edited by Elliot Deutsch and Ronald Bontekoe, 400–9. Malden and Oxford: Blackwell, 1997.

Kasulis, Thomas P. *Engaging Japanese Philosophy: A Short History*. Honolulu: University of Hawai'i Press, 2018.

Maraldo, John C. 'The Alternative Normativity of Zen'. In *Confluences and Cross-Currents: Frontiers of Japanese Philosophy*, 6. Edited by Raquel Bouso and James W. Heisig, 190–214. Nagoya: Nanzan Institute for Religion and Culture, 2009.

Maraldo, John C. 'Zen, Language and the Other: The Philosophy of Ueda Shizuteru'. *The Kuroda Institute*, Fall/Winter (1989): 21–6.

McCarthy, Erin. 'Towards a Transnational Ethics of Care'. In *Neglected Themes and Hidden Variations: Frontiers of Japanese Philosophy*, 2. Edited by Victor S. Hori and Melissa Anne-Marie Curley, 113–28. Nagoya: Nanzan Institute for Religion and Culture, 2008.

Nāgārjuna. *Mūlamadhyakakārikā: The Philosophy of the Middle Way*. Edited and translated by D. J. Kalupahana. Albany: State University of New York Press, 1986.

Nishida, Kitarō. *Hataraku mono kara miru mono e* [*From That Which Acts to That Which Sees*]. In *Nishida Kitarō Zenshū* [*Collected works of Nishida Kitarō*] 4. Tokyo: Iwanami Shoten, 1987.

Nishitani, Keiji. 'The I-Thou Relation in Zen Buddhism'. In *The Buddha Eye: An Anthology of the Kyoto School*. Edited by Frederick Franck, 47–60. New York: Crossroad, 1991.

Nishida, Kitarō. *An Inquiry into the Good*. Translated by Masao Abe and Christopher Ives. New Haven: Yale University Press, 1990.

Nishida, Kitarō. *Mu no jikakuteki gentei* [*The Self-Conscious Determination of Nothingness*]. In *Nishida Kitarō Zenshū* [*Collected works of Nishida Kitarō*] 6. Tokyo: Iwanami Shoten, 1987.

Nishida, Kitarō. *Place and Dialectic: Two Essays*. Translated by John W. M. Krummel and Shigenori Nagatomo. Oxford and New York: Oxford University Press, 2012.

Nishida, Kitarō. *Tetsugaku no konpon mondai* [*Fundamental Problems of Philosophy*]. In *Nishida Kitarō zenshū* [*Collected works of Nishida Kitarō*] 7. Tokyo: Iwanami Shoten, 1988.

Nishida, Kitarō. *Tetsugaku ronbunshū I* [*Philosophical Essays* I]. In *Nishida Kitarō Zenshū* [*Collected works of Nishida Kitarō*] 8. Tokyo: Iwanami Shoten, 1988.

Nishitani, Keiji. *Religion and Nothingness*. Translated by Jan Van Bragt. Los Angeles: University of California Press, 1982.

Nishitani, Keiji. *Shūkyō to wa nanika* [*What Is Religion?*]. In *Nishitani Keiji chosakushū* [*Works by Nishitani Keiji*] 10. Tokyo: Sōbunsha, 1961.

Rahula, Walpola Sri. *What the Buddha Taught* [1959]. Oxford: Oneworld, 2011.

Siderits, Mark. *Buddhism as Philosophy: An Introduction*. Aldershot: Ashgate; Indianapolis: Hackett, 2007.

Ueda, Shizuteru. 'Ascent and Descent I: Zen in Comparison with Meister Eckhart'. *The Eastern Buddhist* 16, no. 1 (1983): 52–75.

Ueda, Shizuteru. *Dōtei 'jūgyūzu' o ayumu* [*In the Course of the 'Ten Ox-Herding Pictures' Path*]. In *Ueda Shizuteru shū* [*The Ueda Shizuteru Collection*], 6. Tokyo: Iwanami Shoten, 2003.

Ueda, Shizuteru. 'Emptiness and Fullness: Śūnyatā in Mahāyāna Buddhism'. *The Eastern Buddhist* 15, no. 1 (1982): 9–37.

Ueda, Shizuteru. 'Jesus in Contemporary Japanese Zen. With Special Regard to Keiji Nishitani'. In *Buddhist Perceptions of Jesus*. Edited by Perry Schmidt-Leukel in cooperation with Thomas Josef Götz and Gerhard Köberlin, 45–59. St. Ottilien: EOS Verlag, 2001.

Ueda, Shizuteru. *Jiko no genshōgaku* [*The phenomenology of Self*]. In *Ueda Shizuteru shū* [*The Ueda Shizuteru Collection*], 10. Tokyo: Iwanami Shoten, 2002.

Ueda, Shizuteru. *Nishida Kitarō*. In *Ueda Shizuteru shū* [*The Ueda Shizuteru Collection*], 1. Tokyo: Iwanami Shoten, 2001.

Ueda, Shizuteru. 'The Practice of Zen'. *The Eastern Buddhist* 27, no. 1 (1994): 10–29.

Ueda, Shizuteru. 'Silence and Words in Zen Buddhism'. *Diogenes* 170, 43, no. 2 (1995): 1–21.

Ueda, Shizuteru. *Zen no fūkei* [*A landscape of Zen*]. In *Ueda Shizuteru shū* [*Ueda Shizuteru* Collection], 5. Tokyo: Iwanami Shoten, 2002.

Watsuji, Tetsurō. *Rinrigaku: Ethics in Japan*. Translated by Yamamoto Seisaku and Robert E. Carter. Albany: State University of New York Press, 1996.

Yuasa, Yasuo. 'Foreword'. In *Encounter with Enlightenment: A Study of Japanese Ethics*, by Robert E. Carter, xi–xxx. New York: State University of New York Press, 2001.

9

Events of excess, being and existence in Jean-Luc Nancy and Jean-Luc Marion's philosophies

Robert Luzar

Introduction: Being, Event, Opening

Such an event gives itself, in effect, all at once: it leaves us without a voice to speak it; it leaves us also without any other way to avoid it; and it leaves us finally without a choice to refuse it or even to accept it voluntarily. Its fait accompli is not discussed, is not avoided, is not decided either.[1]

From Marion's words there are two questions I wish to open with. How does an event take place in this fait accompli? What 'gives *itself*' through an event that seems so absolute? With these I will set up an inquiry that delves into notions of existence, being and excess. I will argue that this excess is related to the concept of event posed by Marion. The inquiry will deal with fields of phenomenology and theology, and how both crossover into a problem of ontotheology. French philosophers Jean-Luc Nancy and Jean-Luc Marion both address this. I will examine the problem of ontotheology as something that has to do with excess – excess as the radical absence of 'being' while existence still takes place. In order to understand why this event is one of excess I will need to further examine concepts of phenomenological 'disclosure' and theological 'revelation'. Marion and Nancy rethink phenomenologies of being through an event that is non-metaphysical. For them, being is empty of internal qualities; nevertheless, the very essence of what one becomes is in excess of who and what one fundamentally is (Self, I, subject, substance).

Let us start by looking at how being is understood as divine, theologically and ontologically speaking. Marion approaches being as, what I wish to call, an *event of excess*. For Marion the excess is 'saturated phenomena', which deals with a religious form of phenomenology. Crudely put, Marion's definition of phenomenology is about the experience of phenomena. The phenomenon experienced is the 'invisibility' of being. This experience deals with ways in which being is given absolutely as 'invisibility'. This invisibility does not conceal a concrete object or actual being; what makes the experience of phenomena excessive and absolute is that there is no substance to render visible. It is through painting that Marion shows how being is an event, the event defined as the experience of invisibility. For him, this has to do with giving, giving visibility to, and thus 'revealing', an excess – excess in the sense that something is profoundly happening (namely God, but without Being). Nancy challenges such experiences of revelation, and religious turns in phenomenology. He instead looks to radical deconstructions of Christian (and monotheistic) traditions, evolving from ancient Greece onwards. A more radical event of 'dis-enclosure', as Nancy calls it, is therefore imperative to approaching being critically, so as to offset any ontotheological event that poses a return to religion.

The context we are dealing with stretches over two millennia of Western philosophical thought, and historically overlaps with Judeo-Christian religion. In order to keep this context succinct, let us look primarily at texts from Marion and Nancy, which focus on problems with ontotheology: Marion's *God Without Being* (1982; 1995) and Nancy's two-part investigation *Dis-Enclosure: The Deconstruction of Christianity* (2005; 2008) and *Adoration: The Deconstruction of Christianity II* (2010; 2013).[2] Both texts are critical of phenomenological approaches to being and existence. It should also be noted that these texts emphasize writing as a critical method of interpretation. For them, writing is a way of interpreting certain limits of language, being, thinking and event.

Here caution should be taken when approaching this debate with secular critique, as in the critique of religion. Both Nancy and Marion are mindful of a certain predicament – overlooked by 'thinkers' who strongly reject religion: that by attempting to critique metaphysics, of trying to overcome substantive notions of Being or of claiming 'God is dead', the metaphysical foundations critiqued are paradoxically retained (e.g. rejecting religious institutions such as Christianity or Islam while advocating 'alternative' spiritual practices). Theology complicates philosophical inquiry. How does someone deal with faith, fidelity or commitment when trying to think more profoundly about existence (with self *and* others)?

So we face a question of theology. What does theology mean in this case? To approach this question we need to understand that theology is an approach that intertwines with philosophical inquiry in its use of 'inscription'. Writing by hand or typing into a keyboard are common examples of inscription; but in theology inscription is an act of writing (e.g. scripture, exegesis) that goes profoundly into notions of faith. This exegetic act also becomes transgressive – 'writing always transgresses itself ... causes him [thinker, philosopher, artist/poet] to write outside himself, even against himself.'[3] Although the theological 'act of faith appears only as a dogmatic and institutional control', the secular approach, in attempting to dispute theology and reject religion outright, has to confront its so-called critical method that 'has no doubt hit the precise spot where the void opened', a void that faces 'the worsening permanence of nihilism'.[4]

The ontotheological problem

How to confront, overcome or even work through such nihilism? The relation between meaning and being can seem tenuous in today's world. We work 24/7, eat, sleep, and live for no reason other than to accumulate wealth, produce and reproduce value; we live in the belief that, out there in the so-called real world, there is some organic principle of life at work; we place 'faith' into individual self-fulfilment, which poses 'a different kind of hell'.[5] Life can become many things, filled with varieties and choices like wandering in a supermarket; but it is a life that can become quite meagre in existence and, worse, meaningless in sense. Nihilism is generally understood as existence that has no meaning; but the real issue at hand is that no fundamental change (in the conditions for the possibility of being) takes place. Which is to say, everything is devoid of an authentic event.[6] Instead it is the individual as just 'me' – some kind of conceptual idol, as Marion would warn – that one ends up supplementing life, not so much with God but with a reductive metaphysical principle of Being (e.g. inner self, Capital, an 'alternative' spiritual deity, mana). All this highlights a predicament. It is a predicament whereby the so-called secular individual wholly attaches himself or herself to higher-order forms of substance so to keep from perceiving Being as purely empty. Instead, 'Being' is perceived as some super-object, out there, infinite and ineffable, as if to be some invisible substance that flows and, in itself, seems organic and rationally whole – when in fact there is no way to rationally question this flow or flux, this principle of metaphysical substance/Being.[7] Each in his own way, Marion and Nancy, fully and radically interrogate this predicament of secular existence.

An 'ontotheological' problem – what does this mean then? Put plainly, as a 'human being' someone exists through and is caused by a certain divine principle that is 'beyond being'. The theological sense, or the more loaded *onto-theological*, comes with how one approaches a higher-order principle of identity (God, sufficient reason, substance) to ground oneself. This principle of identity is Being (with a capital B). Being is distinct from but related to an individual's being. Someone's existence is made possible by some higher Being out there. The 'out-there' would be the sense of something or someone, some metaphysical principle really, that (effectively) *operates* outside each of us. God operates effectively by causing us to be. This transcendence can be interpreted as a condition that is causally at work – and thus operative – by changing each of us, making possible every kind of being (human and non-human). Change moreover expresses a perpetual event – rather than a rudimentary one-time event – the sense that something out there (Being) is continuously transforming all beings *absolutely*.[8] In Heideggarian phenomenological terms, this highlights a 'difference' between Being and beings, or *ontological difference*. Here phenomenology becomes a philosophical approach wherein the very crossover of theology and ontology remains a 'glaring exegetical lacuna'.[9] A critical reading that attempts to question and overcome ontological difference, or religious dogmatism, defines the problem connecting theology with ontology.

What then should we understand by theology? According to Nancy, theology is a means of engaging in a sort of existential faith, where existence is an act of living faithfully within a world shared by things and others, and exist with a sense of nascence and openness.[10] This existential faith is distinct from the interpretation that philosopher Markus Gabriel poses. For Gabriel, faith is more religious, as in having faith in 'an image of a super-object that is worthy of our veneration, while concealing itself behind the appearances'.[11] For Nancy, however, one should exist in such a way that faith is an act but, fundamentally, without any metaphysical super-object. Existential faith happens when there is no real Being hidden and fully there in the first place. To understand this distinction we need to look into a monotheistic theological context. A key figure in this context is the seminal medieval theologian, Thomas Aquinas. For it is Aquinas who employs Aristotelian philosophies of being to vindicate the Christian God as a divine principle: being-as-such is divine in essence (*esse*), causing all things as entities to be what they are – and become. We can rationally demonstrate that God exists, says Aquinas, while at the same time – and here is the paradox – 'God is in no way knowable by us.'[12] Being takes up the form of a metaphysical reality; that is, 'God' is not an actual being so much as an abstract condition that occurs concretely through something causal and infinite in essence.[13] God ought not be imagined as a bearded wise man, but really a more abstract reality that seems 'visible' in nature. Think for instance of patterns that appear throughout nature, from waves to particles or how cells regenerate themselves from an injury: there are abstract principles or laws of nature concretely at play. Aquinas's innovation is in making God a rationally constituted super-object, an absolute principle of reason, or law. This detail is crucial. At best we are what we are (finite created beings) – and become whatever we might be – by engaging with this rationally constituted, self-causing substance, or *causa sui*; in other words, our existence is made possible, and is caused by Being-itself, which is first in kind, unique, wholly subsists, autotelic and transcendent.[14] Such a divine principle is essentially (*esse*) the primordial source that effectively gives each of us – and non-human beings – specific ways of being what each one is (*quidditas*).

Theology employs writing, and speech more broadly, to interpret a word or text that is divine, expressed by God. Language is at the very heart of not only theology but philosophy too. Language is at the heart of being human. In Judaeo-Christian and Islamic (monotheistic) religions language is accounted by 'the Word'. The Word is commonly referenced by God's declaration in Gen. 3.14: 'I am that I am.'[15] Moses hears this transcendent declaration, seeming to come from beyond (this world), an 'outside' that exceeds any real entity (being); and yet, despite 'not knowing', the empirical encounter – the so-called aesthetic experience reduced to one 'moment' – is to be received as given. And this reception of the unknown, of either God or transcendent Being, is the 'event' that ensues from Aquinas to Heidegger. It is an event that Marion queries through a more paradoxical counter-experience of donation and revelation.

Here the theological-exegetical notion of Word, and language as a whole, plays a fundamental role. The Word effectively offers salvation through transcendence. This in lay terms is something like the belief in or feeling that 'outside', out there and beyond one's own being, there is Being, a super-object and principle or Law effectively at work. 'Language permits us to utter, be it by betrayal, this *outside of being*, this *ex-ception* to being, as though being's other were an event of being.'[16] The Word comes not from 'outside', completely other from what one is, but – seemingly – within oneself. And like prayer, ritualistic, repeated, the 'event of being' is perpetuated; there is no one moment to the 'ex-ception'. Here 'event' must be considered more radically.

My hypothesis is that there is a radical event that resonates with the perpetual enunciation and inscription – and exscription, as Nancy will further say – of being open to more than, and thus in excess of, what one originally thinks one is.

In theology the event deals with how one engages with 'Word'. The Word deals with a certain transcendent experience, the enigmatic out-of-this-world experience of opening up 'being' entirely. In a transcendent experience one might say, 'I feel something profound, but I don't essentially know, nor can I put this something (God, substance, the primordial stuff of nature) into words.' The emphasis on feeling or sense thus shifts focus from epistemology to so-called aesthetic experiences sustained by faith in the unknowable.

Here ontology must be thoroughly interrogated for its connection to metaphysical theology. This means interrogating ontological difference. From Aristotle onwards the Ancient Greek notion of being, in its essential specificity (*ontos on*), has been curiously reduced to self-evident forms of essence. Substance (*ousia*) is a key concept here. That one is present to oneself, outside of time, believed – by others as much as oneself – to be fully actualized as 'I' or 'me', completely obscures the ways in which existence takes place (as radical event of excess). Plainly put, and to reiterate the predicament of secular existence, the problem is the sense of living through, and having faith in, a world view or ideology that is *not* sustained by some super-object (substance, divine being). The predicament is in existing with neither a God nor other kind of theological Being. Even if God is rejected the ideology that remains is that in which *one order of Being* is maintained (e.g. the liberal view of natural world as some harmonious and organic flux or becoming). For Heidegger the purpose of an event is to overcome any single order of Being. Difference is the mode in which a kind of phenomenological disclosure comes about; how infinitely different modes and conditions of being open up take place. The disclosure of being takes place through presence (*Anwesenheit*). It is disclosed through poetic forms of language and temporality (*Temporalität*). It is also disclosed through an ecstatic, 'original time' – distinct from linear time, as expressed through a clock – language discloses being, opens it up.[17] Temporality is being's modus operandi, that is to say what someone is – essentially – takes place through a presence that *is* 'time' in the disclosure of being, of what one essentially is. This original-time (*Temporalität*) translates to something of an event that paradigmatically opens being-as-such, opens the essence of what and who one is to total change – rather than retain one order of being, identity or existence. Both Marion and Nancy query Heidegger's notion of event as disclosure and original-time. This is especially the case in what Heidegger calls *ontological difference*: that every entity is disclosed in a way that is qualitatively different to what (*Sein*) seems already there (*da*). I am different to others as well different to myself, because over time I – what I am and who I am – change.

One of the fundamental problems facing the Heideggerian phenomenological event of being is its ontotheological connotation. At the core of this problem is the mode of transcendence as 'beyond being', which is translated from the Ancient Greek *epekeina tes ousias*. That being is beyond anything graspable, non-discursive and enigmatic: this makes phenomenology 'more like a groping about than an inquiry clear in its method'.[18] Other philosophical sources mention this only in passing. For instance, Plato describes how all things exist because they are represented by essences ideal in form.[19] The essence of being 'human', for instance, remains beyond conceptual grasp in that it is transcendent – a conceptual abstraction that curiously remains divine and infinite in form, said to go beyond this world. This binary, of (finite) being corresponding to (infinite) being-as-such, as Heidegger says, is reinterpreted by Christian Scholastic metaphysics.[20] Problematic here is the complete lack of distinction between essence (deriving from the Latin *esse*) and existence (*existentia*): 'that to each being there belongs a what and a way of being, essential and existent – as if it were self-evident'.[21] The 'way of being' describes plainly *how* anything comes to exist and continues to exist. This *how* resonates with the 'mode' in which being-as-such may be empty of inherent qualities and thus exceeding what being *is* (in essence). Metaphysics concerns the nature of all things, the totality that is being. But it holds that every being (I, you, *Dasein*) exists by virtue of a self-causing essence, as in the Latin *causa sui*. This causal principle is conceptually complex. *Causa sui* is an operation constitutive of essence: primordial, first and, most perplexing, beyond or transcendent. In other words, being is the supreme being, whose essentiality is sustained in its divine operation. *Causa sui* connotes what is transcendent yet operative as a metaphysical theological principle of being that causes all finite beings to exist. The problem of ontotheology is precisely here. Metaphysics occludes the ontologically different ways in which being opens, comes into existence, as a *fact*. The fact of existence is in how being comes to be, how someone or something is in the world. The relation between event and disclosure revolves around how being is 'self-evident', or more precisely *given*. Heidegger explains:

> Being is given only if there is disclosure, that is to say, if there is truth. But there is truth only if a being exists which *opens up*, which discloses, and indeed in such a way that disclosing belongs itself to the mode of being of this being. We ourselves are such a being. The Dasein itself exists in the truth.[22]

Being is 'given' in such a way that its 'truth' is disclosed by opening up being in essence. (As I will show later, Nancy argues that being is never given; unlike

Marion, what exists is distinct from any phenomenal givenness of being.) For Heidegger, being gives [*es gibt*] in its openness. And givenness – a key concept for Marion – is the essential mode of disclosure. Such is the Heideggarian event [*Ereignis*]: being-as-such, or essence, ex-ists, disclosing a kind of groundless opening up through which infinite possibilities of existence take place.

Here the event becomes a question of how this disclosure happens aesthetically – Does the actual experience of being effectively and operatively happen? More precisely, what takes place when this aesthetic experience of Being is, so to say, 'inoperative', inoperative in the sense that existence is worked through a non-metaphysical presence?

This question of an *inoperative aesthetics of being* obviously runs counter to metaphysics. The image posed by metaphysics occludes the event of disclosure. If interpreted more radically, an event of excess as 'dis-enclosure', as Nancy will say, is that the beyond-of-being is opened up and created *through* nothing – rather than out of nothing, ex nihilo. That something is created out of some primordial abyss, ex nihilo, correlates to a metaphysical operation that is also called the *ens creatum*. This is a metaphysical operation paradoxically dominated by 'the Christian interpretation of the world, in conformity with the creation story of Genesis'.[23] The *ens creatum* is the divine mode through which being-as-such takes place creatively; only from a divine principle of creation (*causa sui*) can world, reality or existence take place. But this is presuming that God actually is substantive, meaning that God is operative primordially, efficiently at work as the first cause (*causa sui*) – which Marion and Nancy query. There is an ironic twist that secular approaches place on this primordially causal principle that is being. The sense that all beings are created ex nihilo twists the primordial 'nothing' into the most nihilistic of vacuums: 'undoing any premise, including the nothing', as Nancy queries, means 'to empty *nothing* [*rien*] … of any quality as principle. That is creation.'[24] Such a cosmological event is therefore recklessly undermined, since there is no primordial Being, no first and primordially causal principle; nevertheless, as Nancy argues, this sense of nothingness shifts instead into an opening-*out*, an act that defines 'world'.[25] The world is this opening-out, which in principle is a non-metaphysical space of dis-enclosure. In the latter part of this chapter, dis-enclosure will be explained in greater detail; but in the meantime, we might understand this concept as something to do with an act of opening-out. What opens-out is not so much this world as is the sense of a world as 'outside'. It is throughout this outside that someone is exposed to the fact of having to exist and push on with existing. And this is despite the complication that Being is empty of qualities and un-working, that is, inoperative. Existence happens where Being withdraws.

Of God without Being

Only a radical interpretation of essence and existence, *essentia* and *existentia*, 'can provide the basis on which the problem of their distinction can first be posed'.[26] For both Marion and Nancy, this interpretation involves rethinking ontological difference. Methodologically, this means rethinking phenomenology too. It means addressing a radical event whereby being takes place throughout a more singular openness and sense of appearance, or in the case of Marion an event of givenness and saturation. Our inquiry therefore goes into how any event happens experientially and, in terms of a discourse, aesthetically. Here it is important to keep in mind that the event we are investigating concerns how being not only opens but – especially for Nancy – infinitely comes into appearance throughout a certain finite existence. Marion is no doubt important in this regard, since it is he that makes an ontological distinction while still vindicating a kind of theological turn.[27] The turn is paradigmatic in his reinterpretation of *esse*, as theorized by Aquinas. For Marion the Thomistic notion of *esse* 'does not chain God either to Being or to metaphysics', to which he elaborates: 'divine things do not belong to metaphysics as one of its objects; rather, they only intervene in metaphysics indirectly in the capacity of principles for its objects'.[28] What 'intervenes' are the principles of this transcendence, that is the conditions for the possibility of being as *es gibt*, or givenness – 'God gives Himself to be known insofar as He gives himself – according to the horizon of the gift itself ... The gift constitutes at once the mode and the horizon of the gift itself'.[29] God thus intervenes in such a way that 'the gift' fundamentally interrupts a certain introspective look, or vanity, which sustains a metaphysically operative experience of being.

Marion engages a radical form of empiricism in order critically to rethink such experiences of transcendent being. The radical empiricism underlies the notion of event, which is paradoxically prompted by a *non-substantive* being. As Marion hypothesizes through a form of religious phenomenology, the experience of being is fundamentally interrupted because Being is rendered absent, ontologically void. To understand how divine substance is ontologically void, some background must be given to Marion's philosophical enterprise. Marion looks to phenomenology, not so much via Heidegger but to its original founder – Edmund Husserl. Phenomenology is held not as a 'divine' science, as metaphysics is, but rather a critical method – and for Husserl this method is indeed scientific. It is a 'method' in the very sense that the approach is methodical and most of all rigorous – rigorous in the investigation of phenomena that engage a *matter at issue (zu den Sachen selbst)*.³⁰ The paper or computer screen someone faces while writing, for instance, can become something of issue, a matter of curiosity that can grow into questions of 'How did that get there?' or 'What is that?' What becomes an issue then (as ultra mundane as the example of papers and screens might seem) are phenomena that, precisely, *appear* out in the world as 'things'. Importantly, these are *things* that originally and essentially constitute phenomena. 'Back to things themselves' is Husserl's defining dictum. The thing in itself (*Ding an siche*) is the German philosophical conundrum through which Husserl, and Marion, articulate substance and essence, *ousia* and *essentia*. The distinction is that, in strictly Kantian terms, the thing-in-itself can be conceptually thought but the 'thing' (*essentia*, Being, God) cannot be intuitively known. The question of just how 'critical' phenomenological method is becomes tantamount to avoiding any reconstitution of metaphysical theology, evident in Aquinas and echoed in Heidegger's ontological difference. What Husserl calls phenomenological reduction, taken from the Ancient Greek *epoché*, is the method, mode or way through which phenomena, that as matters at issue become things, can be thought essentially. Openly and critically thought. And known indeed through an experience that suspends judgement. Because judgement is suspended, phenomenological reduction is not reductive; rather it critically reduces – or as Husserl says *brackets* – all things as phenomena that, most importantly, give themselves unconditionally. To clarify, and contrary to any connotation of reductive thinking, phenomenological reduction foremost engages givenness in its sense of opening whatever object, thing or essence seems given. That is to say 'giving expression to (eidetic) differences that are directly given to us in *intuition*', wherein givenness prevails by '*completely abstaining from any judgment [sic.]*'.³¹

Phenomenology is therefore legitimized as a *rational* science – rather than divine science – in 'the attempt to think in a nonmetaphysical mode', as Marion says.³² To do this Marion affirms, what is for him, the defining Husserlian proposition: *So much intuition, so much givenness*. '[I]t is a question of showing.'³³ This question is distinct from Husserl's method, which centres upon the individual as 'I'; instead, for Marion, asking about what is shown is a matter that goes beyond looking inwards. Showing means seeing ourselves fundamentally *out* among phenomena. Seeing means seeing phenomena intuitively, absolutely and unexpectedly; seeing beyond the vanity of experiencing oneself inwardly and substantially as some fully constituted 'I'; and indeed of seeing visibility itself, the very mode in which – and indeed how – being takes place.

With Marion we have a methodological innovation: ontology is engaged through a mode of exteriorized appearance. Marion is 'affirming a field of appearance which is to be thought outside of any reference to a hidden or higher realm of reality'.[34] This 'outside' is thought not by God but by finite beings, that is to say anyone and thing that exists and appears exterior to one-self. Existing out there, among others and mundane things; however, existing without being grounded by any metaphysical reality or divine Being. Finitude is the experience of things/beings giving themselves through 'motifs of materiality, infinity, and an ungrounded self'.[35] And every finite being, every Dasein as Heidegger says, gives more, infinitely more. Existing through non-metaphysical excess. This excess is how being becomes more-than-what-one-is, without recourse to some other (supreme) Being. In this way, being is ungrounded existence, infinitely open finitude. Existence means opening up the core of thinking, where divine essence is absent – How? The answer Marion proposes with an astonishing claim: God is without Being.

Though emptied of substance, without Being, God remains *the* theological category. 'Undoubtedly, if "God" is, he is a being; but does God have to be?'[36] Not in so far as Being *automatically affects* (*causa sui*) and self-sustains reality, world or existence, Marion claims. For him, God still remains a phenomenological and theological matter of 'revelation' – arguably Marion's ultimate event; but only in so far as divine essence is *approached* accordingly: 'to go beyond onto-theology, to go beyond ontological difference as well … To think God without any conditions, not even that of Being, hence to think God without pretending to inscribe him or to describe him as a being'.[37] God is given absolutely then in a way that echoes what St. Paul calls *kenosis*: the 'emptying out' of divine Being in the guise of Jesus of Nazareth, the one who dies on the cross. And through this death God is in name and essence crossed out, ontologically emptied of substantial qualities and without return to any metaphysical ground of Being. This Christ event, if one will, becomes that of 'rendering itself unthinkable there by excess … crosses out our thought because he [God] saturates it; better he enters into our thought only in obliging it to criticize itself'.[38]

We now have two implications to contend with. Contrary to the Heideggerian event, of *Ereignis* and ontological difference, there is no poetic form of true, substantial Being to disclose. God is 'the crossing of Being', as Marion says; divine essence is in itself no-thing, ontologically crossed over, totally subtracted. And *perpetually* subtracted indeed. For Marion, this perpetual emptying out of Being occurs actively. It runs contrary to the secular adage of 'God is dead'; theology cannot be rejected from phenomenology. Instead, Marion opens a critique of metaphysical theology – where Being is operative as causal and substantive. This critique Marion works through a rather peculiar concept of 'revealed theology'.[39] It is difficult to say what he is really doing with such a concept, since theology is problematic in Husserl's phenomenology. However, it should be clear that Marion is not rejecting religion; instead he advocates a phenomenology of religion.[40] Though voided, emptied of substantial qualities, God is still engaged through a kind of struggle between visibility and invisibility. Revelation is, if anything, Marion's mode of phenomenal struggle with the excess of being and seeing. Here the second – highly important – implication ensues: ontology is engaged through appearances that are revealed as 'saturated'. All phenomena appear and therefore are given absolutely, given through the excess of being in its unforeseeable yet unavoidable event – fait accompli.

What kind of event, then, does Marion offer us? For Marion painting is one prime example of the event. A 'phenomenology of painting' addresses a kind of phenomenal saturation and paradoxical visibility (of invisibility).[41] Of the numerous examples written about by Marion, there are two works that I believe can help concretize the event of excess – Caravaggio's *The Conversion of St. Paul* (1600) and Raphael's *Marriage of the Virgin* (1504). In the Caravaggio, St. Paul is represented as a figure collapsed on the ground below a horse and surrounded by a number of men gesturing towards him. Each figure is made visible by being painted brightly against a dark background. With hands over his eyes, St. Paul is shown as if unable to take in a peculiar external light. For Marion, what makes this scene evident of excess is the 'anonymous light that seems to come from the exterior of the painting'.[42] The excess 'seen by the light more than he or she sees it' is the way in which the viewer is enclosed by this light – this excess that oversaturates intuition. It is an excess of in-visibility, one might say.[43] The painting itself does not so much give colours that seem visible on the canvas or present representational figures such as people and places; what is given is a paradoxical kind of perspective that happens through in-visibility. It is a perspective that reveals the way visibility itself, and whatever being comes to appear, crosses through the radical absence and guise of Being: invisibility. Marion attempts to clarify this paradox of seeing-through-invisibility in his interpretation of Raphael's *Marriage of the Virgin*. In this case the painting is that of a scene representing a marriage between a man and woman, surrounded by a series of characters: a scene that uses conventions of perspective to focus one's view onto the background of the painting. Behind the group, a walkway stretches towards steps that lead to a door, and through this door a clear blue sky peaking above the horizon. The perspective is made up of these lines and planes, which converge on a point opening onto the sky. It is the sky that is now external, the source of light is viewable – rather than actually out of view, as in the Caravaggio; but does one see something more proper, some spiritual/mystical source or hidden energy for instance? Not at all. No, because in itself this source of visiblity – this standpoint of openness as sky perhaps – is, according to Marion, absolutely *invisible*. The invisible is how Being takes place in phenomenal and thus saturated form, that is, nothing, pure donation, givenness without recourse to some metaphysically onto-theological giver (God, substance). I argue further that this invisibility has no resonance with spiritual sources or cosmic energy.[44] As Marion states, the invisible is put into perspective as a 'strange sky and a real sky', wherein 'the space of the sky encased by the door which is opened onto and by nothing – enables it to be in the open space', there where 'everything visible opens onto the invisible'.[45]

Marion articulates this logic of appearance in relation to the radical absence of divine substance using two concepts: the icon and the idol. Both concepts elaborate Marion's event in terms of how being appears and is revealed elliptically through invisibility. Both concepts have Ancient Greek derivations. From *eidōlon*, the idol is the 'splendor [sic.] of the visible'; and from *eikōn*, the icon is 'the brilliance of the visible'.[46] 'The icon and the idol determine two manners of being for beings, not two classes of beings,' writes Marion.[47] Whereas the icon draws out visibility, the idol dynamically sees the very gaze that reflexively gives what is seen through in-visibility. In this case, the sky is the co-called light through which everything can be gazed and appears with phenomenal saturation. 'The gaze alone makes the idol, as the ultimate function of the gazeable.'[48] The gaze is seen first as whatever appears given to visibility; and gazing is the splendour of visibility giving itself forth. Take for instance the experience of having contemplated something, or viewing a painting. This act of seeing can shift from interest or admiration into something of a singularly blank stare – bedazzled – bringing one to a complete stop. There, Marion states, 'the idol concretises that stop', and 'the gaze's fiery eyes consumed the visible so that each time the gaze saw nothing'.[49] That 'the gaze saw nothing' regards Being/God as how visibility is given through no-thing, emptied of content. Seeing directly *through* God, as Being is disclosed by its non-substantive invisibility. In-visibility is then seeing visibility itself, where what is visible is rendered absolutely invisible (ontologically absent). Seeing through no-thing.

The point to all this highly complicated logic is that appearance is the very how, way, or mode of being (without Being) that takes place in this event. Indeed divine Being radically sustains the idol in its manner of givenness, which Marion articulates in the French as 'la donné'. Givenness correlates to showing how 'the visible dazzles the gaze', and '[t]he idol, as invisible mirror, gives the gaze its stopping point and measures out its scope'.[50] It is here that Marion's phenomenological reduction warrants critical purchase, for whereas the idol gives visibility its aim (gaze), the icon 'is a manner of rendering visible this invisible as such'.[51] Any conceptual judgement is thus suspended and intuition takes precedence, over-saturates visibility and offsets any preconceived concept. For the icon gives too much to see, empties out and therefore renders this excess 'in-visable', as Marion also says. There is no concept as idol that would therefore either precede or come in advance, no ontological difference, no super-object that is intuitively foreseeable beyond anything really visible. As in-visable, Being 'becomes itself visibly laid out in the open'.[52] In such paradoxical ways Marion's phenomenological excess sustains an event of saturated phenomena, and being elicits the appearance of what primordially is not there. Though no-thing Being is nevertheless somehow revealed.

Revelation is Marion's event proper. Givenness (*la donné*) is the act that happens absolutely and unexpectedly, fait accompli. Revelation has three features. (1) It neither can be reversed nor repeated. The light of Being reveals to St. Paul a course from which he feels he cannot turn back from. (2) It cannot be understood through any theological-metaphysical cause. One cannot explain nor show some alternative (false) idol that might reveal some hidden energy or transcendent Being (as there is no primordial and causal principle to reference nor come to know). (3) It cannot be foreseen. It should be further noted that by '*fait accompli*' Marion distances himself from Husserl's notion of horizontality; revelation happens in a rather discontinuous way, interrupting phenomenological concepts of foreseeing and anticipating things as they come and come to be known as they essentially are. Fait accompli is a matter of the absolutely unexpected. The gaze works through the idol, in which what is seen is the invisibility one must continue to view through – and without preconception, without expectation. Upon such features, Marion poses something more perplexing. In actuality, the event is a 'counter-experience'. The actual way one 'experiences' this event extends from the kind of inoperative sense of the in-visible that Being gives absolutely. In plain, what really happens echoes the absence of any hidden source, super-object or conceptual idol: counter to the experience of any spectacle then, the event happens in the excess of revealing what in itself is prima facie, disappointing and prompting resistance – 'a seen not fore-seen by the foresight of any object'.[53] Experiencing this event is quite banal. The so-called moment passed, vitiated. Because there is no primordial substance, no profounder presence even, to intuit or aesthetically experience the event is mundane, so mundane that the experience is un-working. This un-working is, I argue, how the event remains aesthetically inoperative. In other words, the event is experientially vitiated. The vitiation leaves open just how one is to continue to work through the revelation of existing without-Being.

Openness, event, dis-enclosure

So far we understand that the phenomenological event apropos of disclosure fundamentally queries metaphysical being as self-causing, aesthetically operative and transcendent (Heidegger); and that once divine essence is determined as non-substantial, without Being (Marion), a radical experience must fully confront the ontological openness – rather than meaningless vacuum – of existence. The question then is how this event poses something of an open ontology. This openness of what-is does not revert to something as contradictory as pure nihilism, that is, that all existence is empty of meaning. Nancy rethinks this problem in the midst of Christian and monotheistic religion. His 'deconstruction of Christianity' is an ambitious reticulation of ontology and theology. As he succinctly claims, Christianity 'holds us'.[54] And his thesis elaborates this hold accordingly: self-critique, which phenomenological reduction essentially exercises, is definitively Christian. Why? His answer is twofold: (1) Because Christianity internalizes criticality, displaces itself (e.g. kenosis as Being/God effacing itself), and this self-displacement is Christianity's primary mode. Self-criticality is rethinking, questioning, doubting, scrutinizing the essence of things. (2) In this way it produces atheism from within its own tradition. Deconstructed then is the Christian event (revelation) but in such a way that what is revealed are two things: Firstly, this event reveals no-thing, which is to say that God ontologically withdraws from himself and in himself. And secondly, this reveals a kind of mental space that, because Being is self-effacing, opens interpretations and ways of making sense of things as they appear. Disclosure comes from how monotheistic thinking deconstructs it-self. As we shall now see, and to slowly close this chapter, Nancy poses a form of presence and appearance in terms of, what he calls, *dis-enclosure*. Dis-enclosure opens the 'event' as a category, but in-itself is not really an actual event (in Marion's sense) – and this detail I will clarify shortly.

Deconstruction is of course a philosophical approach established by a renowned contemporary of Nancy, and mentor of Marion. Jacques Derrida establishes 'deconstruction' from his reading of Heidegger's overcoming of metaphysics, as in 'the destruction of the history of ontology'.[55] Deconstruction is, quite bluntly, a self-critical approach to thinking and interpretation; more precisely it is an approach that cultivates a radical philosophical approach to any capacity to critique, as in the critique of conditions that make possible thinking and being. Deconstruction is certainly contrary to destroying everything, far from reverting to pure nihilism. Neither concerned with totally annihilating philosophical foundations, nor reconstructing something proper, deconstruction is indeed a radical approach that interrogates phenomenological method, thereby 'taking apart' and, indeed, 'opening' spaces of meaning. Nancy extends this predominant definition by claiming further that 'the gesture of deconstruction' is 'the distension of an opening'.[56] It should be clear though that this distending 'gesture' opens and keeps open, rather than containing or effectively enclosing, the space in which making sense of anything happens at all; dis-enclosure keeps displacing the space through which anything comes into existence. Presence [*parousia*] is of course central to the list of critiqued metaphysical notions; but, more crucially, presence is, so to say, the sense of Nancy's deconstructing event.

For Nancy, dis-enclosure is a kind of *coming into existence*. Dis-enclosure opens and enables meanings to infinitely come, but without presence expressing any substance or subjective condition. Dis-enclosure is the opening of an absence at the heart of presence. '*Parousia* is – to be set apart from the very thing that approaches, to be a gap with and in itself [*l'écart de soi*]. Parousia – or presence close to – differs and is deferred: in this way it is there, imminent, like death in life.'[57] Being is absent by withdrawing and therefore opening up – rather than closing off and rendering meaningless – existence. And existence is what comes and indeed is made into sense. Hence it should be clear for instance that presence is not some (metaphysical) feeling, intuition or subjective sense. Substantive being is 'enclosed' by deconstructing, taking apart and – by ontologically withdrawing – opening being *irreducibly*. Existence is presence in excess of approaching any being at all.

A clarification should then be made as to what Nancy is deconstructing through Christianity. Atheism is one primary result of critiquing and – the attempt – to overcome metaphysics, so to champion Reason. Not to mention a humanist value system, rendering Man – in principle or cause – as some kind of idol of salvation. Monotheism, be it Christian, Judaic or Islamic, engages conceptual foundations, and theoretical foundations that in principle are constituted by notions of Being that are immutable, unifying, homogeneous, non-alienating. And philosophy is also prone to vulgar foundational thinking (e.g. substance proper, Being as one absolute order, Nature as organic flux). With or without God, philosophy erects 'a superior reason equipped with extraordinary properties of omnipotence and omniscience'.[58] An important move that Nancy makes towards atheism is by addressing how Christianity inherently displaces and therefore complicates theistic notions of metaphysics; as seen with kenosis, the place of God is kept absent as a kind of symbolic empty throne. The deconstruction of Christianity works and indeed operates (more efficiently) through the death of God. The notorious claim by Friedrich Nietzsche 'God is dead' is commonly employed for keeping a certain theistic foundation robust, as in the liberal sense of being 'non-religious' (yet, in various degrees, engaging with non-Western spiritual practices like Buddhism or Yoga), although to the detriment of terminating essential sources of will, drive, idea, existence – and event. Dogmatism is one case in point as to why God and religion are to be critiqued and terminated; however, secular thought, I believe, *grossly* overlooks an adjacent claim: 'At bottom, it is only the moral god that has been overcome.'[59] Sure God may be claimed as dead but, as Nietzsche would ask, what do we do now with God's corpse, how do we deal with his abject absent-presence? The gross misperception that ideologically ensues is that of destroying the moral god only to either prompt more extreme world views (e.g. total nihlism, meaninglessness, death), or secular inventions of conceptual idols, as Marion calls them (e.g. universal reason, capital as global market, new age spiritualties). In effect philosophical thinking is embedded in the double bind of 'impossible secularization'.[60] Even Heidegger is ambiguous in his thinking of *Dasein* as some quasi-conceptual idol, wherein existential being stands resolutely towards its rather bizarre temporal horizon of 'the last god'.[61] If not Christianity then another idol takes its place, another metaphysical whimsy of Reason. To keep from reverting to either problem the secular approach must then be reconsidered. And unlike Marion, Nancy stops any further approach towards destroying or reconstructing another substantive Being or super-object. Rather he declares, and to which I completely agree: 'It is not our concern to save religion, even less to return to it.'[62] Dis-enclosure even affirms this lexically; the hyphen [-] separating 'dis' from 'enclosure' opens 'a trace or hyphen drawn to set space between every union, to untie every religion from itself'.[63]

Dis-enclosure is therefore how existence happens. It is where being comes into existence through an ontological openness that, in effect, generates an infinite multiplicity of meanings – and without a primordial meaning tied to any metaphysical cause, ground or operatively efficient Being. It is, if one will, a gesture of ex-istence: the act through which existence comes out (ex-), is exteriorized and exscribed, and thus becomes meaningful. Presence is an event that is made possible by dis-enclosure. Presence is an event however that happens as a counter-experience, an inoperative aesthetic. Take Nancy's engagement with a photographic image. In his photo-essay 'Georges' (2006), Nancy writes about a black-and-white candidly photographed portrait of an elderly man. The man's face is slightly out of focus, appears close up, showing his eyes, nose, mouth and chin. According to Nancy this kind of photo shows not only someone, such as this man (who remains anonymous), but the reality of how one exists through seeing and what is seen – an image. What is at stake for Nancy is how this image as photograph further reflects a radical appearance, and indeed inoperative aesthetic. The man appears in this photograph but, as an image, withdraws any sense or presence of what would otherwise give evidence to someone being fully self-present. The anonymity of Georges further echoes this being-no-one-substantial, a kind of nobody – and arguably someone who resonates with persons dispossessed, like the *sans-papiers*. The image is distinct from the putative presence of something either having-truly-been-there, or expressing someone's so-called (hidden, substantial) inner self. Philip Armstrong clarifies how Nancy's notion of presence and appearance is not about evidencing an 'immediate self-presence' but, rather, *exposes* 'an irreducible excess'.[64] The excess is the exposure that becomes the event in facing and viewing this image, this man, this face; and, moreover, that as an image this face shows someone else, someone other to ourselves. This logic of appearance as excess and exposure opens up a space where meanings can come and be generated. Appearing is the means – instead of one meaning – opening meanings that are in excess of, and without reference to, any substantive Being or inner Self.

Presence opens from what I argue is an irreducible trace. It opens through an irreducible trace that, in a way, points out a space at the very core – and in Nancy's terms bodily form [*corps*] – of existence. Indeed existence is not only for one but the coexistence of many, that is being exposed and shared in common with others. Georges can be any of us facing one another. He is but one image of the *klinamen* – a point at which co-existing with other bodies means being different to and distinct from forming ourselves as One body proper (community, nation, world). The aesthetic experience of this event is thus inoperative. The inoperative aesthetic is, apropos of art, that through which existence happens as a 'vestige'. This vestige of art runs counter to Aquinas's notion of causality, which Nancy queries – 'The vestige does not identify its cause or its model'; in other words, the experience is never of some primordial totality, Being or proper substance (God, Self); rather presence appears in and comes through a radical trace that counters the enigmatic experience of something like a theological fire, the Word of God or Judaic image of a hidden Being within a burning bush – 'In the vestigial smoke, there is no eidos of the fire.'[65]

It should be no surprise then to see just how Nancy makes this deconstructive gesture: an act that traces and affirms a non-substantive presence. Two concepts need to be elucidated here before concluding. Nancy's primary concept is 'sense', which in this case he relates to the Christian concept of 'incarnation'. (Indeed there is resonance between Nancy's sense and the receiving of phenomena posed by Marion's radical empiricism, although with the proviso that sense is post-phenomenological, to which I will comment on shortly.) The body of Christ is a central point of departure here. Christ is said to incarnate the Word of God. 'The Word became flesh and made [Christ's] dwelling among us' (Jn 1.14). Flesh is the body as such, receiving presence – or in Marion's terms, given being as gift fait accompli – by incarnating divine substance in spirit. Flesh for Nancy however is akin to embodying absence radically. Indeed this differs from incarnating some spirit, metaphysical movement or hidden energy beyond one's body.[66] Rather, absence refers to where Christ dies on the cross and, prior to resurrecting from the dead, intermittently becomes inert. *Kenosis* is the term derived from St. Paul that, in Nancy's case, describes this becoming inert, this 'death in life'. Effectively, *kenosis* offsets divine principles evident through operative aesthetic concepts, such as *causa sui*; being exists radically by suspending being, emptying out principles or schemas associated with divinely substantive being. Embodying absence, if one will, is the sense of emptying divine Being. Obviously nothing as crude as 'emptying' actual flesh, blood and organs, leaving a vacuous envelope of skin; instead presence opens by emptying and thus embodying the absence of conceptual objects that totalize being. Nancy clarifies:

> But the man into whom God 'descends' and 'empties himself' (Paul's *kenosis*) is not rendered divine by this. On the contrary. God effaces himself in that man: he is this effacement, his is therefore a trace, he is an impalpable, imperceptible vestige of the emptied and abandoned divine.[67]

Christ's body is dis-enclosed through such an exscribed trace. This self-effacing and deconstructive gesture Nancy calls exscription. Man exscribes by embodying (ontological) absence and – generatively – opening a sense of one's existence. Exscribing this trace of absence means effacing Being in any theological principle. This is how *parousia* thus comes 'to be set apart from the very thing that approaches' (as quoted earlier). The French *l'écart de soi* expresses this incarnating gesture more concretely. 'The "body" of the "incarnation" is therefore the place, or rather the taking place, the event, of that disappearance.'[68] All in all, presence dis-encloses, opens sense infinitely as the fact of existing in this bodily event. And rather than be some imprint or mark made, it is the body that is the trace. Someone exists by tracing how they exist in bodily form, that is appearing and, throughout whatever way of appearing (standing, sitting, laying down), tracing the event of excess and existence. Existence is distinct then from disclosing ontological difference. Neither God nor another idol supplements the infinite sense that happens through 'openness', that is how someone comes into existence by tracing this event of post-phenomenological excess. And to this effect the thesis of this chapter is realized accordingly: not being but existence is the event of infinitely opening oneself up through presence. Existence effaces, traces and thus exceeds being as divine–metaphysical substance.

Conclusion

Each in his own way, Nancy and Marion, convincingly demonstrate that philosophical thinking has metaphysical tendencies that de facto resonate with theology. As I have tried to show, the real task is firstly to understand that the so-called secular method of critique, and Christianity too, sustains an excess of conceptual idols. Both approaches attempt to think through and place faith in transcendent Being. Phenomenology proposes methods, such as givenness, which champion experiences of engaging being in its event; however, the deconstructive gesture rethinks the openness these experiences express. Aesthetic experiences remain equivocal as to what sense this event of excess gives and indeed opens fait accompli. The real merit of the phenomenological event of excess, posed by Marion, is in revealing the possibility of the revelation of the divine through a radical empiricism. God is without Being indeed; his being visible as invisibility echoes a trace that effaces divine substance of its affect. Seeing the invisible means that Being is completely disavowed; indeed there is no essential 'I', or substantial core of identity (inner self, the real me), that need be vainly perceived, felt or generally sensed. What Nancy brings to such an event of excess is a methodology that is post-phenomenological. The event of dis-enclosure concerns existence in the sense of finitude that, by effacing Being, is more concrete, materialist and real. The post-phenomenological sense of this authentic event means that the very divine sense of the Word equally falls under this deconstructive gesture. The merit of Nancy's event is in using dis-enclosure towards making ontology not only distinct from theology (as metaphysics) but also methodologically robust. Throughout events either given by not-being (Marion) or existing without substantive presence (Nancy), aesthetic experiences of Being become inoperative. Un-becoming, the event affirms the empty gesture that deconstruction renders in its address. On the one hand addressing 'the infinite freedom of the Word in our words, and reciprocally', where '[s]o much freedom frightens us, deservedly'.[69] On the other hand, we take up 'a separation and a salutation that is addressed, a separation that renders this address (or its refusal) possible'.[70]

Notes

1. Jean-Luc Marion, *In Excess: Studies of Saturated Phenomena*, trans. R. H. Berraud (New York: Fordham University Press, 2002), 44.
2. Jean-Luc Marion, *God Without Being*, trans. T. A. Carlson (London: The University of Chicago Press, 1995), Jean-Luc Nancy, *Dis-Enclosure: The Deconstruction of Christianity*, trans. B. M. Bergo (New York: Fordham University Press, 2008) and Jean-Luc Nancy, *Adoration: The Deconstruction of Christianity II*, trans. J. McKeane (New York: Fordham University Press, 2013).
3. Marion, *God without Being*, 1.
4. Nancy, *Dis-enclosure*, 2–3.
5. G. Agamben, *The Kingdom and The Glory: For a Theological Genealogy of Economy and Government*, trans. L. Chiesa (Stanford: Stanford University Press, 2011) and K. Malik, 'Yes, We've Lost Our Faith in God, but We've Lost Our Faith in Reason Too', *The Guardian* (1 April 2018).
6. Alain Badiou, *The True Life*, trans. S. Spitzer (Cambridge: Polity Press, 2017).
7. M. Gabriel, *Why the World Does Not Exist*, trans. G. S. Moss (London: Polity Press, 2016), 151.
8. C. Malabou, *The Heidegger Change: On the Fantastic in Philosophy*, trans. P. Skafish (Albany: SUNY Press, 2011).
9. I. Thompson, *Heidegger on Ontotheology: Technology and the Politics of Education* (Cambridge: Cambridge University Press, 2005), 10.
10. Nancy, *Dis-enclosure*, 156.
11. Gabriel, *Why the World*, 163.

12 Thomas Aquinas, *Selected Writings*, trans. R. Mcinerny (London: Penguin Books, 1998), 115; 'The Question of Boethius's On the Trinity', Q.1, A.2.
13 Ibid., 159.
14 Ibid., 36–367.
15 Nancy, *Dis-enclosure*, 156.
16 E. Levinas, *Otherwise Than Being, or beyond Essence*, trans. A. Lingis (Pittsburgh: Duquesne University Press, 2009), 6.
17 M. Heidegger, *The Basic Problems of Phenomenology*, trans. A. Hofstadter (Indianapolis: Indiana University Press, 1998), 318–30.
18 Ibid., 322.
19 Plato, *Republic*, in *The Collected Dialogues of Plato, Including The Letters*, ed. H. C. E. Hamilton and trans. P. Shorey (Princeton: Princeton University Press, 1996), 744; 509b.
20 Heidegger, *Basic Problems*, 88–98.
21 Ibid., 18.
22 Ibid.
23 Ibid., 118.
24 Nancy, *Dis-enclosure*, 25.
25 Jean-Luc Nancy, *The Creation of the World or Globalization*, trans. F. R. Pettigrew (Albany: State University of New York Press, 2007), 45.
26 Nancy, *Dis-enclosure*, 119.
27 D. Janicaud, *Phenomenology and The 'Theological Turn': The French Debate*, trans. T. A. Bernard and G. Prusak (New York: Fordham University Press, 2000).
28 Marion, *God Without Being*, xxiii.
29 Ibid., xxiv.
30 I owe this insight to Nikolaas Deketelaere.
31 E. Husserl, *Ideas – Pertaining to a Pure Phenomenology and to a Phenomenological Philosophy, First Book, General Introduction to a Pure Phenomenology*, trans. F. Kersten (Lancaster: Martinus Nihjoff Publishers, 1982), 33–4.
32 Jean-Luc Marion, *Being Given: Toward a Phenomenology of Givenness*, trans. J. L. Kosky (Stanford: Stanford University Press, 2013), 7.
33 Ibid.
34 I. James, *The New French Philosophy* (Cambridge: Polity Press, 2012), 21.
35 Ibid., 38.
36 Marion, *God without Being*, 44.
37 Ibid., 44–5.
38 Ibid., 46.
39 Marion, *In Excess*, 28.
40 Jean-Luc Marion, *The Crossing of the Visible*, trans. J. K. Smith (Stanford: Stanford University Press, 2004).

41 Marion, *Being Given*.
42 Marion, *In Excess*, 64.
43 Ibid.
44 Tangentially, there are theories and practices in art today that are increasingly, and I argue uncritically and egregiously, advocating reductive mystical tendencies. Such tendencies deal with abstract notions of energy or forces expressed by 'mark', the latter of which is cognate with ways of tracing, recording or capturing. For a fuller account of this issue see Robert Luzar, 'Rethinking the Graphic Trace in Performative Drawing', *Theatre and Performance Design* 1–2, no. 3 (2017): 50–67.
45 Marion, *Crossing*, 7.
46 Marion, *God without Being*, 7.
47 Ibid., 8.
48 Ibid., 10.
49 Ibid., 11.
50 Ibid., 12.
51 Ibid., 17.
52 Ibid.
53 Ibid., 138.
54 Nancy, *Dis-enclosure*, 142.
55 Martin Heidegger, *Being and Time*, trans. J. Macquarrie and E. Robinson (New York: Harper and Row, 1962), 44.
56 Nancy, *Dis-enclosure*, 148.
57 Ibid., 59
58 Nancy, *Adoration*, 32.
59 Friedrich Nietzsche, *The Will to Power*, trans. R. J. W. Kauffman (New York: Vintage Books, 1968), 36.
60 Jacques Derrida, *Acts of Religion*, trans. G. Anidjar (London: Routledge, 2010), 216.
61 Martin Heidegger, *Contributions to Philosophy (Of the Event)*, trans. D. V.-N. R. Rojcewicz (Indianapolis: Indiana University Press, 2012).
62 Nancy, *Dis-enclosure*, 1.
63 Ibid., 60.
64 P. Armstrong, 'From Appearance to Exposure', *Journal of Visual Culture* 9, no. 1 (2010): 11–27, 22.
65 Jean-Luc Nancy, *The Muses*, trans. P. Kamuf (Stanford: Stanford University Press, 1996), 95.
66 The philosophical aesthetics that are operative today in art and culture fall into this dubious metaphysically theological thinking. As a practitioner, I have reflected upon how 'movement', 'trace' and 'embodiment' are interrogated, in practice and theory, by reflecting upon Nancy's praxis of 'exscription'. See Robert Luzar, 'Turning around the Written Mark, Opening from a Weight of Thought', in *Nancy and Visual*

Culture, ed. Carrie Giunta and Adrienne Janus (Edinburgh: Edinburgh University Press 2016), 181–98.
67 Nancy, *Adoration*, 30.
68 Ibid., 83.
69 Marion, *God without Being*, 158.
70 Nancy, *Adoration*, 54.

Bibliography

Agamben, Giorgio. *The Kingdom and The Glory: For A Theological Genealogy of Economy and Government*. Translated by L. Chiesa. Stanford: Stanford University Press, 2011.

Aquinas, Thomas. *Selected Writings*. Translated by R. Mcinerny. London: Penguin Books, 1998.

Armstrong, Philip. 'From Appearance to Exposure'. *Journal of Visual Culture* 9, no. 1 (2010): 11–27.

Badiou, Alain. *The True Life*. Translated by S. Spitzer. Cambridge: Polity Press, 2017.

Derrida, Jacques. *Acts of Religion*. Translated by G. Anidjar. London: Routledge, 2010.

Gabriel, Markus. *Why The World Does Not Exist*. Translated by G. S. Moss. London: Polity Press, 2016.

Heidegger, Martin. *The Basic Problems of Phenomenology*. Translated by A. Hofstadter. Indianapolis: Indiana University Press, 1998.

Heidegger, Martin. *Being and Time*. Translated by E. Robinson and J. Macquarrie. New York: Harper and Row, 1962.

Heidegger, Martin. *Contributions to Philosophy (Of the Event)*. Translated by D. V.-N. R. Rojcewicz. Indianapolis: Indiana University Press, 2012.

Husserl, Edmund. *Ideas – Pertaining to a Pure Phenomenology and to a Phenomenological Philosophy, First Book, General Introduction to a Pure Phenomenology*. Translated by F. Kersten. Lancaster: Martinus Nihjoff Publishers, 1982.

James, Ian. *The New French Philosophy*. Cambridge: Polity Press, 2012.

Janicaud, Dominique. *Phenomenology and The 'Theological Turn': The French Debate*. Translated by T. A. Bernard and G. Prusak. New York: Fordham University Press, 2000.

Levinas, Emmanuel. *Otherwise Than Being, or Beyond Essence*. Translated by A. Lingis. Pittsburgh: Duquesne University Press, 2009.

Luzar, Robert. 'Rethinking the Graphic Trace in Performative Drawing'. *Theatre and Performance Design* 1–2, no. 3 (2017): 50–67.

Luzar, Robert. 'Turning Around the Written Mark, Opening from a Weight of Thought'. In *Nancy and Visual Culture*. Edited by Carrie Giunta and Adrienne Janus, 181–98. Edinburgh: Edinburgh University Press, 2016.

Malabou, Catherine. *The Heidegger Change: On the Fantastic in Philosophy*. Translated by P. Skafish. Albany: SUNY Press, 2011.

Malik, Kenan. 'Yes, We've Lost Our Faith in God, but We've Lost Our Faith in Reason Too'. *The Guardian* (1 April 2018).

Marion, Jean-Luc. *Being Given: Toward A Phenomenology of Givenness*. Translated by J. L. Kosky. Stanford: Stanford University Press, 2013.

Marion, Jean-Luc. *The Crossing of the Visible*. Translated by J. K. Smith. Stanford: Stanford University Press, 2004.

Marion, Jean-Luc. *God Without Being*. Translated by T. A. Carlson. London: The University of Chicago Press, 1995.

Marion, Jean-Luc. *In Excess: Studies of Saturated Phenomena*. Translated by R. H. Berraud. New York: Fordham University Press, 2002.

Marion, Jean-Luc. 'Metaphysics and Theology: A Relief for Theology'. *Critical Inquiry* 20 (1994): 572–91.

Marion, Jean-Luc. *The Visible and The Revealed*. Translated by C. M. et al. New York: Fordham University Press, 2008.

Nancy, Jean-Luc. *Adoration: The Deconstruction of Christianity II*. Translated by J. McKeane. New York: Fordham University Press, 2013.

Nancy, Jean-Luc. *The Creation of the World or Globalization*. Translated by F. R. Pettigrew. Albany: State University of New York Press, 2007.

Nancy, Jean-Luc. *Dis-enclosure: The Deconstruction of Christianity*. Translated by B. M. Bergo. New York: Fordham University Press, 2008.

Nancy, Jean-Luc. *Multiple Arts: The Muses II*. Stanford: Stanford University Press, 2006.

Nancy, Jean-Luc. *The Muses*. Translated by P. Kamuf. Stanford: Stanford University Press, 1996.

Nietzsche, Friedrich. *The Will to Power*. Translated by R. J. W. Kauffman. New York: Vintage Books, 1968.

Plato. *Republic*. In *The Collected Dialogues of Plato, Including The Letters*. Edited by H. C. E. Hamilton and translated by P. Shorey. Princeton: Princeton University Press, 1996.

Thomson, Iain D. *Heidegger on Ontotheology: Technology and the Politics of Education*. Cambridge: Cambridge University Press, 2005.

Index

Achilles 8
Aertsen, Jan 77
akh (Egyptian: transfigured spirit that survives death) 7
aidagara (Japanese: betweenness) 164
Alcibiades 28, 29
Ames, Roger 22, 34
Analects, The 28, 29
anātman (no-self) 51, 113–25, 151–3
Anaxagoras 11
angya (Japanese: wandering in nature) 156
Anwesenheit (German: presence) 180
Appelbaum, David 115, 118, 120, 121
application (Gadamer) 70–3
Aquinas, Thomas 76, 178–9, 183–93
Arisaka Yoko 160
Aristeas of Proconnesus 10
Aristotle 9, 179–80
Armstrong, Philip 192
atheism 191
ātman (self) 51, 151–2
Augustine of Hippo 74, 76, 80
Averroes 91. *See* Ibn Rushd
Avicenna 69, 76–81

ba (Egyptian: a person's soul that may join the gods) 7–9, 13–14
Barad, Karen 26–8
Barth, Karl 132
basho (Japanese: place) 159, 161
bashoteki jiko (Japanese: topological self) 158
being-in-the-world (Heidegger) 159, 160
Betty, L. Stafford 118, 120
Bildung (German: self-cultivation) 30
bodhisattva (Sanskrit: person whose being is perfect knowledge) 153
'body in motion' (Geulincx) 91–104
Bourdieu, Pierre 30
Buber, Martin 162–3

Buddhism 41–62, 191
Burthogge, Richard 99

Candrakīrti 53–5
Caputo, John D. 74
causa sui (Latin: self-caused cause) 179, 181, 185
Chan Buddhism 113–14. *See also* Zen Buddhism
China 21–3
Christianity 75, 129–43, 176–95
Chung-ying, Chen 25
Clauberg, Johannes 101
Collingwood, Robin George 72, 79
Confucian individualism 31–6
Confucianism 21–36
Confucius 29, 31, 35–6
Conversion of St Paul, The (Caravaggio, 1600) 186–7
Corbin, Henry 69
courage to be 141
cultural practice 129–42

daimon (Greek: guiding spirit) 11–12
Dallmayr, Fred 75
Daniel, Joshua 135
Danto, Arthur C. 21
Dao, the (Chinese: the way) 31–2
Daoism 10
daological framework, the 23–8
Dasein (German: being-there) 159, 181
de Beauvoir, Simone 113, 123–5
deconstruction 189–94
de Libera, Alain 78–9
Derrida, Jacques 69, 78, 190
Descartes, René 91–104
desire 42–6
dharma (Sanskrit: the truth about how things really are) 41, 51–60
di (Chinese: earth) 26
Dionysius 8
disclosure 175

dis-enclosure (Nancy)   176, 182, 189–94
Dōgen   153–4
Doppelerschlossenheit (German: double openness)   161

education   21–36
Egyptian philosophy   7
eidolon (Greek: idol)   187–8
eidos (Greek: idea, form)   43–51, 93
Eigenthümlichkeit (German: individuality)   136–7
eikōn (Greek: icon)   187–8
el Bizri, Nader   69
Empedocles   10–11
emptiness   156
Ereignis (German: event)   175–95
erôs (Greek: love)   42–5, 50, 61
eschatology   139
essentialism   1–2
essentialization   139
eternal life   139
ethics   41–62
eudaimonia (Greek: flourishing, happiness)   44
Euphorbus   10
existentialism   113–14, 123–5, 150
exscription   193–4

faith   176–80
falâsifa (Arabic: philosophers)   77–8
Fichte, Johann Gottlieb   132–3
Finagrette, Herbert   21
Flenderus, Johannes   101
friendship   141

Gabriel, Markus   178
Gadamer, Hans-Georg   30, 69–81, 161
gaze, the   187–8
Gelassenheit (German: releasement)   154
gender   140–1
Ge Ronjin   34
Geulincx, Arnold   91–104
al-Ghazali, Abu Hamid   79
Giles, James   115, 117
global universalism   21–36
God   92–5, 98–102, 131, 162, 176
Grosholz, Emilie   95

Harvey, Peter   153–4
Hauerwas, Stanley   130, 134, 142

Heidegger, Martin   69, 79–80, 81, 155, 160–1, 178–80
Heracles   7–9
hermeneutics   70–3
Hermotimus of Clazomenae   10–11
Hesiod   10
Homer   7
horizon   161–2
Hume, David   113–25
Husserl, Edmund   81, 183–4

Iamblichus   10
Ibn Arabi   69, 81
Ibn Rushd   91. *See* Averroes
Iliad, the   3
immortality   11–14, 50
incarnation   193–4
individuality   129–42
inscription   177–9
invisibility   186–7
Islamic philosophy   69–81
I-thou encounter   156, 160, 162–5

Jesus Christ   131
jitafuni (Japanese: non-duality of self and other)   164
Jolivet, Jean   77
Judaism   75

ka (Egyptian: soul)   7–9, 13–14
kagirinai ake (Japanese: limitless openness)   159
kalon (Greek: beautiful, noble)   45–50
Kant, Immanuel   24, 133
Kasulis, Thomas   119, 120, 122, 124
kenosis (Greek: emptying)   185, 193–4
kōiteki chokkan (Japanese: active intuition)   159
Kraut, Richard   49
Kurihara, Yuji   48
Kyoto School   153

la donné (French: givenness)   188
Lebenswelt (German: life-world)   161
Leibniz, Gottfried Wilhelm   21–2, 69
li (Chinese: ritual propriety)   23, 24, 30–1, 34
liberalism   129–42
Liji, The (*The Book of Rites*)   31–2
Linck, Gudula   25

Lindbeck, George 130, 134, 142
logocentrism 78
logos (Greek: reason, word) 75
loka (Sanskrit: world) 51
Lorch, Ingrid Turner 115

Madhyamaka Buddhism 51–6, 61
Mahāyāna Buddhism 42, 61, 113, 153–4
Maraldo, John C. 163–4
Marion, Jean-Luc 175–95
Marriage of the Virgin, The (Raphael, 1504) 186–7
Martin, Craig 91
Master Eckhart (*also* Meister Eckhart) 79–80, 150, 154
materialism 9–10
Mathur, D. C. 119, 120
Meinwald, Constance C. 49
Mengzi 24, 33
Merleau-Ponty, Maurice 56
Mernin, N. David 27
Middle Ages, the 78–9
Milbank, John 129–35, 137, 142
mind-body problem, the 95–102
modes of thinking (Geulincx) 93
monotheism 191
Mulla Sadra 69, 79, 81
mutakallimûn (Arabic: theologians) 77

Nadler, Steven 100
Nancy, Jean-Luc 31, 175–95
neo-Confucianism 26
Nietzsche, Friedrich 150, 191
nihilism 177, 190
nihvabhāva (Sanskrit: no-identity) 51–61
niju sekai (Japanese: double openness) 161
ningen (Japanese: human being) (*also* ninjen) 149, 163–4
nirvana (Sanskrit: extinguishing of suffering) 53
Nishida Kitarō 150, 158, 160, 164
Nishitani Keji 154, 164
Norton, David 114
Norton, Mary 114
nous (Greek: mind) 7, 12–14
Nous, the absolute (Greek: Mind, Being) 12

Odysseus 8
Odyssey, The 7–9
ontological difference 178
ontotheology 176–95
ousia (Greek: substance) 180

Pabst, Adrian 130, 134
Pantham, Thomas 74
parousia (Greek: presence) 190–4
Paul, St. 185
perception 114–18
Pesnau, Robert 96
phenomenology 175–95
phenomenology of the self 149–65
Plato 10–11, 41–62, 181
Platonism 7, 41–62
Plotinus 7, 11–14
Porphyry 13
postliberalism 129–35
pratītyasamutpāda (Sanskrit: co-dependent origination) 51–9, 153
Proclus 14
Protagoras 48
protestant theology 129–42
psyche (Greek: soul) 7–9, 12
pudgala (Sanskrit: person) 51
Pythagoras 11

quantum physics 26–8

Rahula, Walpola 152
relationalism 1–2, 25, 129–42
ren (Chinese: humaneness) 24, 26
revelation 175, 186–8
Rosemont, Henry 22
Rosen, Stanley 47

samu (Japanese: work) 155–6
Sāntideva 54–8
sanzen (Japanese: dialogue with a Zen master) 156
saturated phenomena 176
satya (Sanskrit: The Four Noble Truths of Buddism) 52
Scheffler, Johannes 149–50
Schelling, Friedrich Wilhelm Joseph von 139
Schleiermacher, Friedrich Daniel Ernst 135–42
self-cultivation 32–6

self-transformation 41
sensible species (Geulincx) 93–5
shizen (Japanese: nature) 149
shu (Chinese: reciprocity) 35
Siedentop, Larry 131
Socrates 42, 49, 50
Sophist, The (Plato) 42
soul 7–14, 91–104
Stoicism 10, 13–14
Strazzoni, Andrea 91–2
Suarez, Francisco 96, 100
svabhāva (Sanskrit: inherent existence) 51–61, 153
Symposium, The (Plato) 42, 43–4, 46–50

Taylor, Charles 131
Temporalität (German: temporality) 180
Ten Ox-Herding Pictures 149–65
tian (Chinese: heaven, nature as a whole) 24, 26
Tillich, Paul 137–42
Tolle, Eckhart 14
tradition (Gadamer) 68–81
transcendence 131–2, 181

Ueda Shitzuteru 149–65
upādāna (Sanskrit: grasping instigated by desire and will) 42–5, 55, 61

Vasubandhu 119
virtue 42–61

Waldenfels, Bernhard 74, 79
Watson, Richard A. 103–4

Watsuju Tetsurō 163–4
Weiming, Tu 25–6
White, F. C. 48
Wirkungsgeschichte (German: reception-history) 73–4
world-transformation 41

Xi, Zhu 25
Xunzi 28, 31

yi (Chinese: appropriateness/righteousness) 24
Yijing (*Book of Changes*) 24–5
Yili, The (*Book of Etiquette and Rites*) 31
Yoga 191
Yogācāra Buddhism 55

Zai, Zhang 26
zazen (Japanese: sitting meditation) 150, 155
Zedong, Mao 32–3
Zen Buddhism 113–25, 149–65. *See also* Chan Buddhism
zettai mu (Japanese: absolute nothingness) 149, 156
zettaimujun no jikodōitsu (Japanese: self-identity of absolute contradiction) 159
zhi (Chinese: wisdom) 24
Zhongyong, The (The Doctrine of the Mean) 24, 29
Zigong (Confucius' disciple) 35
Zuntz, Günter 10

www.ingramcontent.com/pod-product-compliance
Lightning Source LLC
Chambersburg PA
CBHW052043300426
44117CB00012B/1945